MARK TAYLOR

A CAPTAIN'S YEAR

BY THE SAME AUTHOR

Taylor Made

MARK TAYLOR
A CAPTAIN'S YEAR

Pan Macmillan Australia

PHOTOGRAPHS COURTESY OF
AUSTRALIAN PICTURE LIBRARY/ALL SPORT

First published 1997 in Ironbark by Pan Macmillan Australia Pty Limited
St Martins Tower, 31 Market Street, Sydney

Copyright © Mark Taylor 1997

All rights reserved. No part of this book may be reproduced or transmitted
in any form or by any means, electronic or mechanical, including
photocopying, recording or by any information storage and retrieval system,
without prior permission in writing from the publisher.

National Library of Australia
Cataloguing-in-Publication data:

Taylor, Mark 1964-
Mark Taylor, a captain's year.

ISBN 0 330 36035 3.

1. Taylor, Mark, 1964–Diaries. 2. Cricket captains -
Australia - Biography. 3. Test matches (Cricket) -
Australia. I. Title.

796.358092

Designed by Liz Seymour
Printed in Australia by Griffin Press

CONTENTS

Foreword 9

CHAPTER 1
A WINTER OF DISCONTENT 11

CHAPTER 2
INDIA
Down and Out in Delhi 15

CHAPTER 3
THE HOME SERIES: THE WEST INDIES AND PAKISTAN
Reflections on a Long Hot Summer 23

CHAPTER 4
SOUTH AFRICA
Victory on the Veldt 41

CHAPTER 5
CALM BEFORE THE STORM 81

Chapter 6
ENGLAND
Beginning the Great Adventure 87

Chapter 7
THE ONE-DAY BLUES 95

Chapter 8
TRAVELLING FIRST CLASS 103

Chapter 9
A TEST IN MORE WAYS THAN ONE 113

Chapter 10
MOVING ON 127

Chapter 11
THE HOME OF CRICKET 131

Chapter 12
TEST OF CHARACTER 143

Chapter 13
HEADING TO HEADINGLEY 153

Chapter 14
ONE UP... TWO TO PLAY 163

Chapter 15
HOW SWEET IT WAS 171

Chapter 16
THE ONE THAT GOT AWAY 179

A CAPTAIN'S YEAR
The Scoreboard, 1996–97 189

*To my two sons, William and Jack,
who have kept my life in perspective
during this challenging twelve months*

FOREWORD
by Richie Benaud

Fewer than 400 cricketers have played for Australia in Test matches in the space of 120 years. One, Allan Border, played 156 times, others less fortunate achieved a single heart-breaking appearance. Luckier are the 39 who have gone on to captain Australia, five of them for only one match, others ranging through a variety of heart-burning, ulcer-generating, but wonderfully rewarding, experiences they will never forget. Sometimes a captaincy appointment has been made by the Australian Cricket Board under its different names, sometimes by the Australian selectors but, irrespective of the method, Australia's record has always been, and remains, outstanding in the cricket world.

So is Mark Taylor's!

He has just returned from one of the toughest assignments of his career, defending the Ashes in England immediately following a three-match series against South Africa, one of the most difficult challenges I have seen in what seems to be an increasing workload for Australia's cricketers. The Australians played nine Tests in this period, with only the washed out match at Lord's a draw. Three games were lost, five were won and Taylor's team was victorious in both series. There are three other captains who have led Australia on more occasions, but in skill, and the priceless commodity of flair, he is right up there with anyone who has walked out at the head of an Australian team. So too in courage—in every respect his and the team's fighting comeback in England was one of the best things I have seen in all the years I have been involved in cricket. This is one of the best Australian teams ever to walk on to any cricket field—strong in batting, nearly a perfect balance in the bowling attack and absolutely brilliant in the field and in the wicket-keeping department. One of the strengths of Australian cricket over the years, from the time the bearded Jack Blackham had the effrontery to stand over the stumps to all bowlers, has been that the 'keepers have been quite outstanding, and now Ian Healy provides such wonderful back-up strength for the bowlers and captain.

There has been much discussion in recent times on the question of how this current team, led by Mark Taylor, rates with some of the great Australian combinations of the past. By common consent, Warwick Armstrong's teams of 1920 and 1921 are regarded as the best combinations prior to Don Bradman's 1948 team, and each of these eras has a common thread—Australian cricket was so strong that many fine players were condemned to a career in Sheffield Shield while the selectors kept to a very small group from which to choose the final eleven.

In Armstrong's great captaincy time the regular eleven was chosen from Herbie

Collins, Warren Bardsley, Charlie Macartney, Charles Kelleway, Armstrong himself, Jack Gregory, Johnny Taylor, Nip Pellew, Jack Ryder, Bert Oldfield, Arthur Mailey, Ted McDonald, Hanson Carter and Tommy Andrews. When the selectors started to build up for the tour of England in 1926 they brought in youngsters like Bill Ponsford, Vic Richardson, Alan Kippax and one not quite so young, Clarrie Grimmett, who promptly took 11 wickets in his debut match. In the Bradman postwar era there was a wealth of talent, Arthur Morris, Sid Barnes, Bill Brown, Bradman, Lindsay Hassett, Neil Harvey, Keith Miller, Ray Lindwall, Colin McCool, Ian Johnson, Don Tallon, Ernie Toshack and Bill Johnston. A tough side to crack for would-be contenders, or for the opposition.

The same applied to Ian and Greg Chappell's teams from 1970 to 1976, combinations of great talent with some fine players, and then others trying vainly to make it into the side. In my opinion the teams led by Armstrong, Bradman and Ian and Greg Chappell have been the best to take the field for Australia. My heart urges me to slip in the era from 1958 to 1961 as well, but my brain holds back a little. We had a wonderful team and no series was lost, but I think we might have been just a fraction short of those other combinations.

But what of Mark Taylor's team? Well, because of the wonderful record achieved, I have them right up there with those mentioned above. Since Taylor has started leading them they have won 18 games and lost 10, some of the reverses when series have already been decided. There have certainly been inconsistencies at the top of the batting order and it is a worry that, at the moment, there is only one genuine Test-class leg-spin bowler in the country, a matter which I hope and trust is a worry for the ACB. It is, though, a splendid team, and it too has a common thread with the other sides, that Australia is strong when the bowling attack is based on skilful and genuine pace plus high-class leg-spin bowling, something good selectors in our country regard as ideal.

Taylor, through both his excellent and not so good batting times, has been a credit to his team, to himself and to the game of cricket, and it has been a pleasure to watch the Australians play under his leadership. No better example of the latter than one of the bravest decisions I've seen when he elected to bat first at Old Trafford in the Third Test of the 1997 Ashes battle. He trusted his team and they trusted him. Another plus mark is his extraordinary record of having only five drawn Tests in 33 matches and nine series, a minute percentage of no results which is approached by no other Australian captain. That is one of the ingredients for attractive cricket for those who pay their money at the turnstiles, and who watch on television, and it seems to me during his captaincy tenure to have been much appreciated by cricket followers around the world. I'm pleased to see cricketers involved in all areas of the media, and I hope this book is a great success for Mark, so too the coming season which, as we rush towards the end of the century, will be all important for the future of Australian cricket.

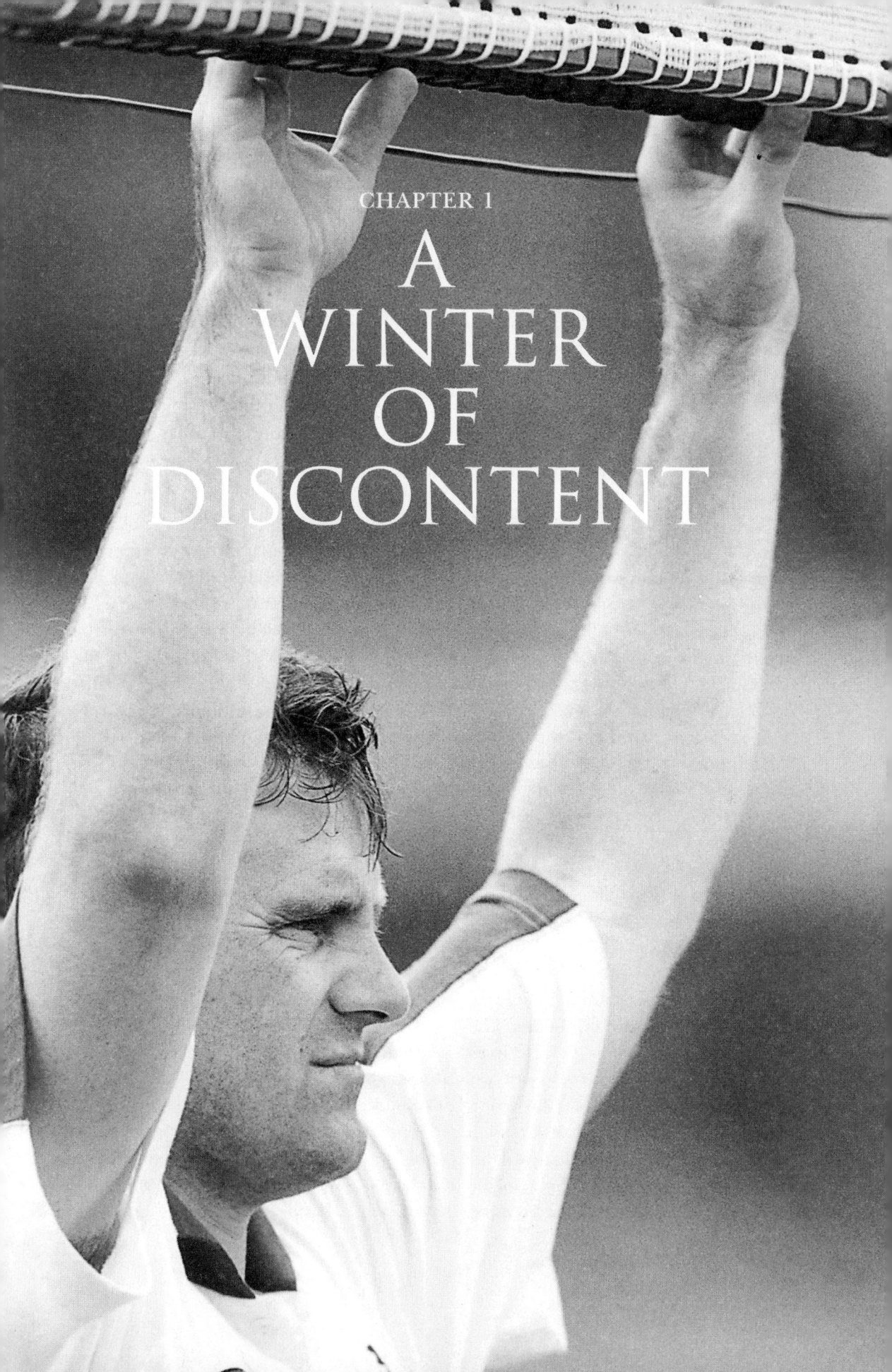

CHAPTER 1
A WINTER OF DISCONTENT

It's something that has happened to just about every one of us. Unconcerned and unthinking, you reach down as you have a thousand times before ... but suddenly this time it's like a knife has been plunged into your back. With me, the culprit was a hefty set of weights. It was a midwinter morning, July 1996, and I had just completed a strenuous set of lifting exercises. It was as I lowered the weights to the floor, knees not sufficiently bent, that I felt that old, familiar feeling. And so it was that my winter of hard work and preparation for maybe the toughest cricketing assignment ever handed to any Australian team became instead the winter of my discontent...

I was injured that July at a place that will almost certainly bring glory to Australia in three years time. After the year 2000, in fact, you can nearly bet it will be forever a sacred place in Australian sport. For weeks I had been working out in the gymnasium at the Olympic Aquatic Centre, Homebush Bay, Sydney. After a lazy, hazy autumn following the demanding season of 1995–96 I had become very serious indeed about getting ready for what lay ahead.

It came in the wake of the disappointment of losing the World Cup final. After one last Shield match, in March '96, I had sat down one morning and mapped out a program. This is what lay ahead: a tour to Sri Lanka, one to India three or four weeks later, confronting the West Indies in a full Test series in Australia plus the one-day tournament (West Indies, Pakistan), then to South Africa and ultimately the big one—the Ashes tour to England in May, June, July, August '97. After that, it would begin again: back home to play against South Africa and New Zealand, followed by a tour of India in '98. I added it up and it came to 20 months of cricket in a 24-month period. For us it was to be an endless summer, totalling 24 Tests and 50-something one-day internationals, taking in four different countries and bringing us up against seven different nations—and with vast differences in the climate and pitch conditions that we would face.

Okay, we had four months off until it all began with the Sri Lankan tour. I would take a month off; a month away from Sydney, from cricket talk, from the demands of the media, from pressure—and then I would begin again. For me, there's no better place to do that than somewhere near my wife Judi's parents' place—Halfway Creek, a tiny hamlet tucked away on the NSW north coast. In late April we packed the car, strapped in the kids—William, four, and Jack, 20 months—and headed off. Fishing, swimming, golfing, eating, sipping the occasional cold ale ... it turned out to be exactly my kind of holiday. That sort of time with the family has become more precious, more necessary as cricket's pressures have increased on me over the seasons. Up north I put on some weight, and shed some stress—and came back to Sydney in the last week of May ready ... for getting ready.

I have the day jotted down when my 'season' began—Friday, 24 May. On that morning I began the haul towards my goal of getting very, very fit. In the weeks that followed I worked out three, often four days a week at Homebush under the direction of a strength and fitness expert, Kevin Chevell, a former first grade fast bowler in Sydney and Perth. The sessions were a mixture of aerobics and weights work, specifically designed for my needs, and stretching over two or three hours. On my days off, I'd go on long bike rides, or ride an exercise bike at home, my eyes glued to the dramas of the Olympics which were unfolding in Atlanta. I was watching my diet, feeling stronger and fitter by the day. As Jack Gibson might have put it, I was doing fine. In 10 weeks I'd shed 9kgs—much of it holiday excess—and I was right on track. Fitness is no guarantee of success—but I've always reckoned the chances improve when you're overfit rather than underfit.

Then came the fateful day in July. I'd suffered varying degrees of a chronic back problem for years, first feeling my back 'go' one day many seasons before when I touched my toes at State training. The feeling I felt that morning at Homebush as I lowered the weights was nothing new. Funnily enough, it didn't feel like a bad one. I was able to straighten up and move reasonably well. For two weeks I set aside

A captain deep in thought. The campaign ahead was both long and challenging.

the gym and weights work, confident I would come good. But the problem seemed only to get worse, my back tighter and more painful by the day, pain shooting down my left leg. I visited the Aussie team physio Errol Allcott and he had a look at me and without too much fussing around sent me straight on for scans and specialists' attention.

I won't go into the full, gory details. Suffice to say that the scans revealed that a piece from the bottom disc in my back had broken away and was sitting on, or very close to, the nerve that ran down my left leg. Complete rest was advised, yet after two weeks, nothing had improved. I had an epidural and another two weeks rest; no change. So they put me into St Luke's Hospital at The Cross and performed a 'partial dissectomy', to remove the errant piece of disc. I was out of the running for the planned Sri Lankan tour, and only an even money bet for India in October. But I wasn't going to give it away without a fight. I had the operation on a Wednesday, and by the following Monday was in the pool, swimming.

I worked hard on my rehabilitation program. A struggling two or three laps in the pool became 10, then 20, then 30 as I gradually made progress. With my left leg still trailing badly in strength and conditioning, I added some bike riding. But at the first State practice I attended I really despaired of my chances of making it for the campaign in India. I tried running for the first time, and felt bloody awful. My leg was so weak—I just couldn't push off it. But I persevered as the clock ticked away towards the tour. As the time neared, everyone seemed keen for me to go, and I was encouraged by the fact that I was at least making (slow) progress.

After a good deal of soul-searching, I made my decision. I would make myself available for the tour. Sydney's spring had arrived, and facing perhaps the most challenging cricketing year of my life, I was 65 per cent fit—and off to face the rigours of a six-week Indian campaign.

It was not exactly the start to the year that I had planned. But as I had told the media looking towards season 1996–97: 'The challenges are there for us'. Indeed they were, and it was time to get going ... even if the skipper was a little below par.

CHAPTER 2
INDIA
DOWN AND OUT IN DELHI

It is not without irony that the Indian campaign of late 1996 proved to be a good deal better for me personally than it was for Australian cricket. I went away well below peak fitness. I had done hardly any running, and was still troubled by the lack of strength in my left leg. Overall, I was significantly underdone. But I came home healthy and strong—not far off 100 per cent fitness again—and having made a reasonably solid personal contribution to the tour, including my first one-day century. For me, the gamble I took in going had paid off.

I'll never forget the first training session in Bombay, though. Errol Alcott put us through some short sprints and I was so far behind, I was almost out of sight. I've never been the quickest bloke in the side, but it really hit home to me then in Bombay's steamy heat how much work I had to do. However, day by day I did it, building strength back into my leg and lungs—rebuilding some personal fitness in the midst of a team in which just about all of us were struggling for form.

The tour provided a brief, undistinguished chapter in Australia's recent cricket history. As a team we were scratchy and below our best, performing at about 70 percent of ability in my estimation. We lost a Test match to the Indians for the first time in 15 years (in three days) and five out of five completed one-day games. After six weeks, we came home winless, despite having had opportunities to win just about every game we played. Teams that are fit and ready have the in-built 'edge' required for them to win the tight ones. We were new to the season and lacked that edge. We lacked our usual killer mentality. The players reacted to the way the tour was set up—just one Test, disappointing travel itinerary and venues, and no matches in

The men behind the scenes—Errol Alcott and Geoff Marsh. An early training session in India.

Calcutta, Bombay or Madras. Minds tended to wander from the job at hand to what lay ahead—to the campaign against the West Indies that we were soon to face back home in Australia.

We even trained that way—like a team getting ready for something down the track rather than being honed for the job at hand. The emphasis was on fitness rather than skill. The spirit in the side was generally good, but we sometimes didn't do the little things that you need to do on a tour. Now and then there was some tardiness in things like getting to training—the small signs of a team not yet fully wound up. We looked like a side suffering from early-season rust.

It was never going to be easy. We were missing Shane Warne after the operation he'd had on his spinning finger, and as someone wrote perceptively early in the tour, the absence of David Boon and Craig McDermott from the equation instantly created an 8000-run, 500-wicket hole in the side. It was a hole we had to work towards filling.

My own tour was reasonably encouraging considering the physical battle I was having. I made 27 and 37 in the Test, which was only average—but not without some promise in view of the long haul ahead—and scored 300 runs in six one-day games. Yet we fumbled opportunities most of the way. Bangalore, where I scored my hundred, was a good example. I had spoken to the guys at length before the one-day game (against India) about lifting our standards and getting out there and showing people what a good cricket team we were ... because we *were* a good team. After a real struggle we got ourselves into a position to win the game, battling to 215 on a slowish wicket on a big ground. Then we had them 8-164 with 47 balls to go. But in front of a seething crowd stirred up by some earlier petulance from Indian skipper Mohammed Azharuddin, we let them off the hook. Tailenders Javagal Srinath and Anil Kumble combined in an unbeaten half-century partnership for the ninth wicket and delivered an unlikely victory. Srinath made a quick 35 or so at the end—about the only time he'd done that in a couple of years. It was the way it was over there—we *let* sides do things to us that would never normally have happened.

It was an explosive match, with the crowd of 55,000 threatening to get out of control on several occasions. Azharuddin's performance when given out lbw to Jason Gillespie was highly irresponsible. The Indian skipper left no doubt he reckoned he'd been hard done by—dragging his feet and alternately looking at his bat and then the umpire. The signals were clear, and sections of the crowd began to bombard the field with bottles and rubbish. I called the team to the centre of the ground and the umpires diplomatically ordered a drinks break. Things eventually quietened down to an extent—only to flare again later following a controversial run-out in which the batsman Jadeja collided with Glenn McGrath. Finally it all finished in an atmosphere of great joy and celebration for the locals with the Indians somehow constructing their victory against the odds. It was another example of us being fractionally out of tune. At full throttle we would have emphatically nailed such a match. It was a disappointing result. I honestly believe that the victory we should have achieved there could have turned the tour around to an extent.

India and South Africa both beat us twice in the triangular Titan Cup one-day

The Feroze Shah Kotla Stadium in Delhi—with its powder-dry wicket.

tournament. Well beaten by the South Africans in the opening game (our 7-219 never looking anywhere near enough), we were highly competitive in the other three games—but still unable to deliver. In the final game against the Indians we put together 284, and while looking like a team getting closer to form, they sailed past us with 6-289. For what lay ahead I was encouraged by history. Against the West Indians in 1995 we lost four out of five limited-overs matches—then beat the Windies in the Tests, on their home turf in the Caribbean.

Travelling through India, we seemed to be on the wrong foot most of the way. In the lead-up to the one-off Test we played only one game, at the end of a six-hour train trip up to a place called Patiala. We lost the first day (of three) to rain, then batted and bowled okay when we finally got on. But it was really only a light workout, less than we would have hoped before a Test. In Patiala we were guests at a colourful evening of traditional dance and local music held in the grounds of the Maharaja of Patiala's palace, just one lingering memory from an extraordinary country of contrasts.

The one-off Test in Delhi was a strange one, played at the Feroze Shah Kotla Stadium on a wicket that was either under-prepared or over-prepared ... whatever it was, the result being a powder-dry pitch on which balls were running along the ground on the first day. Over the whole place hung a haze of pollution, creating a thick and uncomfortable atmosphere. The Stadium is not an appealing place. The dominating grandstand, with its incomplete top tier, broken windows and exposed wiring, is an ugly sight. The wicket, though, was our main concern ...

Even the Indian players were apologising for its state. I had never seen one like it in my career in Test cricket—and it will suit me fine if I never see another. About

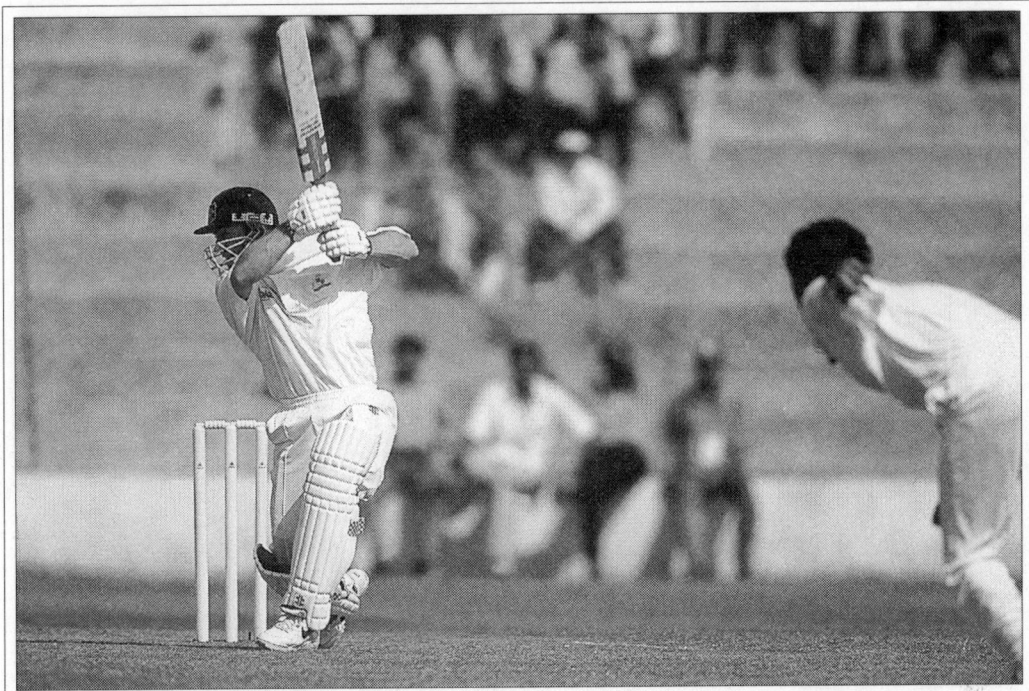
Michael Slater, en route to 44 in Delhi.

the kindest thing I can say about Delhi's pitch is that it was unsuitable for Test match cricket. And about the only thing we did right was to win the toss. Yet having done that we failed to come to terms with the wicket, and the 182 we scratched together was never going to be enough. If we'd managed 300 or so we would have been very tough to beat, with the Indians to bat last on a declining pitch—although despite its appearance the pitch never really did break up. As it was, they showed us how to bat on such a wicket—opener Mongia in particular with his 152—and we were never on track to win the game. India played the sort of cricket that was required in the conditions—calm, tight and calculated—and they beat us fair and square by seven wickets. Their performance under new skipper Sachin Tendulkar was a highly promising signpost for the cricketing future in India.

But a one-off Test is an unsatisfying event at the best of times. For the loser, there is no chance for redemption, and for the winner, no chance to prove that the win didn't come into the category of 'fluke' or 'good fortune'. But that's the way it was in that crowded year—and we had to live with it. Richie Benaud was to pose the question later: 'Why was the Australian cricket team sent to India to play a one-off Test match without proper practice and lead-up to what was always likely to be a difficult assignment?'

We missed Warnie a great deal in that match ... and on the tour generally. He brings so many pluses to a tour—on and off the field. He's a funny bloke to have around the change room—a lifter of spirits—and he's a big wicket taker out in the middle. The conditions in Delhi would have been much to his liking—that dusty, turning wicket on which he would have got bounce and bite. Our two spinners,

Mark Waugh kicks up dust and feels the heat as Australia slides towards defeat in the one-off Test in Delhi.

Bradley Hogg and Peter McIntyre, did their utmost to fill the gap, despite their relative inexperience at that level. It's no reflection on either of them to make the point that neither is at Shane Warne standard at this stage. Who is? Because of their slower pace through the air and off the wicket, neither applied the sort of pressure that India's Kumble, Joshi and Kapoor were able to maintain as they fizzed the ball through. Anil Kumble bowled particularly beautifully, varying trajectory, pace and bounce throughout—and reaped a reward of nine wickets.

Ian Healy especially missed Shane Warne throughout the campaign. The pair of them seem to have been a double-act for such a long time—Heals taking the catches, making the stumpings, cajoling ... encouraging. It's stating the obvious to say that the Australian cricket team is a lesser entity without Shane Warne, whether it's in Bombay, Brisbane or Birmingham.

Having said all that, and accepting that it was a difficult and disappointing tour for us, I never felt any hint that we were seriously down and out over there. It was early days, only the first kilometre or two of the marathon. I knew we had the players and the in-built team quality to do a hell of a lot better in the long haul that lay ahead. I offer no excuses. We should have played better than we did. We deserved a rap over the knuckles, and we certainly got that from various quarters. Journos like the *Herald's* Peter Roebuck sure didn't miss us in their criticism. We hadn't performed well, and we had to accept that. But I'm sure they knew, as we did, that better days lay ahead.

The loss of the Test inside four days prompted a strong reaction from our new

Sachin Tendulkar and the spoils of victory. It was Tendulkar's first win as India's captain.

coach Geoff Marsh, who had been quietly and thoroughly easing himself into the job in those first two tours of Sri Lanka and India in the 1996–97 season. After the Test, Geoff hit the headlines back home with his comments to the media about a perceived 'millionaires' attitude at training. This is what he said:

'It comes down to hunger, doesn't it? I hope the players are hurting, because this was a Test match. I can't say they're all hurting, but I hope they are. You can look for all the excuses in the world why these blokes didn't play well, but they're professional sportsmen. It's an excuse as far as I'm concerned to say it was our first hit-out. We played poorly. One area I've been disappointed in is their training. I think they train like millionaires instead of getting down to business. These guys are professional cricketers, but they've lacked concentration in the nets.'

Geoff's comments coincided with discussion in the press back home on the subject of whether players should be paid more—but in reality his 'millionaires' line had nothing whatsoever to do with money. It merely reflected his belief that we weren't working as hard on our batting as he would have liked. It was a comment about *attitude*. The 'millionaires' line was subsequently taken and used in many different ways. Basically Geoff's words were no more than those of a concerned coach urging his team to put its head down and work harder. I'm sure the two trips away were a valuable foundation builder for Geoff Marsh, bringing him closer to the men who were going to be his charges in the months ahead and giving him an increasingly clear sense of his own role.

In the wash-up I was glad I made the trip to India—for two reasons. I would not have enjoyed the team having a bad tour, and then me coming back in as captain. At least I experienced the lows and disappointment of losing along with the rest of the boys. We also learnt plenty about Indian conditions and Indian life, which will be helpful for the series that lies ahead in 1998. In a way, the Indian experience of late '96 was good motivation for us, steeling us to recapture the winning feeling against the West Indies. We'd had our wake-up call, and we could fight back together.

The real bonus for me was that the personal gamble I took in making myself available had paid off. I went away below par, but came home much improved physically—ready, I reckoned, for any challenge that lay ahead. At the airport press conference I looked ahead to the series against the West Indies, South Africa and England and told the media: 'A pass mark is three wins out of three. I believe this Windies series will be a real catalyst for the next two.'

It was exactly the way I saw it.

CHAPTER 3

THE HOME SERIES:
THE WEST INDIES AND PAKISTAN
Reflections on a Long Hot Summer

The first entry in my notebook as we headed towards our re-match with the West Indies in the Aussie summer of 1996–97 is brief, and to the point. *Major concerns—Ambrose with ball, Lara with bat.*
To that thought, I added the following:
Both teams have had average preparations. West Indies poor start to tour, Australia poor tour of India.

That about summed it up as we squared our shoulders for the long haul ahead: a full five-Test series against the Windies and the challenge of a three-cornered one-day tournament against two of the best teams in the world in Pakistan and the West Indies.

At the Dockside Hotel in Brisbane before the first Test I had a good yarn to the Windies' Courtney Walsh (captain), Clive Lloyd (manager) and Malcolm Marshall (coach). Each one of them seemed genuinely keen to keep good relations going between the two teams, and I was happy about that. It was my wish too.

My captain's log, brief observations jotted down in quieter moments, tells the unfolding story of the weeks that followed:

First Test, Brisbane

Wicket looks flat, but more grass and moisture than in previous years. Go out to toss prepared to bat … because we know they'll bowl. Lose toss.

First session crucial. We're 1-82 at lunch and very happy with that. Ricky Ponting takes attack to Windies and sets the scene for a good day for us. Our 5-192 at one stage ends up at 5-282 at stumps. Great day. Heals kicks on for a superb 161. We all know Heals has it in him, but I don't think any of us believed he could play that well. Make 479.

West Indies' hope...our problem—the enigmatic Brian Lara, a controversial figure in the Test series that unfolded in Australia's summer.

Bowl them out for 277, three runs short of follow-on. For four hours of the day they dominate, with Carl Hooper and Shivnarine Chanderpaul in control, adding 172. Then we rip through them after tea, taking seven wickets. It's nightmare decision-time again. Decide not to enforce follow-on, as wicket is still very good and lead is only 202. With two days to go my belief is that scoring 150–200 runs will be easier in third innings than in fourth. The situation is much the same as it had been against the Poms two years before, except that on that occasion our lead had been substantially more. This time a lead of 202 is not enough. The wicket is good now, and I've got blokes like Shane Warne and Michael Bevan in the ranks. My thinking is

No room for doubt here. The Australians rise as one man as Glenn McGrath bowls Shivnarine Chanderpaul for 14 in the second innings of the first Test.

very much that the best thing is to bowl last on this wicket.

We make 6-217, leaving them 420 to get off 120 overs. They are 1-90 at stumps on the fourth night. I believe we are well placed, although not certain to win. I can't see them making the runs unless Lara cuts loose.

First session of the final day proves crucial. We dismiss Lara in the first hour, and get Hooper just before lunch. There can only be one winner now, although a draw is still a possibility.

Michael Bevan proves to be a very useful weapon and finishes with 3-43. We bowl them out for 296, clinching it in the final hour and win the Test with 14 overs left. Fantastic! The margin is 123 runs, and we lose only 16 wickets to their 20. It's a great way to start summer. The victory anthem in the change rooms is a beauty.

Post-mortem

We played five days of tough Test cricket. Conditions were not always in our favour, especially on day one. We battled through tough times, taking the vital wicket or putting together the valuable stand just when we needed it. Winning that first Test of a series is always crucial—especially against the West Indies. Four years ago we were denied winning the Brisbane Test by just two wickets when the Windies held out for a draw on the last day. I believe we would have won the series if we'd taken that Test.

Ian Healy celebrates the moment as he reaches his century in Brisbane. Healy's 161 not out was the key event in a decisive Australian victory.

Afterwards, I failed to win any popularity polls when I conveyed the news that we were flying straight to Sydney the night of the final day's play. The second Test was to begin in two days' time and my belief was that we had to immediately focus on that, rather than celebrating the Test we had just won. This quick exit, and subsequent denial of the usual celebration night, was a break with tradition. It was a tough call—I feel that the players always deserve to celebrate a victory. But I believed we had to do it. I reckoned if we could win in Sydney, then we would just about have the trophy in our grasp. And I also believed that we needed to get cracking straightaway. The last thing we wanted was to have a good win in Brisbane then blow it away in the Sydney Test.

Despite the victory, at the back of my mind were thoughts for Michael Slater, my opening partner in some 34 Test matches. As an opening batsman you get to forge a special partnership with the bloke at the other end, especially when you've been together for a good while. Slats and I had that. I admit that I was very disappointed when I heard the news that Michael had been dropped. With six Test series under his belt and a Test average of 47, he had been a considerable achiever. The fact that he *was* dropped showed the depth that exists in Australian cricket. I knew the reasons behind it, but the realisation that he wasn't going to be there still came as a shock to me, and a real kick in the guts to Michael. Knowing him as I do, I could see the pain in his eyes when he was told he wasn't in the side. I think it had an effect on everyone. But I felt very deeply for Slater. I know how much Michael loves playing for Australia. I also know that he's too damn good a player *not* to come back. With that footwork (probably more foot movement than any other batsman in modern times) and that eye, he'll be back for sure. And knowing Slats, he'll be back even stronger.

Second Test, Sydney

(EXTRACTED FROM MY CAPTAIN'S LOG)

The SCG is not the West Indies' favourite ground. In recent times, however, it hasn't been ours either. I'm sitting here thinking that we haven't won a Test in Sydney since my first Test against the Windies back in January 1989. In the last six Tests we've played in Sydney, we've lost to Pakistan and South Africa and had draws with England (twice), the West Indies and India. This time too, there's an X-factor. Two Michael Jackson concerts on the SCG have done some damage to both wicket and outfield. There has been late football on the ground too, with the Swans making the AFL finals. The wear and tear factor has been high, the outfield below what it can be and the wicket dry and bare.

We win a vital toss (phew!), and bat. At one stage we're 5-130, but Heals and Greg Blewett are playing well. The tail wags very well and we make 331. Even Glenn McGrath makes 24. He comes in at lunch on day two and comments to the guys: 'I was going to call for my cap'. It gets a good laugh, considering Glenn's reputation in the batting department, which is not exactly sky high. Glenn's 24 is later rated one of the modern

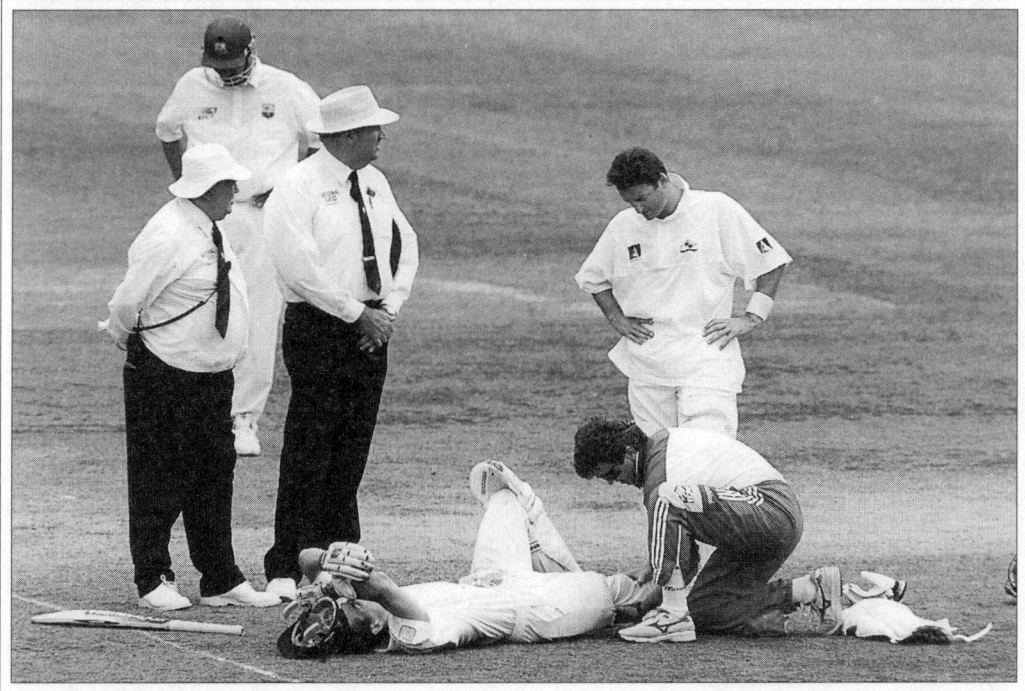

Tragedy strikes the Australians in Sydney. Matthew Elliott (78 not out) is down and out after his spectacular second innings collision with Mark Waugh. A knee cartilage torn, Elliott's home summer of such promise is virtually over.

Was it a juggling act?...or was it a catch? Skipper Taylor *finally* has the ball in his hands after his incredible hands-knees-and-boompsa-daisy catch of Carl Hooper in Sydney. Ian Healy can't quite believe it.

wonders of the world, but the fact is that he has batted well, surprising us—for sure—and maybe even himself. I think it'll be a long time before he forgets the straight drive he played off Ian Bishop. Glenn finally falls for 24, lbw to Jimmy Adams while not playing a shot—a disappointing ending to a classic Glenn McGrath innings.

We bowl them out for 304, with Glenn getting four and Warnie three. It's the first time they've topped 300 against us since the last Test in Perth in the 1992–93 series.

The second innings is both good news and bad. We bat well enough to be able to declare at 4-312. But there is tragedy for Matthew Elliott, who is showing real signs of being a superb Test player as he compiles 78. At that point in his innings he collides with Mark Waugh in mid-pitch, leaving Matty in agony with a torn knee cartilage. It was a freakish moment, showing what an unpredictable game cricket can be. Carted from the field he now faces his greatest test—to fight his way back. I sense that if he does get back he's going to be around for quite a while, because the achievement of winning back a spot in the face of the challenge of guys like Blewett, Hayden and Slater will mean that he wants it really badly.

We set them 340 to win. They're 0-30 at stumps, and the scene is set for a classic final day.

The day does not disappoint. We start with three quick wickets: Campbell, Lara and Samuels. The Lara dismissal (caught Healy) causes waves, as we are to find out later. They are 3-40 when Glenn McGrath drops a caught and bowled off Chanderpaul. He goes on to smash us for 50 off only 38 balls, partnering Hooper who is in a similar frame of mind. The last over before lunch and it's 3-152. At that moment Shane Warne produces a ball that only he can bowl—a huge 'turner' which spins back about a metre from outside off to bowl Chanderpaul middle and leg for 71. It's the turning point ... literally.

At lunch that day we learn the news that Brian Lara has been down at our room yelling at our coach and manager, and that some people at the ground (notably Michael Holding on Channel Nine) had doubts about his dismissal—believing that an edge from Lara hadn't carried to Ian Healy. In his emotional outburst, Lara, still in his pads, announced that Healy was no longer welcome in the West Indies dressing room and that he believed we were cheats.

It was an over-the-top reaction which later brought a letter of apology to Geoff Marsh and myself from West Indies manager Clive Lloyd, which I thought was a fantastic gesture. The disappointing thing was that there was no apology from Brian Lara. Nothing written, nothing face to face. Now, that's never going to worry Ian Healy or the Australian cricket team too much, but in the years to come I think it might worry Brian Lara when he matures a little more. He's a very fine player who's going to be around for a long time, but I think his outburst in Sydney might be something he'll look back on and wished that he'd handled very differently.

We all make mistakes, and sooner or later you've got to stand up for them. I remember Shane Warne making a *big* mistake in Johannesburg in 1994 when he bowled Andrew Hudson around his legs for 60—then went right off the deep end and gave Hudson a big verbal blast. Three or four months later Warnie realised deep down what a bad job he'd done on himself. He was big enough, and man enough, to admit that he was wrong. I hope that one day Brian Lara can do the same thing.

In my view the replay shows that Lara was quite correctly given out caught behind. And if the catch *hadn't* carried I know that Ian Healy wouldn't have claimed it. Even if it hadn't carried (and it did!) there is no way in the world that any player, and especially a senior player, should be storming into the dressing rooms and making the sort of allegations that Brian Lara made. We've all had tough decisions, and generally they seem to come when you're struggling a bit ... a rough lbw, a caught behind when you haven't nicked it. That's the game of cricket.

After lunch Carl Hooper stands as our last stumbling block, and as chance has it, I bring about his dismissal in a moment I won't forget. I catch him at slip—eventually—off Michael Bevan ... via Healy's leg, my ribs, hands, hat and finally foot ... while lying on the ground. In all honesty it was a bit of a stuff up—and if it turned out to be a classic catch, well, it shouldn't have been. After fumbling around trying to get the darned thing under control I *did* mean to kick it, although I had no clue where it might go. I was just hoping to keep the ball in the air so that Heals could catch it. As it turned out it flopped back into my hands—and I finally took the catch.

With Hooper gone, we go right on with it and close them down for 215—a second successive comprehensive victory, by 125 runs. Bevan finishes with two wickets, McGrath three and Warne four. Warnie was brilliant on that last day, notwithstanding the pressure that Hooper and Chanderpaul applied. I doubt there'll be a better ball this summer than the one that whipped out of the rough, bowled Chanderpaul—and turned the match. We're two up ... and very happy to be there.

Third Test, Melbourne

Melbourne was always going to be one of the tough wickets to play the West Indies on. It's renowned for bounce which is both plentiful and unpredictable—and unfortunately the wicket for this Test was no different to what we had seen previously. The wicket actually *looked* very good—but played worse than some of those in the past. By the third day in this Test it was decidedly nasty to bat on. When you're playing the likes of Curtly Ambrose (at his best in this Test) and Walsh, Bishop and Benjamin—blokes who can hit that awkward length—things can get pretty nasty. When balls start bouncing at shoulder height, then the next one goes through at ankle level, it gets very difficult to play.

If this is the Melbourne Test...it must be Christmas season...and the snappers get into the spirit.

The Melbourne Test had more than a few things in common with the third Test in Trinidad during the 1995 series. At both places we had the chance to clinch the series. And at both places we struck a difficult wicket on which we were competitive and in a position at one stage to go on and win ... only to get beaten comprehensively. In Melbourne we made 219—50 or 60 less than we would have liked—then had them 9-233 at stumps on the second day, with Glenn McGrath striking back for us. That was a darned good bowling effort, considering we lost Jason Gillespie with injury in only the third over of the game. They ended up with 255, so led us by 36. Back in the change room we figured that if we could knock up a lead of around 200 we'd have a great chance of winning the game. As it turned out they bowled us out for 122, with Ambrose getting four wickets and Walsh and Benjamin three each. They knocked off the necessary runs for the loss of four wickets and suddenly the game was over—and the headlines were 'Massacre at MCG' and 'Calypso Kings'. From 2–0 and going strongly, we were 2–1 and nursing our wounds.

I missed out in both innings—and that was disappointing. I made seven in the first innings when one from Ambrose hit me in the midriff and dropped onto the stumps. In the second, I was there for an hour or so, had scored 10 and was just beginning to feel that I'd go on and make some vital runs when I edged one off Courtney Walsh. So far, it had been a reasonably disappointing series personally—40 and 30 in Brisbane, 20-odd and 17 in Sydney, and now Melbourne. I had made a start each time, but not gone on with it. I was disappointed I hadn't made a 50 yet. I was a *little* concerned about my own form, but not overly worried. I was confident I could get out of it. And in my chat with the media after the game I was pretty buoyant. Two of the wickets so far had been suited to the West Indies (Brisbane and

Whooo! The celebrations unfold behind as skipper Taylor is on his way, bowled by Ambrose for 7. First innings, third Test, Melbourne.

Melbourne) and we had squared accounts with them on those, plus picked up the Sydney Test. A game score of 2–1 wasn't looking too bad at all.

It was at about that time that the media focus on me began to intensify. There were headlines along the lines of 'Tubby's Drought' and 'Mark Taylor's Year of Living Dangerously' which recorded that I had made 264 runs at 24 in my last five Test matches. It was a pretty narrow focus, and fairly misleading—taking in a dead-rubber Test against Sri Lanka, then the one-off Test against India. Before that I'd had a very successful 1995–96 summer, probably ranking as one of our top two or three batsmen of the campaigns against Pakistan and Sri Lanka. Bill Lawry chipped in with an opinion: 'I don't think he [Taylor] has any problems because he is a winning captain. It was different with me.'

The One-Dayers

The hard fact of it was my hope of lifting myself out of my batting rut did not eventuate in what was a disappointing one-day campaign for Australia against the West Indies and Pakistan. A pattern developed—I'd make a start, then as soon as I tried to accelerate the pace there'd be a slip up, and I'd be out. In the first game in Sydney (v Pakistan) I was run out for 11, in the second in Brisbane I was gone just when I was settling in on a good wicket (we made 281).

The series produced its usual mix of volatile and dramatic moments. The Sydney

Christmas in Melbourne—and Matthew Hayden, Mark and Jack Taylor and Justin Langer gather under the tree.

crowd was on its worst behaviour for the New Year's Day match against Pakistan. There were pitch invasions, some 87 arrests and later some large and lingering headlines when it was revealed that a group of North Sydney rugby league stars had run into bother, with their skipper Jason Taylor being escorted from the ground by the police. We lost there, then lost in Brisbane too when our 281 was insufficient against Brian Lara's 102 and Carl Hooper's 110.

On a terrible wicket in Hobart, Pakistan beat us 149 to 120, and at this point the realisation was starting to sink in that we were likely to miss the World Series play-offs for the first time in 17 years. The media focus was now intense … especially on me. At the conference after the Hobart game I was asked whether I had given any consideration to standing down from the last couple of one-day games, and going back to play a scheduled Shield match. I probably made a mistake when I told the gathering that I *had* considered that option. Well, the fact was, I had. But I had rejected the idea pretty quickly. There was big cricket ahead—the fourth Test in Adelaide, the fifth in Perth. I figured that going back and playing a Shield game against some lesser quality attack was not what I needed. I needed to hang in there and try and get myself out of the rut by playing against the sort of bowlers I was going to face in the big games. My frankness led to headlines such as 'Test Skipper Considers Return to Shield Cricket', probably adding a little uncertainty to the mix at a time when I had made up my mind very firmly to press on.

The one-dayer in Perth was about the last straw. Our batting had been poor through the summer, but we did a good job there, making 267 for 7 (Mark Waugh

92). It was a good score and for much of the way we had the Windies down and out. But we let them off the hook when we dropped Brian Lara a couple of times and he punished us spectacularly, scoring 40 runs off the last 24 balls. Next day we read assessments like: 'Brilliant Brian Lara yesterday force-fed Australia with the shattering message that they have become a cricket team who can lose a game from anywhere'.

We were out of the World Series finals—and it's never nice to be captain of a side that misses out on something. We were hurting, but we regrouped and went to Melbourne and beat Pakistan there, showing that rumours of our demise as a one-day cricket team were somewhat exaggerated. The one-dayers of early '97 were a frustrating experience for the team, and for me personally. At different times we were in a position to win just about every game we played, but we kept letting them slip through our fingers.

The good thing that came out of us missing the finals was that it gave us all three or four days off—a chance to go home, put the cricket gear away and think about what we had done so far ... and what still remained to be done. Every one of us knew that the Adelaide Test was the Big One. Perth [the fifth Test] was going to be tough. The West Indies love Perth and we knew how hard it would be there. Being at home while the one-day finals were being played gave us all the chance to refocus, to think about that 'extra five percent' which could make the difference between winning and losing in Adelaide.

The following excerpt is taken from my notes written on the plane from Perth to Melbourne after the fourth one-dayer:

> Changes have occurred to both the team and to me—notably that we are now on a serious losing streak ... and I'm not making any runs. We have now lost our last five games (one Test, four one-dayers) and the fact is that we have not scored enough runs in either form of the game, with yours truly as one of the chief offenders. I believe our batsmen have lost confidence in themselves; we are now looking for the ball to do things rather than getting out there and hitting it. Of all the batsmen only Stuart Law and Mark Waugh look to be in good form, with Steve Waugh and Greg Blewett not looking too bad. Michael Bevan and I are the main strugglers at the moment. But I won't accept that all is lost. I have always believed as a batsman that you are only one innings away from being back in form. For me, that might be my next time out in the middle ...

My thoughts went back to my first tour as an Australian player, the Ashes campaign of 1989, when I spent the first month batting terribly—with a top score of 11. In the second last game before the first Test, against Somerset, I played a very poor cut shot which came high off the bat and floated towards the fieldsman in the gully. I don't know what happened then. But somehow he lost sight of the ball and didn't even get a hand to it. From what should have been a regulation catch, I picked up two runs. I went on to make 98 and 58 in that match. All of a sudden I was seeing the ball better and getting my feet into position quickly. From the moment of that dropped catch I went on to have an excellent series as we beat the

Poms 4-0. The tour was the turning point of my entire career—and when I think about it, the whole thing swung on that catch missed in the gully at Somerset. It happened once for me. I knew it could happen again ...

In trying to find an answer to the batting slump (my own and the team's) I have come up with two answers. The first lies in the continuing slide in the standard of pitches around the country. An easy excuse from a batsman struggling for form, you might say? Well, it's a bit more than that. In many conversations I've had with prominent people in the game there's general agreement that formerly first class wickets, such as Sydney's and Melbourne's, are becoming more and more uneven in their bounce every year. I believe this is the reason that most top order players in all three sides this summer are struggling, with the majority of runs scored by middle order players who face a ball that has become older, with the bounce therefore a little more consistent.

The second reason for our batting problems centres on a lack of self-confidence and self-belief among players in our team. An increase in the standard of bowling we are facing is one factor; a fear of being dropped in the face of competition from so many good young players is another. Players have to confront this anxiety, at all levels of the game at all times. It is the tangible that separates the State player from the Australian player. Good players find a way of handling it; others fall back to the next level. One thing never changes—it is always up to the individual player to confront this reality of the game and make what he can of it.

I am buoyed by the memories of what happened after we lost the third Test in Trinidad in 1995. As with this Melbourne Test we were positioned to win that game. But we lost it, badly and suddenly—just as happened in Melbourne. But after Trinidad we regrouped to win the next Test of the series. That's exactly the plan this time, and I am sure there is the quality in the side to do it. We must overcome our batting woes, however ... especially me.

Fourth Test, Adelaide

Looking back, the only thing that could have been better in Adelaide would have been for Mark Taylor to make some runs. I managed only 11 and that was disappointing, because everything else went absolutely superbly.

There were tough decisions to be made before the game. I went to Adelaide honestly expecting to play three fast bowlers. The Adelaide wickets I'd seen in the past always required three quicks and my initial gut feeling was to include Paul Reiffel and leave Michael Bevan out. But down there I was getting a lot of advice from people telling me that the wicket was now not conducive to fast bowling, and that it was the spinners who were getting the wickets. It was a good wicket with just a tinge of grass on it—very flat, and very even-looking. I had a good look at it and reckoned that three quick bowlers weren't going to do any more damage than two. An added ingredient was my doubt about Reiffel going the distance—he had been battling

Michael Bevan beams from a cluster of team-mates after dismissing Jimmy Adams for a duck (caught Mark Waugh), second innings, fourth Test, Adelaide.

injuries and was only just back in cricket. So, after due deliberation, we went the other way, picking Bevan at seven and naming just the two quicks—Glenn McGrath and Andrew Bichel. A gamble? Well, maybe... but it couldn't have worked out better.

The plan was to win the toss and bat first. It was about the only thing that didn't go right (apart from my batting struggle). I lost the toss, and they batted. But by halfway through the first day on one of the best wickets I've seen in Adelaide in the last five or six years, the match was gone for the Windies—and the Frank Worrell Trophy was in our grasp.

Truly excellent bowling, particularly from Glenn McGrath up front with the new ball, and then the spinners, Warnie and Bevo, destroyed the Windies for 130. Michael Bevan—our 'late thought'—took 4-31. By stumps we were 2-139 and on our way. At the close of play on day two we were 5-434, with Matthew Hayden contributing 125, then the next day we extended to 517 (Blewett 99, Bevan not out 85, Mark Waugh 82).

Michael Bevan will probably never get a closer encounter with the glorious uncertainty of cricket than he did in this match. In the second innings, with Australian domination of this Test absolute, he took six more wickets (for 82). An unbeaten 80, 10 wickets, named man of the match—what a game it was for him, and what a timeless example of the ebb and flow of the game of cricket. We had the Windies 6-154 by the close of play on day three and wrapped it up the next day, their last four wickets adding another 50.

It was a fantastic result for Australian cricket. Four years before we had lost the corresponding Test by one run, and that had cost us the series against the West Indies. Now we were home safe with the Frank Worrell Trophy in under four days of a Test we had dominated from the first ball to last. The feeling was one of enormous satisfaction, and sheer relief.

The aftermath of a Test victory—and especially one like *that*—is an intriguing time. The media are there pretty quickly after the game, expecting to witness great scenes of celebration and joy. And when they come into the room I find that you do put on your big smiley face and pretend you're really happy... and of course you *are*. But my preference after a game like that is to sit for an hour or so and just soak it up. Many things run through your mind. In the dressing room that afternoon my mind went back four years, to Craig McDermott being given out by Darrell Hair caught behind off Courtney Walsh, just two runs short of victory. Now we had beaten the same side by 383 on the same ground. We'd all worked bloody hard for that and there was a deep, almost numbing, feeling of satisfaction.

Through all the celebrations though (and they were long and loud!), something nagged. We had retained the Trophy, and wore the unofficial tag of 'world's best', but just down the track was a dead-rubber match against an opponent who was hurting badly after what we'd done to them in Adelaide. And, to make it more difficult, it was to be held in Perth, where the Windies love to play...

Fifth Test, Perth

Cricket has a habit of bringing you crashing back to earth at times. And so it was in a Perth heatwave, in this fifth Test of the summer—played on a pitch that was dry and cracking before the first ball was bowled, looking certain to fall apart.

We got smashed—I can't put it more plainly than that—and my bad trot continued. My first innings dismissal (for 2) sort of summed up my season. After we had won the toss and batted (which seemed to me the only choice), Matthew Hayden was gone second or third ball when he nicked one to slips. I was there with Greg Blewett, trying to dig in, and Greg hit one nicely off the middle, behind point. The ball was travelling, but flew straight into Chanderpaul's hands. I hesitated, just for an instant; both Greg and I probably reckoned it was heading for three or four when it left the bat. Then I'm off and running, and Chanderpaul's throw comes in as straight as an arrow a fraction above the stumps. Jimmy Adams flicks off the bails and I'm out... by a couple of inches.

I watched the replay on screen as I walked off. I didn't throw the bat. I didn't carry on; maybe deep down by now I was resigned to the fact that this was going to be a pretty ordinary series for me—that, in football parlance, the ball wasn't destined to bounce the right way. It doesn't mean that I wasn't deeply disappointed. It was that sort of summer. I had missed opportunities all along to break this so-called drought. It seemed that every time I'd gone in with a new, fresh approach I'd found some damned-fool silly way of getting out. Now it had happened again.

Our innings was a struggle, although Mark Waugh batted really well. There were some lazy shots played—one of them was Mark's, bringing about his dismissal—which were indicative of the sort of shots that can creep into a match that is really of no consequence in the big picture. Shots that wouldn't have been played in Adelaide. We made 243.

Is that wicket with a 't'... or a 'd'? Spectators crowd to get an up-close on the dry and cracking wicket which hosted the fifth Australia–West Indies Test at the WACA.

In reply the Windies built a total of 384 on the back of Brian Lara's 132 and Robert Samuels' 76. On a declining pitch, their lead of 141 looked formidable.

We awoke on the third morning not only with a mountain to climb out on the cricket field, but also to be confronted by comments in the media from Lara labelling us sledgers and pointing the finger at his 'mate' Shane Warne as the ringleader. It was very disappointing stuff, and especially so from a senior member of the side like Lara, the West Indian vice-captain. I really think that if a player of his standing had a problem he should have come and seen me as captain—or taken it to Shane Warne, a guy with whom he is supposed to be on very friendly terms. It was a case of a player using the press, and I have to question the motivation behind what Brian had to say.

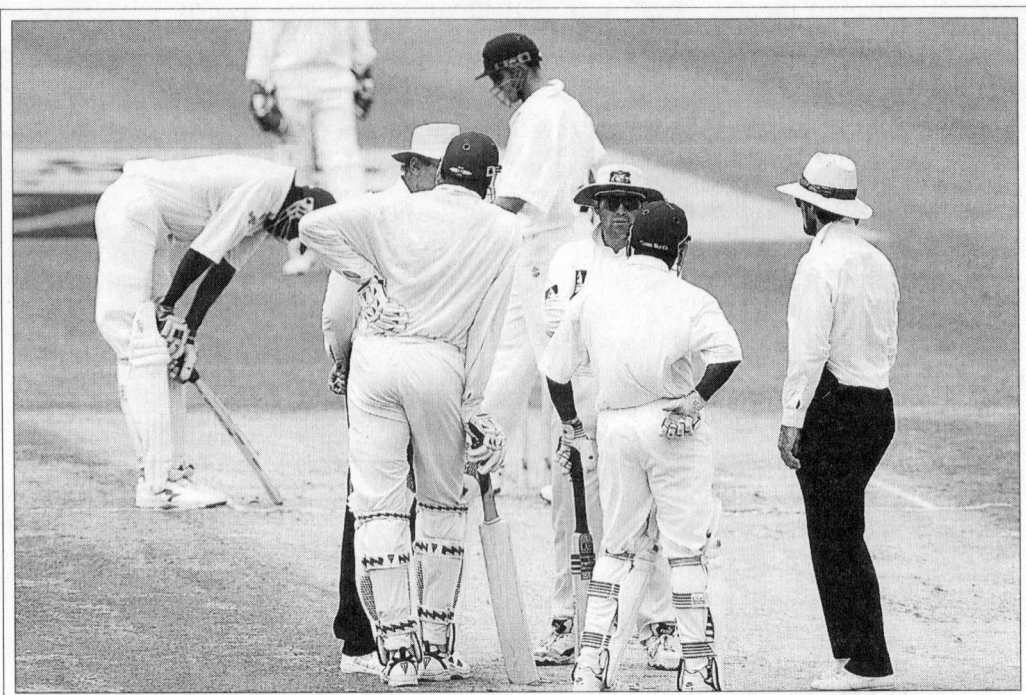

Mark Taylor and Brian Lara (right of group) exchange words on the second day of the fifth Test in Perth. The West Indian vice-captain hit the headlines during the Perth Test when he labelled the Australians 'sledgers'.

The fact is that it had been a pretty tame series; about the only drama had come in Sydney when Lara stormed into our dressing room and called us cheats. Now the bloke had made a century, after a largely disappointing summer for him, and had decided to have a go at us. I seriously question the reasons behind it. I think he was trying to take some pressure off himself and put it back on us. It was disappointing stuff, adding a nasty and unnecessary edge to the end of the series.

The Test match ended on a disappointing note for all of us. We could muster only 194 on a pitch that was deteriorating rapidly and the Windies knocked off the 50-odd needed for victory in just over 10 overs. Greg Blewett was bowled by one that pitched just over halfway down … and ran along the ground. Curtly Ambrose got me for 1, with a good ball that caught the edge. It was with an air of resignation that I walked off the WACA. We remembered tough days against the Windies and we had wanted to nail them 4-1, Steve Waugh as much as anyone—our best player with the bat over the past two or three years. But Steve made a duck and 1 in the game, and as much as we talked about wanting to drive home our advantage, we couldn't do it. We had played our grand final in Adelaide.

At the press conference after the game I fielded many questions about what Brian Lara had said. I called him an 'antagonist' and reckon that was about right. Brian had talked about playing the game 'the right way'. Well, I think that generally the Australian team *does* play the right way. We play it tough, sure—and the odd word is said out in the centre. But in the three years of my captaincy we've only had one guy reported—Joey Angel in my first Test, who was reported for showing dissent at a decision, but it was a fairly minor incident and he received no more than a warning. It was the only time we had had any problem in my time as skipper.

My regret with Brian Lara is that if he *did* have a problem out on the field on the second day when he and Robert Samuels were batting, the right thing for him to have done would have been to come to me, or the umpires, and make his point. That was the right forum. I think if we're going to keep the game the way we all want it, as much as possible has to be solved out on the field—and not debated endlessly (and sometimes inaccurately) or over-emotionally in the press. I don't think the problem was that great in Perth. Brian Lara made a big deal of it because he set out to make a big deal of it. He wanted to take the gloss off Australia winning the Frank Worrell Trophy—and that's what he did.

A strange summer for me, I suppose … an up and down summer. Yet I reminded myself as the dust settled on the Perth Test that we had become only the second side to win consecutive series against the West Indies. In my own personal disappointment at the continuing struggle I was having, that gave me a great deal of joy and solace. There had been disappointments, sure: the snail-slow start in India, Melbourne, and Perth, as well as becoming the first Australian team in 17 seasons to miss out on the one-day finals. But the Big Prize had been won … the Main Game had had its desired result.

And I knew that in the passing of time when I looked back on the Aussie season of 1996–97, I would forget about my run of low scores. I would forget about the fact that we missed out on the one-day finals. Instead, I would remember that we had taken on the might of West Indian cricket through a long, sweltering summer. And won.

CHAPTER 4

SOUTH AFRICA
VICTORY ON THE VELDT

Thoughts from the Captain's Notebook

It's going to be tough, that's the first thing to be said. I know that. We're coming off a hard series against the Windies, but we can't take our foot off the pedal one fraction. The South Africans are like us—they play tough, and they play to win. I want a tour on which the guys enjoy the experience and enjoy each other's company, but one where all the necessary steel is there when the going gets tough. Which it will.

At least there was a plus out of what happened to us in Perth. The early finish meant we all had a couple of extra days at home—days to switch off from the West Indies campaign and to start focusing on South Africa. I'm confident. I know that we have a very, very good cricket side with plenty of options. Warnie had a fairly flat period around Christmas, but he seems to have come out of that. Glenn McGrath was nothing short of superb in the Windies series. I know we have the bowlers to bowl them out and the trick is for us batsmen to tame their attack. I need to get back into form, and Mark and Steve Waugh need to be firing. For the new players like Matty Elliott, Matthew Hayden and Greg Blewett, it's a great challenge and a great chance. And we've got the best wicket-keeper in the world.

Player for player we're stronger than them—but they're at home, and the qualities of toughness and pride will lift them every day they're out on the field. I think South Africa's strength lies in the fact that they're a good all-round side, batting down to eight or nine. There won't be too many cheap wickets for us. If they do have a weakness, it's the fact that they don't have a Steve Waugh-type player or even a Mark Waugh-type player who averages high 40s or 50s in big cricket. All their players average in mid to high 30s in Test cricket which suggests to me that they're good players, but short on someone who's in the habit of making big scores at the right time.

Their bowling will be steady. Allan Donald is their danger man. Watching him in the recent series against India he bowled very well. He generated real pace and got a lot of wickets. Blokes like Lance Klusener and Shaun Pollock will back him up along with Paul Adams, the left-armer with the freakish action who none of us have yet faced. He could be a shock tactic for them. But I think we've got the high quality players in our top six, then down to Heals and Warnie at seven and eight, to combat them.

Australia's strength is that we really haven't got too many weaknesses (notwithstanding what happened in Melbourne and Perth this summer). We've got quality batsmen who have done well over a number of years in Test cricket, and we've got good young players coming through. I think Matthew Elliott has the technique to be a very, very good player for Australia. Matthew Hayden made a century in Adelaide and looked even better in his 40-odd in Perth in the fifth Test. Greg Blewett had a very good series, and will be a good player for years to come. We've got good pacemen in McGrath, Gillespie, Reiffel and Bichel. And we've got Warnie and Michael Bevan, plus Heals to tie it all together. We're strong all round. Not unbeatable, but very, very capable of winning the series if we get the feeling right.

Getting there

For me, the toughest day of these tours is always the one on which you leave. Leaving Judi, William and Jack was as hard as I expected it to be. William's nearly five now and Jack has just turned two. They are both starting to realise where I'm going, and that I'll be away for a while. So, as usual it was tough saying goodbye at the front door. But I'm a cricketer, and touring is part of what we do. Life is short at the top, and you know you're going to be back with the family before too long, so you get on the plane and go.

We travelled via Hong Kong, then had the long haul across to Johannesburg. Dr Ali Bacher, who just about runs cricket in South Africa, was there to meet us. We touched down at 6am and I was very thankful that my first 'meet the press' exercise was not scheduled until 4.30pm that afternoon. So I was fairly fresh and ready for the press conference, at which there was a good deal of questioning on the subject of sledging. They asked me about the Perth Test, and I told them I didn't believe the sledging had been bad. If I had, I would have done something about it. I said I didn't believe it would be a problem on the tour, even though the series brought together two teams of similar qualities—teams that played it tough, and to win. But I told them too that it didn't matter who the captain was or how good he was, sometimes it was hard to put the lid on a player in the heat of the moment. There were no guarantees.

All the players in our team know the deal, and our record over the past two or three years has been very good. I resent the 'Ugly Aussies' tag that is put on us at times. I don't think we're any better or any worse than a number of other cricket teams.

Getting ready

We're off and running with some intense training under a new physical fitness conditioner, Steve Smith from Perth. It's a real mix—gym sessions, bike riding and power walking to support the usual net sessions at the Wanderers ground. There has been the usual whingeing from everyone (including me!) but deep down I know we're all enjoying it. My plan is to keep working hard physically throughout the tour to get sharper. Hopefully it will help my batting form.

On an afternoon early in the tour, a big storm brewed over the Wanderers

Normally you wouldn't be seen dead in a shirt like this (or a cap like this!). But the Social & Fines Committee's 'Funny Shirts' project in South Africa produced some real shockers, adding some fun to a tough tour—including Glenn McGrath's floral number.

ground. We kept an eye on it, but stayed out there working on some fielding and catching practice. All of a sudden there was a flash of lightning and the bolt struck a light tower only a hundred metres or so away from where we were. It scared the hell out of us. Don't think I've ever seen a practice session finish so quickly.

The Social and Fines Committee of the tour (comprising Steve Waugh, Shane Warne, Justin Langer and Matthew Elliott) came up with a pretty dastardly idea, involving 'funny' shirts. They had a hat draw so we could each pull out the name of a bloke to buy a shirt for. A significantly bad shirt. The deal then is that you have to wear the shirt to the fines meeting, which is to be held once a week. The fines meeting covers such blunders as being late for the bus, wearing the wrong gear or general tardiness. The only stipulation with the shirts was that they have to be as horrible as possible, and they had to have a collar. Well, I can tell you there are some real shockers. Ian Healy bought mine—a cream crocheted blouse which is something less than flattering. But it's a bloody sight better than some of them. I can't begin to tell you how horrific some of them are. The good news for people back in Australia is that meetings of the fines committee are not covered by television.

The Campaign Begins

We started casually and enjoyably with a match against the Nick Oppenheimer XI on his personal cricket ground. Oppenheimer is one of the richest men in South Africa (and one of the richest in the world), with his family involved with the formation of the De Beers diamond company. Nick is a cricket buff, and picks an invitation side which includes his son Jonathon. Nick himself played in the game when we were over here in 1994. It's a sort of limited overs game, and we batted for approximately 50 overs and made 290 odd. Matthew Elliott made a very good 90, Steve Waugh a quick 70 and Matthew Hayden 60. I batted down the list and was out there for quite a while for 20-odd. I'm still not overly impressed with my form, but it's not too bad. It's just nice to get a bit of time in the middle. They got pretty close—280-odd before we knocked them over. It was a good game, if a little light-hearted. I'm a bit disappointed; we should have cleaned them up an hour or so earlier, but the atmosphere was casual and we probably slackened off a bit. All in all a reasonable start to the tour.

There's some news on left-arm spinner Paul Adams. On the advice of the South African Cricket Board, the Western Province selectors have left him out of the team we'll meet in the opening first class match. There's some good and bad in this. In all honesty it would have been good to have a look at him. But the other side of the coin is that I reckon he's going to be pretty disappointed too. He hasn't played a lot of cricket lately. In fact, the word is that by missing this game, he'll have been without a game for three or four weeks by the time the first Test comes around. It's something of a punt. Maybe he'll come into the Test fresh, or maybe he'll come in rusty. Time will tell.

Western Province

I honestly couldn't have asked for a better start to the tour proper. I won the toss on a very good pitch, we batted, and we all made runs—including yours truly. I made 85 and probably should have scored 100. I wonder if things are turning for me? I had a big stroke of luck early on. I was on two or three when Matthew Hayden called me through for a run ... then sent me back. I was in trouble, but Herschelle Gibbs missed with the throw, and I stayed out there. It's amazing how much impact those 'small' moments can have. I'm not kidding myself that the 85 was anything like super form. But I started to play a few shots—something I haven't done for a while. I started to play better off the pads, which is always a good sign and I middled a couple of cover drives as well. It wasn't sensational. I'm still a few digs away from that but it was fantastic to have four hours in the middle and to have a really good workout. We declared at the end of day one around 4-400.

We ended up winning the match. When they were 5-260 at tea on the second day, I had a word with their skipper John Cummings and we decided we would try for a result—a hard thing to do in a three-day game on a good wicket. They declared, so we went out there and played some shots. We set them 350 to get off 81 overs, which sounds formidable but in fact was a reasonable ask on an excellent wicket on a ground with a quick outfield and one very short boundary. To their credit the Western Province guys really went for it—there was some dashing stuff and the crowd got their money's worth. We ended up winning by about 30. The crowds were excellent (12,000 on one day) and the match an excellent opener. Our bowlers had to work hard at bowling a good line and length on such a wicket.

Boland

This was a minor, 50-overs game at a place called Paarl, some 45 minutes from Cape Town. It brought another useful hit out—and a comfortable win. We made 320 off our 50 overs, with everyone getting 50 ... including me. Once again I felt reasonably good without feeling tremendous. Glenn McGrath and Shane Warne made their first appearances as bowlers on tour, and both were a little rusty. Glenn got hit a bit and so did Warnie at times. But we restricted them to 260-odd, so enjoyed a nice win.

Natal

The shift up the coast to Durban was very welcome. We all got in some swimming and surfing around the game against reigning provincial champions Natal. We went in with a team fairly close to our likely first Test outfit, although without Greg Blewett who should be in the team.

We lost the toss and they batted, which was fine. I felt our bowlers needed the hit out and hoped we would get two good bowls at them. The first day turned out to be a real wake-up call for us. After having them around 4-80 at lunch they knocked us around rather severely in the afternoon with their captain Dale Burkenstein belting a quick hundred and one of their openers also making a very good century. Scoring around 330 at just under four an over, they then put Matthew Hayden and myself in for seven overs at the end of the day—and bounced the hell out of us.

Our batting on the second day was no more than reasonable, apart from Mark Waugh who cashed in on the good wicket with a fluent 120. All the rest of us seemed to make 20 or so—getting a start, then getting out. I made 20, Steve Waugh 22, Matthew Hayden 28, and Matthew Elliott 38. And this against a Natal attack missing two key men, Lance Klusener and Shaun Pollock, who had either been rested because of the heavy workload in the season so far or because they were being tucked away from view for the Test. A bit of both, I reckon. With Klusener I suspect there's a fair bit of the 'mystery' approach in it. He's a bloke we don't know too much about and no doubt they want to keep it that way. The word is that he can bowl as fast as Allan Donald. I suspect he's been placed in cotton wool. We ended up making 370 to lead by 35 in the first innings, although it was nearly even at the end of the day when they knocked off 21 for no wicket.

On day three against Natal, we started thinking 'Test'. I made the point to the guys in the dressing room before play started that the Test was nearing, and it was time to switch on. The response was tremendous. Glenn McGrath bowled beautifully without getting a wicket, and Shane Warne bowled very well before he had a twinge in one knee, and I took him out of the attack as a precaution. Jason Gillespie chipped in with a couple of wickets, and Michael Bevan grabbed four—and we ended up knocking them over for 115 on a darned good wicket. We needed 78 to win, and got them for two down, with me unfortunately one of the two, caught in slips for one trying to glide a ball from their off-spinner. A really excellent win, and just what the doctor ordered.

The lead-up

We're in good shape for this first Test with plenty of blokes in form, even if the skipper is still a little short of it ... but getting there. The only problem we've got is that Paul Reiffel is out of the running for the Test thanks to a recurring problem with his lower back which affects the hamstrings. Steve Waugh trod on a ball and has a slightly swollen foot, while Warnie has a sore knee. But apart from 'Pistol' there's nothing major, and we're close to ready.

We're playing good cricket, and we're enjoying the tour. South Africa is easy to enjoy but as I told the guys at the start of the tour: 'Cricket tours are only enjoyable if you play good cricket on them'. You can have a wonderful time in places like England, the West Indies and South Africa. There's great camaraderie, the odd game of golf... but if you're getting beaten or playing poorly, you're never going to enjoy it much. Our goal on these overseas campaigns never changes: play good cricket and have a good tour.

FEBRUARY 26, 2.30PM

It's two days before the Test and we're just back from practice. We've got a bit of a tummy bug going through the team, which seems to happen over here, but generally things are fairly good.

I'm feeling fine—a little sharper and fitter than when we came away, and I've worked hard on that. I'm hitting the ball quite well in the nets and I'm looking forward to the Test, which is something I lost a bit in the Australian season. In the last couple of Tests against the Windies I was looking forward to them for the wrong reason—mainly just to try and wrap up a series, rather than a chance to score some runs and enjoy myself.

The team is just about sorted out. The wicket on the Wanderers ground in Johannesburg has some grass, but not much, and apparently it's been taking turn all year. I dare say we're going to play Michael Bevan, who will bat at seven.

FEBRUARY 27, 10PM

Test eve, and if I had to find a word to convey how I feel, it would be 'satisfied'. The bookies have us at 9/4 outsiders for the series. But the fact is that things have gone brilliantly for us so far, and if I was allowed to bet (which I'm not), I'd be having something on us. I believe that if both sides play to the best of their ability, then we're going to win. At 9/4 the odds are generous. We've narrowed the side down to 12 men. Paul Reiffel is out of the running as I mentioned (although he's back in the nets bowling, and that's good news) and the other player to miss out is Justin Langer. I'm yet to have a chat with Justin, but I'll be doing just that. It seems that during my years as Australian captain he's been the unlucky one. Probably I've had more chats with him over missed selection than with anyone else. Yet he's going just fine—he's played very well on tour so far, and has done all that I could have asked of him. But with Matthew Elliott having proved that he's back, someone had to miss out, and Justin is the guy. I'm going to tell Justin to keep hanging in there, and that his opportunities will come. There'll be a time in the future when guys like myself and the Waugh brothers won't be around, and he's got to be ready to put his foot in the door when that happens. Justin is a better player now than he was two or three years ago when he was also in and out of the Australian side. He's a more aggressive player; a batsman who looks to take the bowling on and dominate. My feeling is that we'll go with only two quicks and that Andrew Bichel will be 12th man.

The wicket looks good. I don't think it will be what they call a 'raging turner', but it will get slower and slower as the game goes on. I'm quietly confident, and hoping for a good night's sleep.

First Test, Johannesburg

MARCH 3

It's the third night of the Test and we're looking good. I have just watched a day's cricket during which not a single wicket has fallen. Steve Waugh and Greg Blewett batted right through the six hours, just as Geoff Marsh and I did at Trent Bridge some seven years ago. It's been a fluctuating Test; we had them 8-195 on the first day on a pretty good wicket, but the tail wagged and they got to 302 which I suppose was a reasonable score. On day two we were 4-190 at stumps, with the last session washed out. I only managed 16, but unfortunately (or fortunately ... I'm not quite sure how to look at it) hit the ball really well. I was feeling comfortable—then one from Shaun Pollock kept a little low, took the bottom of the bat and found its way back on to off-stump. For the time I was out there I felt I was seeing the ball as well as at any time this summer. The scorecard didn't look great, but there was encouragement in it for me.

At the end of day two it was pretty much level-pegging. Not any more. Greg Blewett and Steve Waugh have batted superbly. Blewie's on 150-odd and Steve 130; we're 4-480, 170 runs ahead with two days to go. We're in a wonderful position to press home the advantage on a wicket that will offer some more turn to Warnie and Michael Bevan as the hours go by.

Skipper Taylor got a start in the first Test at The Wanderers Stadium, only to play on, when 16, against Shaun Pollock.

The hero of the hour...Greg Blewett leaves The Wanderers after yet another unbeaten session. Blewett's mighty knock of 214 was the foundation stone of Australia's victory.

MARCH 5, 5.30PM

I'm in a hotel room in a place called Sun City, famous for its championship golf course and casino. We're here for a couple of days R & R and to have a look at the wildlife. I reckon we've earned it. Earlier this afternoon we beat South Africa by an innings and 196 runs, which is a hell of a big win whichever way you look at it. The foundation was Greg Blewett and Steve Waugh's fabulous partnership of 385, just 20 runs short of the fifth wicket record set by Sir Donald Bradman and Sid Barnes back in 1946–47. At the end of day four we had them 4-99, needing 320-odd to make us bat again. Today we just wrapped it up, bowling them out for 130 in an hour and 15 minutes. Shane Warne took 4-40, including four of the top five wickets and Michael Bevan 4-40 too; it was a swift and sweet conclusion.

And that's why we're at Sun City—to play some golf, and try our luck at the tables. We drove up with John Williamson's True Blue blasting on the bus's PA system, plus some Cold Chisel and Joshua Kadison, with everyone singing along and enjoying each other's company. It's times like these you're glad you're playing cricket for Australia.

At the press conference this afternoon, someone asked me if this is the best cricket team I'd played in. I tried not to give too much away, but you know what? It probably is. We have no real weaknesses. We've got balance and enthusiasm and the sort of team spirit that special teams need to have. Three years ago the South Africans beat us in this same Test at the Wanderers ground. This time we smashed them—Greg Blewett with 214, Steve Waugh 160, and Matthew Elliott 85. We're playing very, very close to our potential. My only concern is that maybe we won the

Jacques Kallis, one of South Africa's new breed, ponders the task at hand in the nets at Port Elizabeth.

game too easily. There's a lot of cricket to go, and the South Africans are going to come back at us. There is now some pride at stake and you can never underestimate that.

But I can't see us getting beaten. I really can't. And this is something I have never experienced before. These guys should not beat us in a Test match. But my task is to make sure we don't drop our standards and make ourselves vulnerable. A great bonus for us is the fact that Shane Warne is back near his best. If we can keep him going the way he is and Bevo keeps coming on nicely the way he is, then we've got the spin strike power we need. I honestly don't think Bevo wants to be known as a bowler, but his left-arm wrist spin is really doing the job for us. A couple of years ago Warnie would have taken six or seven wickets in the second innings, but he only got four because Bevo cleaned up the tail so well.

MARCH 8, LATE MORNING

I'm lying in my hotel room watching NSW play Waikato in the Super 12s rugby game at Sydney Stadium. The reason I'm not doing something a little more active is that I twinged my back at the start of the warm-ups for the three-day game here in East London (a three hour drive from Port Elizabeth) against Border. It was a simple thing—just run-throughs and running between wickets as we always do. I was scheduled to play in the match, but my back was feeling pretty tender and I had no choice but to pull out. I had some x-rays and spoke to an orthopaedic surgeon yesterday. The damage is nothing serious, but the advice from both the doc and Errol Alcott is to take it easy. And that's what I'm doing. The injury is to the right side of my back—not on the side which needed surgery last year. It's a disappointment. No, it's worse than that—it's a pain in the butt (literally!). About the only thing left for the Australian cricket team at the moment is for the captain to get the monkey off his back and start making some regular runs. I felt I was edging up on that and was looking forward to this game, then the Test which starts next Friday. We have a one-dayer in Port Elizabeth on Tuesday, before the Test. My fingers are crossed.

I've been flicking through some of the newspaper clippings. The South Africans seem to have gone overnight from potential world champions to 'overrated'. It's amazing what one Test match can do in the columns of the press ... and we've all been through that. Before the Test, Kepler Wessells, former Australian player and South African captain, was tipping a comfortable homeside victory in the series. One match later he's questioning the courage and commitment of the team—and the captaincy of Hansie Cronje. Wessells says he can't figure out why the South African team is playing so badly considering they're lined up against considerably weaker Australian opposition than in 1994. The comment is typical of a bloke who has played through a particular era and suffers from somewhat blinkered vision. Wessells looks at players such as David Boon and Allan Border—very, very fine players and household names in Australian sport—but he doesn't pay due accord to someone like Greg Blewett who has just made 214 in a Test match and averages 50, or Steve Waugh, who averages 50 in Test cricket, or Mark Waugh (44), or Matthew Elliott, who has made an outstanding start to his Test career. In Wessells' eyes these blokes don't rate alongside those who went before—and I think he's wrong. The sort of comments he offered are tough on Hansie Cronje too. When you have a disappointing loss the last thing you need is fellow players (particularly ex-captains) coming out and having a go at you. This is a time when you need your troops to rally around you.

Having said all that, from Australia's point of view it's great. All Wessells' words have done are to build more pressure on the South Africans, and that's to our benefit. It seems that a lot of people here expected that they were going to win the series pretty comfortably. Among the few people who rated us a big chance were the South African players themselves. Cronje is on the record with his opinion that we are entitled to be rated as world champions.

Anyhow, here I am injured, and that's not too brilliant. It means that just at the moment I'm not around the guys as much, or having my usual input. But looking at this team I'm consoled by the fact that I doubt the players need my presence or that of the senior guys as much as on some other tours. They are keen, hungry, motivated and tough.

MARCH 9, LATE AFTERNOON

We've wrapped up the match against Border in a couple of days. Blewie made a century, the bowlers all got among the wickets (Jason Gillespie getting seven in the first innings), and we just annihilated them. Border are supposedly the third strongest provincial side—we've now played the top three and beaten each of them, with two of the games finishing in two days.

And I'm on the mend. I've been for a walk and swim with Errol Alcott and I'm feeling stronger and freer. The Test is five days away, and I'm going to be okay, although I'll miss the Tuesday one-dayer. The plan is to get to the nets Wednesday and Thursday. Things are going fantastically well. I couldn't be happier.

Second Test, Port Elizabeth

MARCH 14
It's the morning of the second Test and for everyone except me, the preparation has been great. I'm still a bit stiff and sore, and I'll know about it running between wickets, but I'm feeling more than good enough to play.

There is a theory here now that we're just about unbeatable on flat or normal Test wicket, and that the best chance for them is on a green-top. The wicket here at St George's Park, Port Elizabeth, has *plenty* of grass on it, in line with that theory. The problem for them of course is that we have Glenn McGrath and Jason Gillespie in *our* ranks.

If I get the chance I won't hesitate to put them in and put the pressure back on them.

My own theory is that the wicket is a little under-prepared for Test cricket. It's not as hard as a normal Test pitch, due to the fact that it hasn't had the amount of rolling that a wicket should get for such a game.

I think though that a good touring side is one that can handle all conditions, and so I'm still very, very confident of us winning this Test. I just know that the people who have been involved in the preparation of this particular wicket have done their best to offer something that suits the South Africans with their three or four seam bowlers.

MARCH 15
The first day is over, and I've got to be reasonably happy. As I'd hoped, I won the toss and sent them in, which is something I'm not sure I've ever done before in my Test captaincy career.

At a couple of different stages—at 4-22 and 7-95—we really had them on the ropes. At 7-95 we had David Richardson caught behind by Heals off a fair dinkum edge—but the umpire ruled it had brushed the pad. At 8-95 with Allan Donald and Paul Adams to come, I reckon we would have bowled them out for 120-130. As it was they battled to 209. In the big picture, that's good for us ... but it could have been better. In reply we're 1-10. Matthew Hayden nicked one early and was on his way.

I think the wicket will be a little flatter tomorrow—it won't have as much zip, or take as much seam. But it will be pretty juicy first thing after sweating under the covers and the first hour could be crucial.

I had no idea how I would go after my time away from the middle with this sore back, but I batted 50-odd minutes (for seven) and felt reasonably comfortable, albeit in a fairly defensive mode. I was just trying to get through to stumps.

The state of the wicket is a subject of considerable debate. Geoff Marsh fielded a number of questions at the press conference about its condition, but when you're in this situation with the game in progress you tend to be pretty reserved about what you

Jason Gillespie shows his delight as he snares the wicket of Adam Bacher (49), second innings, second Test, Port Elizabeth.

say. You don't want to give the impression you're looking for excuses for what's happened ... or what may happen. Must say, though, that I felt sorry for blokes like Adam Bacher, their opening batsman, and Herschelle Gibbs and Jacques Kallis, young fellas starting out on their Test careers. From their point of view I think it's very unfair for them to come out on a wicket which the groundsman—for whatever reasons—has prepared as a green-top. My sentiments would have been exactly the same if we had batted first. The wicket is under-prepared—and I think that's grossly unfair.

I don't expect flat wickets all the time. People are calling us the 'flat track team'. Well, I think that means we're a good cricket side—that when the wicket's even and fair, we play the best cricket on it. This juicing up of wickets ... or dare I say it ... 'doctoring' of wickets ... is just not on. Anyway, the bottom line is we're in fair shape to go on and win the Test match. But I just wonder if some of the younger blokes don't go on and make it in international cricket, whether they'll look back at this game's wicket and wonder if they got dealt a fair hand.

MARCH 16

I'm back at the pub—and boy, have we had a bad day at the office! We went into the day knowing that a good batting performance could just about wrap up the series. Instead, we were bowled out for 108 and at stumps they were 0-83 in their second, so an overall lead of 184 with all 10 wickets in hand.

I'm trying to figure out what went wrong. Basically I think we just weren't positive enough—we faced some 70 overs for our 108 runs, and that's not really our style. This evening we had a meeting about it and I think we all agreed that we just weren't mentally aggressive enough in our approach. They bowled very, very well—a tough, disciplined line, with the wicket helping a bit and the ball swinging around.

I went early, and disappointingly. After toughing it out last night, I was gone for 8 on about the 10th or 11th ball I faced this morning. I chased one, nicked it, and was on my way. Bloody disappointing—I had set my goals to be very positive today and unfortunately I probably set the tone for the innings by getting out so early and cheaply.

The reality for me is that it's another failure in a lengthening list this summer. I keep thinking I'm going to come out of it, but I suppose if it doesn't end shortly, it might be time for me to step aside and give someone else a go at the captaincy. Honestly, there's no way I could really pick myself in the team at the moment apart from the captaincy—and I have always believed that no player should ever just be picked as captain. I don't think anyone deserves to be picked *only* as Australian captain. If I don't turn it around I'll think very seriously of standing down.

Time is running out. I've probably got the second innings of this game, then the two innings of the third Test to find the form I'm looking for. I have already decided that in these next three innings I'm going to be very positive. I'm going to try and play some shots and get the feet moving. I think that has to be the approach.

Physically, the back injury has checked me just when I felt I was making progress. I've been going to the gym—doing a bit of boxing and skipping, but the week away from the crease with this back thing hasn't helped.

MARCH 17

What a difference a day makes. Just 24 hours on, we're right back in the hunt. We talked last night about being a little more aggressive and more positive in our approach, as well as being a little more patient with our bowling. The goal was to put them under the sort of pressure to which they had subjected us. And it worked like a dream! We were on top all the way. An early run-out (of Kallis) thanks to a great piece of fielding by Greg Blewett was followed by a great team effort by the bowlers—especially Jason Gillespie, who picked up three more wickets to add to his five in the first innings. With a bit of luck he could have had 10 or 11. They lost 10-85. We couldn't have hoped for anything better.

Things were going okay in the chase until we got to 23, at which point I was out lbw to Brian McMillan for 13. I *was* probably out—the ball hit me a fraction high,

Mark Waugh in full flight on his way to 116 in the thrilling second Test at Port Elizabeth. Setting up Australia's victory, it was one of the great innings of Waugh's career.

This is the moment! Ian Healy raises his bat in jubilation after swatting Hansie Cronje for six to win the second Test for Australia.

but was more likely going to hit leg stump. It was just a bit disappointing. There have been a plague of lbw shouts in this game, and as is often the way when you're struggling, you're the one who gets given out. The one thing I know is that there have been a lot of closer lbws given *not* out in the game.

At stumps we were 3-146, chasing 270 to win. In a day's cricket we went from being 10/1 outsiders to slight odds-on favourites to win the Test. The first session tomorrow is the key. If we can see off their initial burst and get on top with the bat we can win— and win comfortably. If we lose early wickets, they're going to put pressure on us. The game is there to be won by both teams, which does make it a darned good Test match. For all my earlier comments, that's the thing about under-prepared wickets. You often get low scores, but sometimes you get great Test matches too. With its fluctuating fortunes, this one is a beauty. My next entry in this diary is either going to come from a very disappointed Aussie captain … or a very jubilant one. Victory in this one would be a special achievement, considering where we stood at the end of day two.

MARCH 18

It's 6.50pm, the evening of the fourth day's play, and we've just won a Test match and clinched a series. Phew! I think you can put it down as a Test which only comes along every 20 or 30 years. It certainly wasn't all smooth sailing. We lost Steve Waugh just before drinks in the first session, then Greg Blewett just before lunch (5-205), leaving us 65 to win.

After lunch things went beautifully. At 5-258 with Mark Waugh and Michael Bevan at the crease, we were cruising to victory. Although maybe we started to think too soon about the celebrations. Suddenly Mark was out, bowled by Kallis, then Michael, caught at first slip. Shane Warne donged one over the bowler's head but was out lbw soon afterwards and we were 8-265. Things were suddenly very tense indeed. The end came with spectacular suddenness. Jason Gillespie faced five balls of a Kallis over after Warnie was out, and Ian Healy shaped up to Hansie Cronje. With all the field out, including a deep forward square leg and a deep fine leg, Heals picked the ball up and planted it over the deep backward square leg boundary for six. What a shot! We had won by two wickets.

This was my 80th Test match for Australia and I cannot remember a win that comes close to this one. To climb off the canvas the way we did was very special. I doubt if I'll ever play in a bigger Test victory than today's. It was a win that has surely proven beyond further debate that we do not deserve to be regarded as a 'fair weather' cricket team. I went on to the front foot with the media after the game to drive that point home. Essentially I told 'em a few things that had been bugging me and the team. Every time we have had a bad day—and cricket teams have those—people have written us off, claiming we're a 'fair weather team'; 'flat-track bullies' who 'can't chase totals', or 'a two-man team' (meaning Shane Warne and Steve Waugh—that if Steve doesn't make runs or Shane take wickets, then we can't win). We proved *all* of that wrong this Test and I told the media so. I really

Mark Waugh has a victory hug for Ian Healy as the Aussie wicketkeeper and batting partner Jason Gillespie leave the field after the extraordinary ending at St Georges Park.

spoke my mind, and made the point that I was disappointed in what some of them had been writing. Probably it will backfire and they'll have the last word, as always. But it sure felt good to get it off my chest. I'll be interested to see the papers these next couple of days. I'm sure they'll find a way of saying that Taylor was out of line in what he said and that we're an arrogant team or whatever. There won't be any apologies. But we showed 'em today … we showed 'em this game, and I don't care what anyone thinks.

So now, at about 7.00pm on of the last day of the second Test, we've all had a celebratory drink or two, and I really am proud and delighted. For us to chase and get 270 in a tough Test on a challenging wicket—a Test in which neither team had scored more than 209—was a wonderful achievement. The ending provided by Heals was spectacular, but above all else I'll remember Mark Waugh's 116, one of the truly great Test match innings.

Again today I have been asked about my position in the team. As I have written here, my form has been ordinary, and worrying. I did some sums the other day about my form and the form of my partner at the other end. In the last eight or nine Tests I have averaged 18.2, while my partners, including Michael Slater, Matthew Elliott and Matthew Hayden, have averaged around 25 at the other end. It has been a tough time for opening batsmen.

I've been giving it a lot of thought and I'm thinking, bugger it! I'm the Australian captain and at the moment I'm the best man for the job. I'm going to keep doing it until I'm told that someone else can do a better job than I can. I know we're the best Test cricket team in the world at the moment, although there is room for improvement in the one-day game. We're not unbeatable, but if you're going to beat us you've got to play bloody well for the entire game. That's not arrogance talking … I've never been an arrogant person. I'm a realist, and I know it's the truth. I believe we are the only team in the world that could have come back and won from where we stood at stumps on day two. We won a Test match that no other side could have won, and as captain of that team, I'm proud tonight. I feel renewed. I know that with the players we've got there are going to be some great years ahead. I look forward to those years … and I want to be part of them.

MARCH 19

A few observations here, offered in the clearer light of day. There are sore heads around, and the mists of a great celebration are lifting. What a day it was. I won't soon forget the way we boomed out 'Beneath the Southern Cross' in the change room after the game. Best rendition ever, I reckon. The guys had their arms around each other and it's very hard to put into words just how fantastic the feeling of victory was.

This team is probably the best I've played cricket for Australia with … or at least equal to the best. The spirit in the side is nothing short of fantastic.

The individual elements of the Test are now taking clearer shape in my mind as they tend to after the glorious jumble of a victory like yesterday's. The last 20 minutes of the Test was about as nerve-wracking as anything I've ever experienced. I watched some TV footage today of how I looked during that time—I was a nervous wreck! Several times my head was in my hands. Seated alongside was Steve Waugh, who I have decided to blame for the collapse that turned it into such a nail-biting finish. At 5-258 we were sitting there, revelling in Mark's magnificent century. I was still doing it tough—I wasn't going to be happy until we got there. Then Steve poked me in the ribs. 'Wake up to yourself, Tubby,' he said. 'We're home here ... we won't lose five for 12!' Almost as he spoke, Mark was out ... then Michael Bevan ... then Shane Warne. I blame Steve Waugh.

Tummy exercises, designed to keep a wonky back in fair shape, were part of the Taylor training regime through the long season. The back problem flared again during the South African campaign.

Afterwards I was talking to Heals about the shot that won the match. He told me he was actually thinking of playing a square cut, because he thought that was the best chance of hitting Hansie Cronje for a boundary. Then Hansie drifted one on to his pads and Heals didn't even think about lifting the ball over backward square for a six. It just sort of happened ...

Heals told me about Shane Warne's arrival at 7-258, when he'd barely been out there more than a few balls himself. Warnie was nervous, as he sometimes can be—especially when it comes to batting. It certainly wasn't a case of a pair of Mr Cools out there. 'What are we gonna do, Heals?' asked Shane. Heals' answer was a classic: 'I don't know. I haven't worked it out for myself yet ... how can I let *you* know what to do?' Replied Warnie: 'Well, I can't feel my legs.' So we had a couple of nervous wrecks out there ... but we got the job done.

The celebrations were long and late. We ended up at a pub called Toby Joe's listening to the band. I think it was about 3.30am when they finally kicked us out, with Heals and I the last two to leave. I haven't had many late nights in recent years, but the boys reckoned it was very difficult to get me home last night. I was in a very, very buoyant mood.

This morning some thoughtful tradesmen decided to do some repair work on the stairs right outside my door at around 8.00am. I had to get up anyway, to get to the SABC studios to do a live TV cross to Ray Martin back home. Under the weather, I think, was a fair description and I don't much like doing interviews when I've had a night out. But I hope it came over all right.

Later we headed to a wonderful game reserve about an hour's drive from Port Elizabeth. Even on a couple of hours' sleep it was a fantastic day, observing lions, rhino, elephants and giraffe.

As captain and (struggling) batsman I'm constantly buoyed by the support I'm

At the top of the stairs their captain waited...as Ian Healy and Jason Gillespie made their joyous progress back to the dressing room after the winning of the second Test.

getting from home. It hasn't been a great time for Mark Taylor, opening batsman for Australia, although it *has* been a great time for Mark Taylor, captain of Australia. The messages from home don't differentiate. They are wonderfully positive, all the way from Prime Minister John Howard down. The PM has been a great supporter and I value his messages before and after the big games. After the Port Elizabeth Test the faxes have been rolling in from everywhere: 'Well done', 'Congratulations', 'Hang in there'—they all bring messages of positive support, and when you're far from home you appreciate them greatly. They came from both people I know and people I don't know. A swag of them. One that I treasure which arrived before one of the Tests was from my son William. It read: 'Dear dad, I hope you get 100 runs. Have a nis (sic) day out at South Africa'.

As for me—well, about all I can say for sure is that I *will* be 'hanging in there'. I know I'm a better player with the bat than I've shown in recent times and I told the press that at yesterday's post-game conference. My form is about the last thing they have to pick on in this team. At the moment, My batting is the only weak link. I reckon just about all the other bases are covered. So that's the task at hand—for me to make some runs in the next Test. When we fly back to Johannesburg tomorrow I'm going to knuckle down and just work on my own performance. Making some runs would make me feel a lot better—and I know it would please a lot of people who are cheering for me back home too.

MARCH 20

It's the evening before the third and final Test—a dead rubber, but a game we want to do well in, all the same. Today at the team meeting I spoke about the lack of motivation which is often a problem when you win a series and then go into a dead rubber Test. The fact is that in the past few years we've often played poorly in these games. I asked the guys to search for some individual motivation—to find some individual goals they want to achieve over these next five days.

I also found out today that no Australian side has ever brought off a clean sweep of an away series—that is, won every Test of a series away from home. Now, that's something to shoot for. The feedback from the players was good, especially the younger blokes. They really want to play well. Matthew Elliott, for example, has played four Tests for four wins, and is keen for five.

We trained well at Centurion Park today and I'm satisfied the preparation has been good. The task now is to get the job done. The wicket looks a little uneven, but doesn't have the same coverage of grass that we struck at Port Elizabeth. It looks a good Test wicket—a little more in the batsmen's favour, but offering some potential for the bowlers too.

Trevor Hohns, the chairman of selectors and a good friend of mine, is in town. He's here to discuss possible changes to our side for the one-day series which follows the Test. Trevor informs me that there *will* be changes and one of them might be me, although the ball is my court, and I'm appreciative of that. My back hasn't been great. The choice is either that I stay on and play at least some of the one-day campaign, or head home and get an extra two weeks' rest prior to going to England.

Trevor assured me today that I will captain the side to England, and that is a relief—although it will be an even *bigger* relief if I can score some runs in this Test. I know I'll be doing everyone a favour if I can manage that. There's nothing worse than the captain of a sporting side being out of form. I'm encouraged by the fact that plenty of people will be cheering for me to do well personally.

To take the team to England was, of course, a goal of mine—and it will be an honour. Right now I have some thinking to do about whether to stay on here or go home. I'll monitor things during the first two days of the Test to see how my back's going. That's how long I've got to decide—48 hours. The selectors' recommendation is that I go home and get myself right—but I know it would be an uncomfortable exercise to leave my team halfway through a tour. I've got a tough call coming up. My inclination is not to go home unless I'm going to get some genuine advantage out of it.

Third Test, Pretoria

MARCH 21

The end of an even first day of the third Test. They sent us in on a wicket that was doing a bit. It's a little uneven ... a bit of seam for the quick bowlers and later even some turn for Pat Symcox. I wasn't unhappy about batting first; it would have been my choice to bat if we'd won the toss. We're all out for 227 and I would have been far happier with another 40 or 50. We looked set to get plenty more at 4-190, but Steve Waugh was given out caught behind down the leg side in a decision which most people felt went the wrong way. We struggled from there.

I made 38, having batted for more than three hours. I'm still struggling, but it was good to spend some time at the crease. My main problem is that I'm still not *quite* in the position I want to be when I'm trying to play shots. The timing is just that fraction off. But I'm working hard, and I'm getting there. Regular walking and bike riding are playing their part after the struggle I had with my injury. There was some grudging recognition from the media of my long, if struggling, innings. But they were quick to also point out that I had now gone 19 innings without a Test half-century.

After today, my inclination is to tell Trevor Hohns that I won't be going home. I'm more than prepared to miss a few of the one-dayers, but I think to stay here and work is the best way I can get right for England. Here I'll have the chance of a few more digs, and also the chance to work with Steve Smith, our trainer, and get myself as fit as possible.

MARCH 22

Back from Ellis Park, the rugby union ground, where we've just seen the NSW team go down narrowly to Transvaal in the Super 12 series. A good match, with the NSW boys fighting back to trail 27–26 late before going down 37–26. They were a bit stiff. The NSW misfortune pretty much sums up our day on the cricket field. At close of play the South Africans were 3-240 and in a pretty good position. We didn't have a lot of luck—the bowling was better than the score would indicate, but absolutely nothing went our way.

I don't think I've spent many more frustrating days in the field than today. So many times their batsmen played and missed. I reckon it must have happened 60 times or more. From all that we only got one edge all day, when Gary Kirsten got a touch that was gratefully accepted by Ian Healy. It was a great moment for Heals—

Congratulations all round as Ian Healy takes his 300th Test wicket (Gary Kirsten)—c Healy, b McGrath—first innings, third Test.

Adam Bacher's 96 was a key contribution to South Africa's third Test win.

his 300th Test dismissal, putting him second on the all-time 'keepers list to Rod Marsh. It was the highlight of the day (for us) by a fair margin. We all thought Heals would probably get the record on the green-top at Port Elizabeth, but he had to wait a little longer. Now he's off on the next quest—to break Marsh's record. There's not much in it: Heals' 300 dismissals have come in 88 Tests; Rod got 355 in 96, so he's a tick ahead on the averages. A couple of great 'keepers.

Anyhow, we're in a spot of bother. Their opening batsman Adam Bacher is 96 not out, and the way this match is running, we're going to need a change of fortune. So far it hasn't gone our way at all.

MARCH 23

We're a fair way behind the eight-ball. They made 384 and we're 4-94-odd... in other words, about four wickets for minus-70. We didn't have a lot of luck. A very confident shout for a caught behind off Brian McMillan was turned down—he went on to make 50, then Hansie Cronje whacked a quick 80. I missed out, making only five, and it was like a flash of *deja vu*. I nicked one pushing forward off Donald and got caught behind. It wasn't a great shot—sort of a half-and-half effort as I tried to defend the ball.

Funny thing was, I wasn't as disappointed as maybe I should have been. In a way there was a sense of relief as I walked off. I thought to myself, 'Well, that's the end of that... thank God!' It's been a tough summer; a disappointing summer on a personal level. My woes have been well documented. I'd like answers, but I'm certainly not looking for excuses. The fact is that it's been a testing summer for opening batsmen generally: Matthew Hayden was out for a duck today and Matthew Elliott, at number three, scored 12. The wickets have had plenty in them for the new-ball bowlers—and when you're struggling, as I have been, it makes it tough to get your game back on the rails. I'm glad it's over. The first class southern hemisphere is finished for me and my next first class bat will come in England where I'll be looking to turn it all around.

I had a net session after the day's play and asked Greg Chappell to come down for a chat. I was happy to see him—there have been articles in the papers here suggesting that Greg thought he might have an answer or two for my batting problems. Things were awkward for a time between Greg and myself. A few seasons back he had put his name to an article in the *Courier-Mail* focusing on my batting form, and suggesting that I shouldn't be in the team. In the wake of that came a piece in which he suggested I had won the Rip van Winkel award, waking from a deep sleep I'd been in. This second piece came after I'd made 170 against the South Africans in Melbourne. I was disappointed with that and told him so. I told Greg that I'd always be prepared to listen to what he had to say and if I didn't agree, well, I'd make my own judgment. I believed (and still do) that any past Australian captain—and especially one of the stature of Greg Chappell, one of the greats of the game—should offer any advice he may have face to face, rather than through the columns of a newspaper.

This looks suspiciously like out...Allan Donald blasts one through Greg Blewett's defences and bowls him for a duck. Second innings, third Test, Centurion Park.

Anyhow, this time Greg had written a good positive piece on some thoughts about my batting problems. We had a yarn at the nets and it was interesting stuff, although largely in the area of things I was trying to do anyway. Greg talked about watching the ball *very* closely—something that Bob Simpson taught me to do when you're struggling. He also suggested I should be trying to get forward more—something I've tried to do in my batting throughout my career, but something I *haven't* been doing over the past three months. He talked about accentuating my movements in playing forward and playing back—and to really work on it. I'm going to work on getting forward—even if I have to wear a couple on the bloody helmet!

The other tip that Greg gave me was to go away to a darkened room somewhere and just think about my good innings—to try and recreate my thought processes on those days. As Greg said, when you're playing well, there are only good things going through your mind. It's true. The funny thing is that when things are going badly, every ball seems to be a beauty, right on the spot you don't want it. I'm going to take Greg's tip and go away and think about some of those good innings. Hopefully I'll break this bloody spell—because it's giving me more grief than all the people back home writing about, reading about and watching what Mark Taylor's doing over here. As Greg Chappell said to me, it only takes a few little things to go right and you're back on track. He believes that I haven't 'lost' it—and I agree. I've gotta keep believing in that ...

MARCH 24

It's over. Day four of the Test, and we've lost by eight wickets. We were bowled out for 185 today and the South Africans got the 29 runs required, losing a couple of wickets on the way. Allan Donald bowled very well and another controversial leg side catch decision (against Ian Healy) didn't help our cause.

Heals was very, very unhappy with the call against him and stood his ground for a time. When he came off the field he waved his bat at a spectator—then threw it to the top of the stairs and into the change room. This brought a report from the match referee Raman Subba Row, and Ian and I were called to a meeting after the press conference obligations were completed. There wasn't a whole lot said—the atmosphere of the meeting was pretty light. So it came as a big surprise to Healy, our manager Col Eagar and me when it was announced that Ian had been given a two-match suspension. This came pretty much out of the blue. It's a fact that Raman Subba Row had said at the start of

Cricket balls spell out the message for the popular 'Heals'.

the series that he would not look favourably on any form of dissent. But in the context of this match, I honestly believed he would take a lenient stance.

It had been a very frustrating game—for both teams. There had been a number of contentious decisions and the frustration levels were high. We had gone into the game in a good frame of mind. Ian Healy had said a number of times: 'Let's just keep cool, have a good time and see how we go ... because we've done the business.' From that, it had come to this. At the end of day four we had lost the match, and I had also lost my wicket-keeper for two of the one-dayers.

Steve Waugh is named man of the series after the third Test, adding another laurel to a glittering career.

It provided a sour ending for us. Earlier I had been in a positive frame of mind in my chat with the media. I told them we had come over here to win a Test *series* and had done that, even if there was disappointment in this individual match. Tonight, I'm not overly disappointed about the loss—I could feel this one slipping away and sometimes in cricket it's like that.

But I'm *very* disappointed in the Ian Healy situation. I don't for a minute condone the lapse in behaviour on this last day. Neither does Heals for that matter. He's regretful and disappointed. I just think he's been a bit hard done by. Considering the circumstances of the match I reckon a fairer penalty would have been a suspended sentence—sort of putting Heals on notice that if anything else untoward happened in the next year *then* he would get a couple of matches tacked onto any sentence. Two games straight? That was very, very tough.

Reflections on a Tough Summer

A meeting with some of the English journalists looking ahead to the Ashes series has prompted me to produce my 'third term report'. The journos came up with the stat that in the last 17 Tests we've played we have won ten and lost seven. On paper that's good, but not terrific. However, a couple of those losses were dead rubber games, so if you cross them off that makes it 10–5 which is a fairer reflection of the way we have played. I think one of the great things about the statistic is that the Tests in which we have been involved have either been won or lost—not drawn. People want results in Test cricket, and they want to be entertained. We, as players, want people to come and watch us play, so we make a conscious effort to get results. I reckon it's a wonderful statistic that in our last 17 Tests we have produced a result. We'll probably get a draw somewhere along the way, but rain will more than likely play its part in that. The way we're playing we're either going to be knocking sides over and

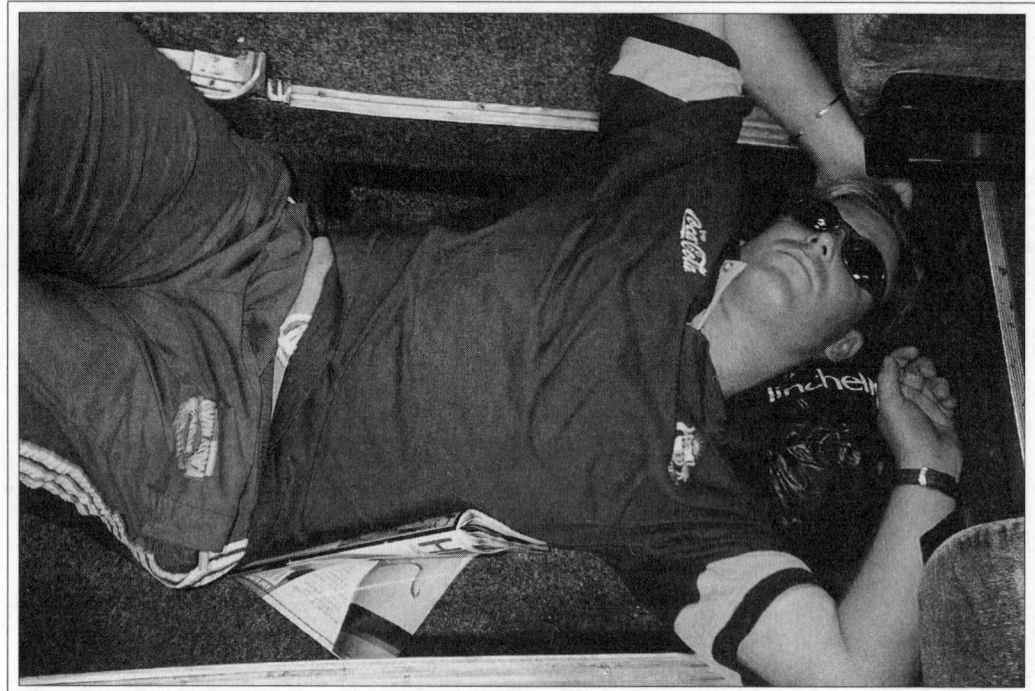
Boy—that leg-spinning is hard work! Sunnies still in place, Shane Warne grabs 40 winks.

winning ... or getting knocked over. Fortunately at the moment, we're doing more of the former ...

I'm very, very pleased with the way the team is going under my captaincy. We've played ten games over here, won nine of them and lost one. No draws. Along the way we have played some excellent cricket. The side in South Africa has been as good a team unit as I've been with. Before we left Australia a mate of mine rang to tell me he had taken odds of 11/4 on us winning the series. He collected in two straight Tests. The bookies obviously saw things very differently from the way I did. Before we left I stacked our team up against their team and was very happy with what I came up with. The series went pretty much the way I thought and hoped it would; we won most of the big moments and that was the difference between the two sides.

My batting form remains the unanswered question. I have just been reading an article by Peter Roebuck who writes: 'The moment of truth is about to arrive for Mark Taylor in the Ashes series'. Well, he's spot on with that. He reckons I could do more—but makes no suggestion of *what* more I could do, apart from recording that I'm in a slump. This is hardly fresh news. I've been saying that at press conferences for the last couple of months. Maybe Peter hasn't been listening.

The thing is I don't really know where to turn. I figure that I've spoken to just about anyone who might be able to offer something of value. I've talked to Greg Chappell and Neil Marks; I've talked to my father and my wife. Yet still I can't quite nail it. The thing I'm going to keep doing though is working hard—maintaining and building on my fitness. The back problem I have had over here in South Africa certainly hasn't helped. It checked my progress just when I felt I *was* making progress. I made 80-odd in Cape Town, then hit the ball well for my 16 runs in the first Test. I don't think I played and missed once in that innings. I just got one that kept a bit low, took a bottom edge and rolled back onto the stumps. I really felt I was on the verge of something that day.

But it was before the next game that my back went and suddenly I was struggling again. Anyhow, I've got to draw the line on all that and start afresh. I'm going to work hard on the things I do and try to relax. I generally am a pretty relaxed person, but there's a lot to this job as Australian captain. Pressure is never far away. The fundamental thing is that I don't believe that at 32 I'm washed up as a batsman. I probably never thought I was a batsman who was going to average 50 in Test cricket as I did in my first 30 or so Tests. My early goal when I was starting out was to average 45. Now the average has dropped down to 42, so I've got some work to do. The target is to bump that up—to average around 50 in my remaining Tests … however many that may be.

The task at hand is to find my way out of the maze, and the best way to do that is to keep working at it and to keep as fit as I possibly can. I know one thing for sure—the Poms will be targeting me in England. They'll be focusing on me as a weak spot in the side—if they can keep me down their hope will be that they can bring the team down. My goal has got to be to not let that happen. If I can come back, and come back stronger than I've ever been, then there's no barrier to Australia doing exceptionally well in the Ashes series … and looking down the track to many good seasons ahead.

One-day Avalanche

Phew! Seven one-dayers in thirteen days—it's going to be bloody hard work. That's the task at hand as we set up camp in East London and ready ourselves for the blur of cricket which ends a long, tough summer for both the South Africans and ourselves. The programmers are certainly getting their pound of flesh—frankly, I reckon five one-day games would have been plenty. Anyhow, it's carved in stone. We're cricketers, and play cricket is what we have to do.

For my own part, I'm going into the two weeks determined to enjoy myself. I'm going to be aggressive and try to play my shots. And I'm not going to play all the games. I'll have some R & R time and get some mental rest. I'll play four or five games, to try to use the series to get back some confidence and fluency.

MARCH 28

We've had some time off, played some golf, and relaxed. We're a team with a different look thanks to the arrival of fresh troops from Australia—Adam Dale and

Michael Bevan takes it to the South Africans. He was to play an important role during the one-day series.

Stuart Law from Queensland, Brendan Julian and Adam Gilchrist from WA and Michael Di Venuto from Tasmania. Picking the first side wasn't easy in the circumstances—pretty tough in fact. After a great deal of deliberation we slotted new-arrival Adam Dale into the team ahead of Andrew Bichel. Adam has had an outstanding year for Queensland—particularly in one-day cricket where he's been very miserly with his bowling—and he's just come off an excellent Shield final in which he took nine wickets.

But it was a tough call for Andrew who has been with us all the way, suffering an injury problem early, then missing out on the Tests through our policy of having two quicks and two spinners. With Paul Reiffel and Andrew not having bowled a lot of balls in a match situation recently, we were reluctant to take a stab at having two underdone quicks to support Jason Gillespie, so Adam Dale got the nod. Andrew Bichel is disappointed—and understandably so. We've all had a good yarn to him—Geoff Marsh, Heals and myself—and being the sort of bloke he is, he's accepted it well. Being a selector is never easy—sometimes you have to make tough decisions; decisions that hurt. Today we did that.

So how are we going to go? Well, I don't really know, to tell you the truth. The South Africans have an excellent one-day record, winning around 80–85 per cent of their games in the last 12 months. They're a disciplined side—they bowl good line and length, their fielding is excellent and their batting very solid. They don't seem to have a lot of flair players in their side, but they do play good steady one-day cricket. In contrast, our record is pretty poor, and we've got some ground to make up. But we have the talent, and I'm feeling pretty good about our chances. To win it we're going to have to match them in the area of discipline and patience, then get the edge through our individual flair and talent—which I feel we have more of.

MARCH 30

We're one-down, after a game in which we had our chances. At 2-125 off 25 overs, then 4-163 we were looking pretty good—but then three run-outs, particularly those of Steve Waugh and Greg Blewett, proved costly. We ended up struggling to 9-223, which was probably 20 or 30 more than we should have got, as at one stage we were 9-178. They got the runs four wickets down after giving us a bit of a sniff early. We had them 3-50, but missed a couple of chances that could have had them five for less than 100. Kallis and Cullinan went on with the job, with 122 for the fourth wicket and they got the runs.

I made only seven, which increases the pressure on me and the team, I suppose. As mentioned, my plan in these games is to relax, enjoy myself and play some shots in the hope that things will click. But there was some disruption before the game which created a bit of tension right at the start. On the morning of the match, Mark Waugh unfortunately had to pull out, which didn't help our preparations—or my own as his opening partner. Then I made the mistake of leaving Michael Bevan's name off the

Skipper in the stand. Mark Taylor sat out some of the one-dayers to give himself a chance to freshen up before the Ashes Tour.

team list I handed Hansie Cronje at the toss. I gave him only ten names.

I went out to bat in a reasonably relaxed frame of mind, looking forward to having a bit of a whack on a pretty good wicket. In the middle, Cronje asked me: 'Is that your team that's been listed on the board?' I replied: 'Yeah, of course it's the team.' The penny dropped when Cronje had someone bring me the team list I had given him ... a list with only ten names on it. I suppose if Cronje had wanted to be pedantic he could have made us play with only ten men, although anyone in cricket would have realised it was an honest mistake, and that Michael Bevan has been a certain starter in Australian one-day teams over the last two or three years. The fumble I made at the toss took a little of my focus about what I was out there for—to bat well. I was quietly stewing over something I had never done before. At seven I got a leading edge to a ball and was well caught at backward point by Jonty Rhodes. I had let myself down. I had let something bother me when the plan was not to let *anything* bother me and to just concentrate on the job at hand.

The minor stuff-up convinced me of one thing—that I could do with a break from the game. I have always felt pretty much in control of things through this long summer, but the incident at East London convinced me that I'm just about ready for a spell. I'm going to play tomorrow's game—the second one-dayer—and hopefully get some runs. But I probably won't play any more games after that. That's the sort of advice I'm getting from Geoff Marsh and other people I respect, and I'm taking it on board. In my own heart it's what I feel too.

The plan is this: I'll play tomorrow, and try to relax and enjoy myself in what will probably be my last bat of the tour. At the start I'm going to make sure that I write the list out correctly! Then, when it's over, I'm going to stand aside and let Heals take the reins for the last five one-dayers.

Of course it doesn't sit comfortably with me. The fact that I've lost it—temporarily—as a batsman hurts down deep. I remain convinced that I'm going to find 'it' again before long. I'm not washed up. I don't believe my eyes are gone (a suggestion apparently made one day by an ex-international in the press box). I'm just in a slump that has gone on far too long. The task is to change my frame of mind, to get back to being the Mark Taylor of old, the opening batsman who has averaged 45 for the last eight bloody years ... but for some reason can't do it this year ...

I remember back ten years or so to some advice that Neil 'Harpo' Marks (NSW

Skipper Healy leads the Australian one-day side into battle. Match three v South Africa at Cape Town.

Sheffield Shield manager/selector) gave me during a season in which I was really struggling with the bat. 'Mark, if I were you,' said Neil, 'I'd get your cricket bat, your pads, your gloves, put 'em all in a big bag, and stick 'em under the bed. Pull out your golf clubs instead, and have a month away.' I did that back then, and it worked. It's time for me to go back to something that worked in the past.

MARCH 31

We're one-all. I won an important toss in Port Elizabeth today and sent them in to bat. We had them three for about 30 and kept them down to 8-221, which was a good effort. The energy level was higher—we fielded better, and generally played better. We still missed a couple of chances—I missed a couple of tough ones in slips—but keeping them to 220 was a pretty fair effort, with Adam Dale picking up 3-18. We did the business by seven wickets with five overs to go, with Mark Waugh contributing a super 115 off 125 balls and Steve Waugh 50 off 52. It was South Africa's first defeat in the last 14 home one-day internationals.

I made a swinging (literally!) 17. I decided that I'd been batting so badly I'd just go out and have a bit of fun. I just swung from ball one. I didn't hit too many but I think at least I set the tone for the way we wanted to play out there today—to be positive and aggressive. The ever watchful media didn't approve. In the *Daily Telegraph* Robert Craddock wrote: 'Yesterday he (Taylor) came out swinging in an out-of-character innings of 17 when he resembled a beaten boxer throwing punches from crazy angles in the knowledge he is about to hit the canvas. The harder Taylor tried to slog the bowling, the worse he looked.' Hmmm.

The fact was I enjoyed myself, especially batting with Mark Waugh again. I get a kick out of batting with Mark in the one-dayers. We know each other well, having played a lot of partnerships together in both one-day and Test cricket. It was pleasing to finish what *could* be the end of my campaign over here with a victory.

At the end of a comprehensive and impressive victory I fronted up at the press conference. The first question thrown into the ring was about my form. It's moments like that that make me wonder whether I'd ever want to be part of the cricket media when my playing days are over as has been suggested now and then. If that's what you have to be like, I'm not sure I want to do it. We had won a good game of cricket, Mark Waugh had played a truly magnificent innings—yet the first question was about my form.

They all know I'm batting badly. *Everyone* knows I'm batting badly. Yet they harp on it. Endlessly. I know it's only blokes doing a job, but jeez it wears me down sometimes. Anyhow, I handled it okay. I was feeling pretty relaxed about the win and about things generally. I don't know what they'll write about though. That's out of my hands, so I won't worry about it. The main thing is we're back in business. We've shown the South African team and the South African public that we can play one-day cricket. Now I'm ready to hand over the reins to Heals in Cape Town and I'm going to try and relax a bit and enjoy the tour. If I'm needed for another one-dayer, well, I'll be ready.

Michael Bevan lofts one away, en route to 82 in the third one-dayer at Capetown.

APRIL 4, DURBAN

We're heading into match four, down 2–1 after being clearly beaten in the third game. They got away from us when we looked like pinning them down to 220 or so, but they took 57 runs off five overs and 45 off the last three to set us 246 to win. Worse, we were without Mark Waugh who split the webbing between his little finger and ring finger on his right hand, needed six stitches and couldn't bat. We started badly, slumping to 4-25 in the eighth over. Michael Bevan put some starch in the middle with 82, but we were never really in the game and finished 47 short of victory.

I sure didn't enjoy the loss, but I must say I didn't find it overly difficult just being a spectator. I enjoyed the break from all the pressure—from trying to score runs, from being out there constantly monitoring the bowling, setting fields, making decisions, etc. Now and then through the game I had itchy feet to be out there. But only now and then. I recall Sir Donald Bradman's words on the art of captaincy: 'I don't know any game which entails such a severe and prolonged strain on the skipper, but, like the master of a ship, he must exercise control and accept the responsibility.'

We had a day off after the game and went cray fishing at a place called La Med at Clifton Beach. We had dinner and a few drinks there at a place right on the beach. Days like that are an important part of the fabric of any tour. Some of the guys took helicopter joyflights to have a look at the sights of Cape Town. I declined—I'm scared of heights, and helicopters have never really been my scene.

With Mark Waugh out, I toyed with the idea of playing tomorrow. I decided against it for a couple of reasons—firstly because the rest is doing me good, physically

Michael Di Venuto—a fine 89 at The Wanderers in the fifth one-dayer.

and mentally, and secondly, we've got Adam Gilchrist fresh and fit over here, and he can do the job. Frankly, my back is still not great. Errol has been working on it daily and recommends continued rest. So I'm settling for the grandstand again.

APRIL 7, JOHANNESBURG

It's two-all. We had a strong win in Durban after an indifferent start in which there were silly run-outs and in which we lapsed at one stage to 4-50. Thanks to a good innings by Adam Gilchrist—77 off 88 balls—and some good support play by Heals and Andrew Bichel, we struggled to 9-211 on what was probably the best batting wicket we've seen in the whole campaign. I thought we were perhaps 20 or 30 short of what we needed. But cricket is a funny game ...

After the best part of 30 overs they were 1-81, with their run rate starting to improve. Suddenly they lost four wickets in 20 balls, and it was 5-89. They never really looked like winning from then on, although the last pair put on 31 to get them to 196. Our guys bowled straight and well. Andrew Bichel was really steaming in at the batsmen in his first game for about a month. His first spell wasn't great but his second was full of life and enthusiasm, rewarded with a couple of key wickets. We ended up winning by 15 runs with an over and a half to go. It was a bloody good effort considering that we were defending such a modest total.

I'm taking it pretty easily, limiting myself to some basic training. My back is improving and the main pain I'm experiencing is provided on a regular basis by the media. I'm not getting much rest there. There is still a great deal of speculating about my form, my future, and my place on the Ashes tour. To get away from all this was part of the motivation for me when I stepped down from the one-dayers. But I didn't get away from anything. It's still there … it never goes away. Even when I took this break on the advice of people like Trevor Hohns and Geoff Marsh, I knew deep down that the media wouldn't leave me alone. The demand of the media is a daily one, and its appetite voracious. The 'Mark Taylor out of form' story is still big news. I'm not doing *anything* at the moment, but they're still chipping away. I've tried to talk to a few of the guys privately, but it's like talking to a brick wall.

For tomorrow's game we've kept Andrew Bichel in the side at the expense of Paul Reiffel, who has been battling the 'flu. I know Paul will be disappointed. Mark Waugh is still out with his finger problem and there's a genuine lack of experience in our batting lineup. Steve Waugh and maybe Stuart Law at number three are the only truly experienced players. We're a fairly inexperienced side, but the spirit is good. On the other side of the fence I remain perplexed why the South Africans aren't picking Gary Kirsten, a bloke who averages around 46 in one-day cricket. I think it's a poor selection on their part—but we're happy to see him out of the side. At the moment both sides seem to be bowling and fielding better than they're batting.

A spot of cray fishing was the perfect break in the middle of a hard fought one-day series.

APRIL 11

It's a few days and a couple of cricket matches on since my last entry... and we've just won the one-day series. Beauty! At the Wanderers, Johannesburg, we won the toss, scored 7-258, and kept them to 8-250 in reply. It was a really good all-round team performance. Everyone made a few runs, and Michael Di Venuto played particularly well, with 89 up front. It was a tense, see-sawing game which provided plenty in the way of thrills, and little in the way of relaxation. On several different occasions I thought we were gone... then not long afterwards I'd be thinking: 'Hey, we're gonna win this!' And so it went, right down to the wire.

Last night we topped off what can only be remembered as a marvellous tour by winning again, on Centurion Park, Pretoria. They set us 285 to win—a gettable target on a smaller ground like Centurion Park. But chasing 285 in 50 overs is tough, no matter what ground you happen to be on. The guys really played superbly. When Mark Waugh was out for a duck on the third ball, I think most people were writing us off. But Michael Bevan (a century off 90 balls) and Steve Waugh (80 off 100 balls) played superbly and we won the game with an over to spare for the loss of five wickets. I don't think we played perfect one-day cricket. I've seen us bowl better and I've seen us field better. But the batting was just terrific, and everyone chipped something in to the win. It was the sort of performance that reinforces my feelings about this team—that it is truly an excellent outfit, with wonderful team spirit.

The last ball of the South African tour. Allan Donald bowls Steve Waugh in the seventh one-dayer at Bloemfontein, clinching victory for the home side but leaving it 4–3 for the Aussies at the end of an immensely successful campaign.

When you're trying to rate this side against another, it's very hard to put a figure on the quality of team spirit. But it's been a big factor in what we achieved over here, that's for sure. The win at Centurion Park has rounded off the campaign beautifully, no matter what happens in the last one-dayer. We came here primarily to win the Test series, and the one-dayers if we could. As of last night we have achieved both goals—notwithstanding the fact that the captain has been struggling to make runs. That's a reality, and so it was last night that Mark Waugh got a duck. But the thing that matters is how the team goes, and the answer to that is... bloody well. It's a team that relies on *everyone* to do his bit at certain times and that lifts the individual pressure. Everyone of us can say that we're going to go out there and give it our best shot—to make runs or take wickets. It's a nice feeling to know that if it happens you don't manage it on a certain day in a team such as this, someone else will.

APRIL 12

The night was a big one. The clock showed 4.45am when I finally crawled into bed. We were due to fly out this morning for the last one-dayer on Sunday. But that plan was canned somewhere along the track as the celebrations unfolded. Now we're going by bus and if a few ales aren't consumed along the way... well, I'd be very surprised.

Mission accomplished...and the celebrations are about to begin. The Australians have completed the 'double' in South Africa by taking the one-day series and gather here for a happy celebration shot in the dressing room at Centurion Park.

Reflecting on the tour, I feel for my own part that it has been both tremendous, and testing. We fly home in three days time, with both trophies packed in our luggage. And that is Mission Accomplished. As seems to be our way in dead rubber games we lost the last one-dayer fairly comprehensively, falling 109 short of South Africa's 6-310 at Bloemfontein. Now I'm looking forward to getting home, although I know the airport will be a minefield. I can picture it now—the opening words of the press conference: 'Well done, Mark—fantastic tour ... blah, blah, blah ... now, what about your own form?' You can bank on that and 20 more questions in the same vein. I summed it up this morning in an interview I enjoyed doing with Tim Lane of ABC radio: 'It's simple. Mark Taylor doesn't pick himself as Australian captain. The Australian selectors pick the team and then the selectors pick the captain who has to be approved by the ACB. At this stage I am that person—and I'll be that person as long as those people I've mentioned want me to be that person.'

I'm not getting any contrary messages. I'm going home as captain of Australia, and I'm sure I'm going to be captain of the side to England. I'm looking forward to that—a chance to win some more games of cricket, to make some runs...maybe to shut some people up. For all my personal problems I look back over this summer and the only thought is: 'Phew! It's been a goodie. A real goodie!' Only in the one-dayers in Australia did we play poorly. That aside, we've scooped up the trophies we wanted to win. As skipper, I'm very, very happy about that. The challenge in England is to keep the winning spirit going...

Peter McIntyre sends one down in the Test match in Delhi.

Mohammed Azharuddin, a controversial figure in the one-off Test.

Mark Taylor pushes one past Vikram Rathore at short leg at the Feroze Shah Kotla Stadium.

Shivnarine Chanderpaul is bowled for 71. Second Test against the West Indies at the Sydney Cricket Ground.

Matthew Hayden in attacking form, fourth Australia v West Indies Test in Adelaide. Hayden made a major contribution with his innings of 125.

The Test match is won ... and so too the series. Fourth Test Adelaide, and the celebrations begin.

Mark Taylor, his Australian team and the Frank Worrell Trophy—in Perth at the completion of the fifth Test.

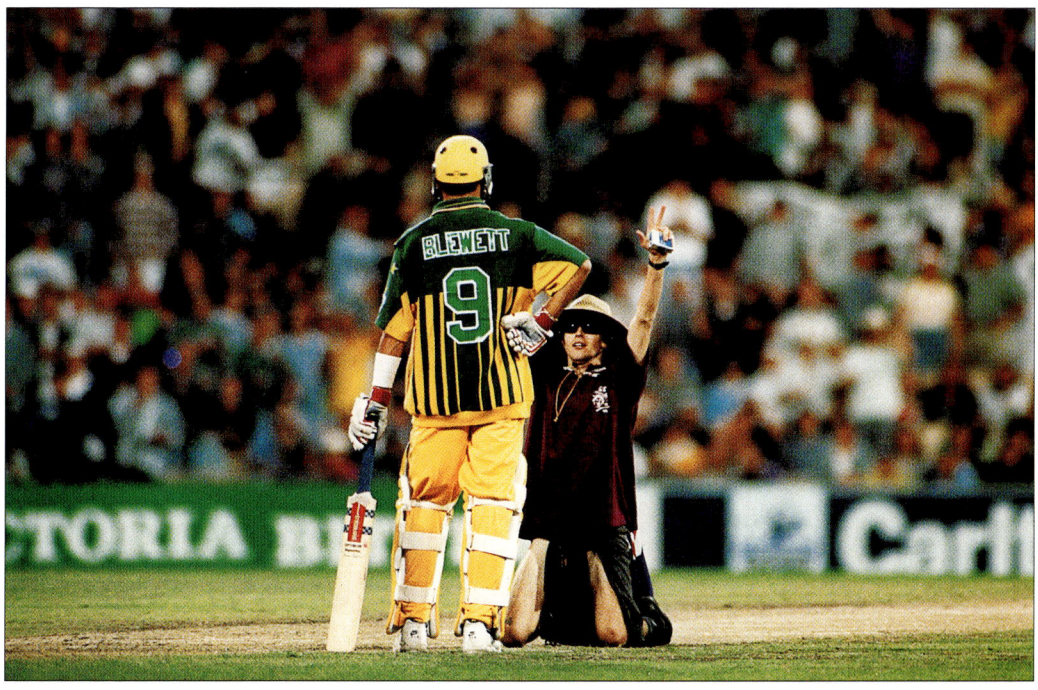

A Sydney Cricket Ground pitch invader hails Greg Blewett during the Australia v West Indies one-dayer. Blewett (12 not out) was at the wicket when Australia, 2–162, topped the Windies' 161.

The skipper departs, dejected, out for 11 in the one-dayer against Pakistan at the SCG on New Year's Day, 1997.

It's helter-skelter as Aussie heroes Greg Blewett (left) and Steve Waugh chase the runs against South Africa, first Test, Johannesburg. Blewett scored 214 and Waugh 160.

Mark Waugh and fan club—Australia v a SA Invitation XI in Port Elizabeth.

The setting at St George's Park, Port Elizabeth—venue for the second Australia v South Africa Test.

Hansie Cronje's jig signals the departure of Mark Waugh, for 20, first innings, second Test in Port Elizabeth.

Skipper Taylor is deep in thought as the Aussies edge towards victory in the nail-biting second Test at St George's Park.

A joyous moment of victory—second Test in Port Elizabeth.

Any tour to South Africa has its spectacular sidelights—and here a jeep-load of Aussies go 'on safari' to meet a special inhabitant.

A panoramic view of Centurion Park—setting for the third Australia v South Africa Test.

The fiery Allan Donald bounces opener Taylor in the third Test.

Another series ... another trophy. The Aussies with the spoils of victory at the end of the South African Test campaign.

The 'bad shirts' escapade provided some fun among the Aussies on tour in South Africa ... and Justin Langer had one of the baddest.

Classic action from the dashing Mark Waugh, en route to 115 in the second one-dayer at St George's Park.

Under the lights in Cape Town ... the picturesque and dramatic scene at the third one-dayer.

An exultant Andrew Bichel captures the wicket of Dave Richardson in the fourth one-dayer in Durban.

It was a season in which Mark Taylor more than ever needed some time off to ease the pressure. Here on the South African campaign the skipper is coasting, doing it easy on a day out on the water.

CHAPTER 5

CALM
BEFORE
THE
STORM

Home safe, and happy to be here. I've managed some R & R with the family, a brief holiday, and a spot of fishing. No cricket, no media, and an easing of the pressure that has been my constant travelling companion these last few months. But all the while, of course, cricket has been there in the back of my mind—thoughts of things past in South Africa...and the challenge ahead in England's summer.

These few words will be the last I write on the South African campaign. It's now in the realms of history and I don't wish to dwell. Looking ahead must be the way for both me and the team. Suffice to say that it disappoints me greatly that in South Africa I didn't manage to dispel the cloud, and end the persistent rumour that my career was over. Now, I must carry all that with me to England and I wish it wasn't that way. The sure thing is that the speculation and questions won't stop until I make a big score in a major match. Those who have me under the microscope will want a 50 from me at the very least in a Test and preferably a century. Runs in a county game won't be enough.

The pressure is certainly on, as there's been so much media speculation about me and my future. Much of it has been fair. The fact is that I haven't done the job as an opening batsman. My record over the past five months is not what I would have wanted. But it's only five months—not 12 as has become accepted lore in the papers. My troubles have been in the period post-India. That's five months—long enough, but not the end of the world.

I have no doubt there has been an element of bias in some of the reporting. I don't reject the criticism. I haven't made the runs and I've got to live with that. But it seemed to get to the point where there was a Mark Taylor obsession. The journos and their editors were on a roll...they must have reckoned that I was selling newspapers.

During the one-day series I had a chat with one of the Aussie journalists. I hadn't played for a week and a half yet his back page lead story the previous day had been almost entirely about me. I asked him: 'When's it gonna stop?' He answered: 'It won't stop until you make runs in a Test match.' The story he had written had suggested that my one-day career was over. It came after the match in which Adam Gilchrist made 77. His theory was that Gilchrist, my replacement in the match, had succeeded—and therefore I wouldn't get back in. I pointed out that Adam in fact was the reserve *middle order* batsman (he batted at six) and reserve wicket keeper—not the replacement top order batsman. I said to him: 'If you had a certain bias *towards* me and not *against* me you could have written an article suggesting that the Australian one-day side needs Mark Taylor back at the top of the order as we were 4-50 in the match when Adam went in. 'Good point,' he replied. Finally he came clean. 'Mark, my own view is that *you* shouldn't be in the one-day team.'

Well, it was an honest opinion and one that I'm sure is shared by a number of people. But such an opinion reflects a certain bias. Obviously when he's writing any story about me for his newspaper, that personal bias is going to come through. That was my concern.

More worrying though were articles which suggested that there was turbulence within the team—with me as the focus. When I discussed those with the journalists involved, they were vague. There were suggestions that there had been 'a bit of bar room talk' centring around whether I was any longer entitled to a spot in the team. The stories contained no quotes. Again, it was mildly concerning. Obviously you can of read whatever you like into bar talk—and particularly if your own bias happens to have a particular slant. Suggestion of this 'trouble' surfaced towards the end of the tour when in fact the support for me was fantastic from senior players like Ian Healy and Steve Waugh.

The job of being Australian captain is a complex one. It's not just a matter of setting fields and working out a batting order. It's about so many other things—about handling media responsibilities, working with administrators, and taking on a host of off-field obligations. With the pressure I've been under, I've probably learned even more about the job these past five months. It hasn't been easy at times, and I've learnt a lot—but I don't think I've lost any friends. I know that the journos are out there trying to do the best job they can, often under pressures of which other people are unaware. And as I have said to them, I'm just trying to do my job.

England, here we come

The team for the Ashes tour is out today, April 17, 1997, and I guess a reasonable assessment would be that it's fairly predictable. Of the 17-man squad, only reserve 'keeper Adam Gilchrist hasn't played Test cricket. But he's been nicely blooded by a couple of tours and five or six one-dayers. It's an experienced side, although I wouldn't call it an *old* side. Heals is a couple of months older than me at 32, and together with the Waughs (31), we'll be the senior members. All of us have played more than 60 Tests, and three of us more than 80. So, a team with experience—but no 'Dad's Army', and a very solid squad. 'Taylor given final chance' was the *Sydney Morning Herald*'s headline assessment.

The big talking point is that Ian Healy has been dropped as vice-captain, with Steve Waugh getting the job. I know Heals will be very disappointed at that, and the thing that I have to come to terms with is that his sacking is partially my fault. It's not that I had any input on the matter, but my batting form and a perceived instability in the side has dictated the decision. With the cloud over my own future—if my form doesn't improve—the selectors wanted the vice-captain to be the next captain of the side. They obviously didn't see Heals at 32 as the next captain in the post-Taylor era, so they gave the nod to Steve on the chance that my form won't come good. It was a tough call for everyone involved, but I know that Heals will take it the way he takes any setback—on the chin. Then he'll settle in to do the best job he possibly can behind the stumps, as he has for years. The irony of it was that the controversy about Heals missing the vice-captaincy temporarily took some of the heat off me.

I'm happy to see 'Slats' (Michael Slater) re-instated to the side. It has been a difficult year for him, struggling to come to terms with his exclusion from the Test side. Some people are surprised he's back. I'm not. I have always liked his sense of adventure as a batsman. He's not an opener from the old school, but a bloke who will play his shots and entertain. Sometimes he'll disappoint, but other times he'll get out there and win you a game in the first hour or two with his aggression. Some of his hundreds have been made at vital times in crucial matches. I think back to his 170 in Brisbane against England in the 1994–95 season, and to his 150 at Lord's in his second Test match in 1993. He can put bowlers on the back foot as well as anyone, and the fact that he's back will only enhance the side. I've enjoyed our association, and I'm looking forward to batting with him again.

There's no doubt that the unlucky player on selection day was Paul Reiffel. In his last Test match he took five wickets in the first innings against the West Indies in Perth and bowled well. But then injury in South Africa, plus the balance of the side we chose against them (two quicks and two spinners with Michael Bevan batting at seven) meant that Pistol didn't get to play, and therefore didn't get the chance to either enhance or harm his chances. For England the selectors have gone for Michael Kasprowicz and Andy Bichel, blokes who have done the job in Shield cricket. Andy didn't get too many opportunities in South Africa, but when he did get the chance he played well, particularly in the one-dayers.

It must have been very tough for the selectors to leave Pistol out. I'm sure the injury problems he's had now and then have been a factor in that. There is certainly no questioning his ability. On his day he's a very, very good bowler, and especially in English conditions. He's unlucky.

I'm really looking forward to this tour—the chance to get back and play at cricket's 'home'. We've got a very solid outfit, although some people will say we've got too many batsmen in the squad. And we *have* got a lot of batsmen, so it's going to be difficult to give everyone a go. I can see already there'll be some tough decisions to make over there as a selector and captain. There are going to be players who are going to miss out to some extent and not play as much as they'd like. But the task at hand is to maintain and build on what we have achieved over these last six months. We've got to keep that going, and keep the team spirit rolling.

The opportunity is there for us to re-confirm our standing in world cricket—and also to hold the Ashes for five series in a row ('89 in England, '91 in Australia, '93 in England and '94–95 in Australia). I understand that if we win in England this time we will be the only side to win five successive Ashes campaigns. I'd love to be part of an achievement like that. I played in the other four, as did Ian Healy and Steve Waugh—and we're hell bent on making it five.

It's a tour on which we have everything to lose ... while they have nothing to lose. We're the form side of Test cricket over the last couple of years, while they've been struggling and copping their fair share of criticism. The expectation on them winning the series will not be high—the latest betting has us 4/1-on favourites to hold the Ashes. So they'll come in with an attitude of nothing to lose and everything to play for. That could spell danger for us—a two horse race in which everyone is tipping the same winner.

The tour will unfold at its traditional leisurely pace—four one-day games against County sides, then the three one-dayers against England for the Texaco Trophy. By the time the summer is done these early games will pale into insignificance, lost in the shadow of the Ashes series. For all that I'll be disappointed if we don't win the one-day series against the Poms. But whatever happens will have no real bearing on the Tests that lie ahead.

One body of opinion is that there'll be turning wickets in England again—that they fancy the chances of Phil Tufnell and the newcomer Robert Croft being the ones to get us out. Well, I'm not too bothered about that. I'm happy we've got Shane Warne and Michael Bevan in our side and if we are faced with turning wickets we have the option of playing Bevo at seven and going in with two spinners and two quicks. If it turns out that the wickets are more geared to the seamers, then the choice will become whether we play Michael Bevan in the top six and add an extra seam bowler, or leave Bevo out. Form and wicket conditions will dictate.

Form is the key—and that applies to me as much as anyone. Basically, spots in the top six are up for grabs. Frankly, I don't want to be picking myself in the form that I've been in lately. I'm captain and a selector, and that's a big leg-in—but the way I'm going to approach the first four weeks of the tour is this: I want the openers, whether it be me, Matthew Elliott or Michael Slater, to be the in-form openers and the same to apply to the next four middle order players. I want us to build stability in the side right from the start. The only thing that can undermine us is instability—and that applies from the captain down.

For my own part, I won't be going to England to make a million runs. I want to improve on recent events—and I've said that enough times now—but that doesn't mean I have to make two or three thousand runs on tour and 900 runs in the Tests. I just want to play solid cricket, to help lay down a foundation for us to retain the Ashes. If it happens that I do make a lot of runs in the Tests, fantastic. But if it means me making 400 runs and solid, regular contributions, then I'd be happy. I'm certainly not putting huge pressure on myself to emulate what I did in 1989, when I went over there relaxed and hopeful—and scored the second most runs in an Ashes series, behind only Don Bradman. I'm going over there to work hard, enjoy myself, and hopefully play well in an Australian team that brings home the Ashes.

I believe that if we play anywhere near our potential in the next three and a half months, we'll win the series. I think that we have the better all-round side. The task is to allow no complacency to creep in, and to maintain and build on the momentum that has swept us through this last southern hemisphere summer. What lies ahead in England for us is a fairly jovial first two or three weeks, backgrounded by the hard physical work that our trainer Steve Smith will put us through. Then, the serious stuff will begin …

CHAPTER 6
ENGLAND
BEGINNING THE GREAT ADVENTURE

The Ashes tour for the 1997 Australians has begun ... in Hong Kong, half a world away from England's green swards. This is PR stuff, spreading-the-message work—a match against a Rest of the World XI as part of Australian cricket's development programme. The weather is tropical and wet and we're to play on a synthetic wicket. The footwear in the circumstances will be rubber soles or running shoes. It's gonna be a casual, low-key way for an Ashes tour to begin—but we're up against a more-than-useful side comprising players from South Africa, Sri Lanka, Pakistan and India. There'll be nothing wrong with the standard of cricket.

The last 36 hours have been tough—the usual mix of great anticipation and lump-in-the-throat sadness at leaving home and family for a long spell. We met at the Quay West Hotel in Sydney's Rocks district to pick up our gear, and go through the tour briefing. I was sitting there at one stage signing some autographs when Justin Langer leant across to me. 'Gee, it was hard saying goodbye to Sue [his wife],' said Justin. The Langers have a six-week-old baby which doesn't make farewell time any easier. 'Mate, the only thing you can be sure of,' I said, 'is that it only gets tougher the older you get.' I meant every word. It does.

The older the kids get, the more they understand just what you're up to. It's always been tough for the wives and partners—left behind to hold the fort, keep the spirits up, keep the kids going, to keep explaining why dad's missing for such a long time. I did my best the other night to explain it all to William, five. I told him I was going to England again to play cricket and he just listened to the first few words of it, then sort of switched off. It was interesting ... his way of coping, I suppose. I could see by the way he looked down that he *knew* dad was going away again. 'I'm going away for about 50 sleeps—then you and mum and Jack are coming over,' I told him. 'Fifty sleeps?' he replied. 'That's a *long* time!'

Before one of the tours a year or so ago I remember telling him that I was going away for 70 sleeps. 'Seventy sleeps,' said William thoughtfully. 'That's not very many.' These days he knows a bit more about figures. Two-year-old Jack doesn't grasp it yet. There's just the reality that when he wakes up in the morning ... and the next and the next ... that dad won't be there. That makes it tough for Judi, having to handle that. But she's fantastic at it ... tougher than I am, and better at parting than I am. She'll do as she's always done—be a fantastic mother and look after herself and the kids while I'm away. I know they'll all be looking forward to coming over to England around third Test time.

It was great to catch up with all the guys at the hotel yesterday. The buzz was just terrific, and spirits were as high as they should be. This is *the* tour. If you're an Australian cricketer, this is the one you want to be on. We've drawn the line on all that has gone before. It's nil-all in the Ashes series, and that's the way we're approaching it.

Touchdown

We've made it. It's May 12, early springtime in England, and I'm in my room at the Westbury in London, shuffling some gear and getting ready for the first gym session of the tour. The Hong Kong game was something of a farce, played in wet weather on a synthetic pitch with covers all over the ground. There's not much to say: we kept them to 240 off 40 overs, an ordinary score on a very small ground. We got the runs for six or seven down in about 29 overs.

The big talking point no doubt will be that while on four I slashed at a wide one from a bloke named Mosin Kamal from Pakistan, missed it, and was given out, caught behind. At the press conference afterwards I was asked in varying ways whether this was a continuation of my slump. I tried to explain—and I doubt the media accepted it or believed me—that as far as I was concerned this wasn't part of the tour. For me, the Australian Ashes campaign starts at Arundel Castle this Thursday in our match against the Duke of Norfolk's XI.

A captain in focus. Mark meets the press at Heathrow and the first shots in the Battle for the Ashes are fired.

It's great to be in England. If there was ever going to be any doubt that I would be in for some stick over here, it was dispelled the moment I bowled up to the immigration counter at Heathrow. 'Ah, Mr Taylor,' said the bloke behind the desk in a pukka English accent. 'The captain?' he enquired. 'Yes, that's right,' I said. 'Hmmmm, for how long?' he offered. It was on already. The first bloke I'd met in England—and he was straight into me!

But I wasn't about to let some airport johnnie blacken my mood. I had a couple of hours at the hotel to freshen up before meeting the press—and I must say I wasn't overly looking forward to that. But the conference turned out to be quite enjoyable. I was feeling very relaxed as I introduced the team to a very large gathering of the media, then settled back to field the questions. Of course I got some questions about my own form, but I've become pretty used to those. Generally I felt completely in control. As I said to the ladies and gentlemen of the fourth estate, it was good to be back in England. And it was. There was a mist of light rain on the windows but, well ... that's England.

In my mind during the day was the thought of getting to the nets, of getting back to famous Lord's. Net practice hasn't been something I've looked forward to much in recent times. Going to the nets has just been another chance for me to bat badly. But I'm looking forward to walking into Lord's, to plonking my bag in the change room and heading out to the nets at the nursery end. I'm feeling good. My back's okay and I'm pretty relaxed. As I told the media, I'm going to give it my best shot. If it doesn't work out and I don't play every Test match and I'm no longer captain of Australia—so be it. At least I'll know that I've tried my damndest.

Before I left Sydney I had a chat with Raelene Boyle at a function for the Sporting Chance Cancer Foundation, of which I am a founding member. Raelene, of course, has been fighting her own battle in that regard. 'How're you going?' she asked me. 'Fine,' I said. She obviously was pretty tuned in to my plight. 'Get out there and enjoy it ... have a bit of fun,' she advised. 'Do what you've always done in the past.' And that's exactly what I'm going to try and do. Today wasn't half a bad start. Imagine having *fun* at a press conference! But I did. I'm going to do my best to keep this spirit of positive enjoyment going all the way. I hold on to a vision—I've got the Ashes Cup in my hands, I'm back in form and still captain of the Australian cricket team. That's my personal quest ...

MAY 15

It's early morning on the day it all begins, the day of the traditional tour opener at Arundel Castle. We play an invitation XI captained by 44-year-old John Emburey, in what is always a good-spirited easing-in to the tour. Must admit I've got a few butterflies. A few runs would be nice, even in a lighthearted game such as this. I probably won't be quite as relaxed as the Australian captain generally is in such a game. I can remember AB (Allan Border) playing in these sort of games and batting at about seven or eight—just coming in for a bit of a swing. I won't be doing that. I'll open—view it as an opportunity to make some runs and break the drought.

The start to this tour has been excellent. The vibes are good and the sun has been shining these last couple of days. I think we've all relished the pleasure of some net sessions at the home of cricket, Lord's, especially for the players making their first Ashes tour. I've been hitting the ball well; my feet seem to be moving better. But I know too that *runs* are what I need. I'll be trying to get some of those today.

As always the first week of the tour is pretty much full-on. We had an enjoyable *Coke* function at a place called the Cafe de Paris, then, last night, the traditional MCC dinner at Lord's. As captain, I have a role to play at all these functions—introducing the team, saying a few words. It goes with the job. We have set about creating a very positive image for the team. We make an effort at all times to look good, to look smart. We have made ourselves very available to the media and I think that's impressed the local scribes and got us off to a good start. People see us as polished, and ready for business. It's exactly the way we want it—to be perceived as the professional, responsible Aussie sporting team that we are. Our goals for the tour have been set: to take every game seriously, and to try and win every one of them.

We are carrying some injury niggles, which is about the only downside to these early days. Greg Blewett is having problems with a knee, Andy Bichel has a back problem, Michael Bevan is a bit below par with a groin strain and Warnie's getting some work done on his right shoulder. Both spinners are missing from today's opening match, so we're a bit down in that department. We need them back soon. I sense that the spinners are going to have a lot of work to do on this tour and especially so if the weather stays the way it is now.

Jeremy Snape is the man underneath as the Australian captain crashes over the top—an incident from the one-dayer at County Ground, Northhampton.

MAY 16

We're off and running—and the opener at the beautiful surroundings of Arundel was a raging success, or about as good as a low-key game can be, anyway. I made 45 and while it wasn't a dazzling 45, there were some glimpses of good form in it, with a couple of nicely struck boundaries. We made 235; Mark Waugh made 46 and hit 'em very sweetly while Michael Slater made a good 50. Then we had them 8-59 at one stage, with wickets to everyone. Jason Gillespie got one with his first ball on English soil and ended up with four. It was a great start for him—he bowled with good pace, swung the ball away and maintained good line and length. It was an impressive debut which suggests it may be a great tour for him. In the end they made 120, so it's strike one to the Aussies.

Tonight soccer is jostling with cricket for the premier spot in my mind. A bunch of us are just back from Coventry City, a 45 minute drive up the motorway, where we watched a benefit game in which Manchester United played Coventry. Phillip Neville, the son of a good pal of mine, Neville Neville, organised the tickets. Phillip and his brother Gary both play for Manchester United and England.

I met their dad when I was playing in the Bolton League years ago. When Judi comes over with the boys she'll be staying at a house the Nevilles own at Bury. They are a terrific sporting family; Phillip's twin sister Tracey is currently playing netball for England. Tonight's soccer was a nice diversion as we ease ourselves into a programme that will get heavier and heavier.

There's rain on the wind tonight, but we're looking forward to our second one-dayer against Northamptonshire.

Northamptonshire

The first fairly serious game of the tour turned out to be a pretty good one for me. Winning the toss and batting on a wicket that looked as though it would do a bit early (and it did), we were helped by some pretty scratchy bowling in the first few overs. Slats (33) got away to a flyer, while I got away slowly. Mark Waugh chipped in with 38 in the middle, and Adam Gilchrist with 40 at the end. I ended up with 76 off 121 balls—not what you would call a scintillating innings, but a promising one. We made 232, batting only 47.4 overs. With clouds gathering over the ground, we bowled well. Michael Kasprowicz got some really good late outswing and Jason Gillespie, Brendon Julian and Warnie all made contributions. We had them 5-130 when the rains came. When the sums were done, we were winners on run rate. This northern summer has a rainy look about it.

We drove to Worcestershire straight after the game, through persistent rain. It's now Sunday morning, May 18, and the sky is steely grey and the ground sodden underfoot.

Worcestershire

A brief, early nightmare for us ... but maybe a blessing in disguise, too. Sent in to bat on a wicket that was doing a bit we were bowled out for 120. The Worcestershire bowlers were steady medium-pacers who nagged away with good line and length. Ragged batting which lacked commitment let us down. It's early days and probably most of us are focusing on trying to click into some individual form, rather than address the match situation. We were well beaten. They got the runs in about 40 overs and taught us a lesson or two. Mainly they showed us that we just can't afford to rock along to every match and expect to win it. The work has to be done. Adjustment has to be made in approach depending on the wicket and the conditions. We got it wrong today, but hopefully we'll learn from that. I made 14, gone the instant I tried to play my first really aggressive stroke. Trying to drive down the ground I got an inside edge and was caught behind. I'm not disappointed with my start to the tour—I feel I'm going reasonably well.

Durham

A win for the English weather here, and that's a shame. The skies are weeping rather badly and play never looked much of a chance. It's disappointing. With the one-dayers approaching, the match was a chance for us to work out one or two minor puzzles in the side. The skipper, for example, would have loved to have picked up some more runs here. And the plan was to try Michael Slater at six, where he batted particularly well in India in the three-cornered series against the Indians and South Africans. The rain has washed away that plan and on the eve of the first one-dayer we have to pick a side on what we *think* is merit and form. One more game would have been handy.

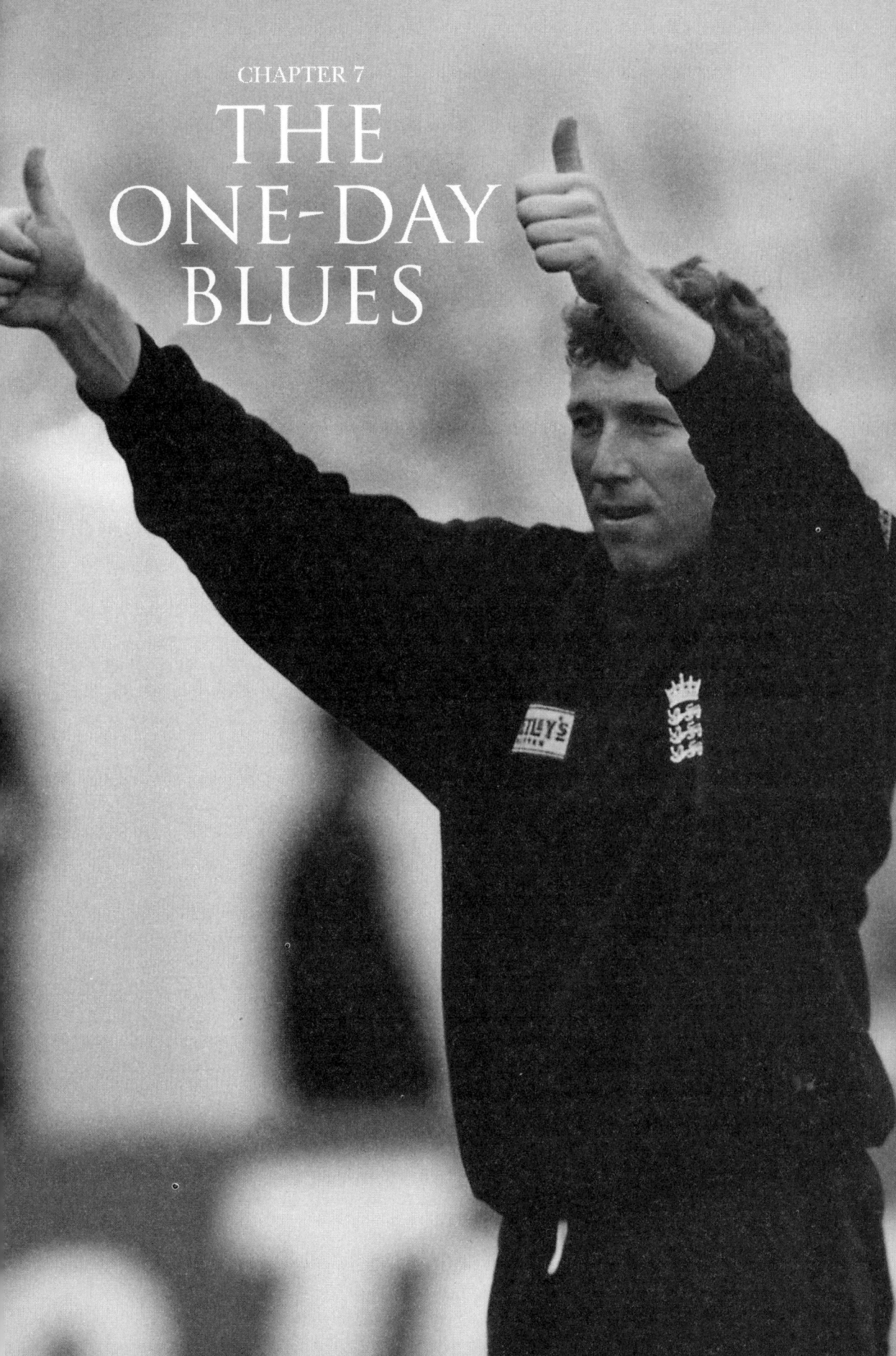

CHAPTER 7
THE ONE-DAY BLUES

Praying...or hurting? The skipper in the nets at Lord's.

In Leeds, Yorkshire, on the evening before the first one day international, the whole team went for a meal at a place called Dino's. At the next table were none other than Mike Atherton, Darren Gough and Robert Croft—blokes we are going to see a lot of in these next few months. The exchanges were cordial; there is respect between the two teams.

Our team selection is not going to be easy. I'd like to think that I've done enough to justify being there—or made enough strides in the right direction, anyway. Hopefully I can go out and play a 'Mark Taylor innings' and put everyone at ease. Michael Kasprowicz and Brendon Julian were duelling for a spot, but BJ has a neck problem and that will probably rule him out. Michael Slater will bat six—I'm sure he's looking forward to grabbing the chance.

This is an early chance for one team or the other to put their stamp on what may lie ahead. We have come over here as favourites and if we can get away to a good start in the one-dayers it will trouble the Poms a good deal. At the back of their minds will be the thought that we are likely only to improve as the tour unfolds. A good start for them will give *them* the confidence they need to muster a big challenge in the Tests. I think they have more to lose in the one-dayers than we have. A loss would really rattle their cage, considering that we are warm favourites to retain the Ashes anyway. Conversely a loss for us would be effectively not much more than a further jolt after a slowish start to the tour—a signal for us to work even harder.

We don't want to think about losing though, and the last couple of days have been good. There is a spring in the step of this cricket team. Our team meeting before the final training session couldn't have been more positive. I spoke to the guys about being a bit tougher, about squeaking out as many runs as we can in that middle order. I'm hopeful that we're going to play well, but time will tell ...

The slight worry is that a few of us are perhaps physically below par. A lot of the guys have had the 'flu so far—in varying degrees. And right now I'm battling a throat complaint myself, hoping that it won't flare into something worse. The weather in Leeds is shocking—freezing cold, with a sharp wind blowing. About the only thing it's not doing at the moment is raining (or snowing!).

I accept that the pressure is on me. I'd love to get away to a reasonable start, to get my own confidence up—and to get people to stop talking about me, and my form. That talk has been less of late, but I know if I can stop it altogether it will be just one less distraction the Australian team has to worry about.

The One-Dayers: Match One

Under cloudy skies at Headingley and on a wicket that was doing a bit we were given a rather loud wake-up call. It was a match in which it seemed we were never in the ascendancy, apart from a period when we cut into their top order for not too many runs. We started badly—losing the toss, and struggling on a wicket that was seaming around. I edged one early from Darren Gough, a ball that decked away. Should have played it tighter to my body. But not one of us managed to take it by the throat and we really struggled to 8-170 off our 50 overs, with Bevo top scoring with 30. In reply we had them 4-40, but couldn't ram home the chance. From that point onwards the bowling and the fielding were both untidy and they got the runs with nine overs to spare, four down. You could call that a convincing win.

We were a bit scratchy; a bit rusty—maybe short of a little match practice. But the worrying thing was that we were down on enthusiasm. Back in London, we've talked about that. After a practice session for the second one-dayer we sat around the change rooms and had a good yarn about what went wrong in Leeds. The general feeling was that although we're struggling a little for form, it's more the lack of urgency in our play—a vital ingredient in one-day cricket. The fact now is that we must win tomorrow—otherwise the series is gone. Yesterday the Poms topped us on the score of enthusiasm. Today the headline in one of the papers is 'The Ashes are coming home'. It's a premature reaction, of course—but the fact is that England have taken a lot of heart from their win. It did them plenty of good. Maybe it did us some as well, signalled for us to tighten up, toughen up—and lift the intensity. The hope is that we'll do all of those things in Game Two. The English press really are amazing. Today they had the Ashes heading back here. But it's just as certain if we win the next two games that they'll be calling for heads to roll in the England side.

I'm heartened by the fact that our team harmony is especially good. One small factor in this is the regular card 'school' on board the bus whenever we travel. We spend a lot of time on the bus, and more and more it becomes like a second home as we criss-cross the countryside. I've teamed up with Michael Bevan to take on Shane Warne and Matthew Elliott at 500. I can report that after the trip from Leeds to London, about a four-hour haul, the score stands at Bevan–Taylor 36 games, Warne–Elliott 23. Pretty convincing, I would suggest. Warnie and I used to be a regular team but we've split up this tour to educate Bevo and 'Herb' Elliott in the art of 500. The score suggests that Bevo has been a quicker learner than Matthew. It's a good way to pass the time, although not all the guys are card players. Warnie loves 'em—I think it's the gambling side of it. I'll keep you posted on the ongoing battle; however I get the feeling there may be a change of personnel. I think we're starting to lose Matthew Elliott's interest and that at some stage down the track we may have to find a new partner for Shane.

Another fact of touring life in England is the ever-present, devout autograph (and memorabilia) hunter. Actually 'collector' is a better word. People here have a genuine love affair with the game of cricket—and many people seem to go to an

Texaco Trophy Match One, Headingley—and Darren Gough makes an impassioned plea for Steve Waugh's wicket. The appeal was turned down and Waugh made 19 in Australia's disappointing start.

enormous amount of trouble in preparing things they want signed. Over here it's not just a rough piece of paper that's thrust into your hand—often it's something ornate, and obviously special to the 'collector'. Wherever we are, I get regular letters every day from people wishing us well, and people looking for an autographed team sheet or some memento from the tour.

On arrival in London I had a big package waiting for me from the kids in first grade at Denmead Prep School in Hampden. The kids are about six, and they all wrote nice little cards welcoming us to England. They've all done little drawings, told us about their favourite sports and so on. This *passion* that exists for the game over here is one of the reasons that blokes like myself and the Waughs enjoy coming to England so much to play cricket. The love for the game that exists among so many people is very genuine, and very deep.

The One-Dayers: Match Two

Well, two strikes and you're out. I'm sitting in my hotel room contemplating the fact that we have just lost the second one-dayer and that the Texaco Trophy has gone to England. It was a disappointing day all round, although we certainly played a lot better than we had in the first game. For me there was personal disappointment in my run-out at 11, just as I felt I was starting to get going. There was a mix up involving Mark Waugh and me and I got stranded—about half a pitch short of making my ground. It was a bad day for run-outs; we had four of them but still managed to muster 250, with Michael Bevan getting a very good 100 and Adam Gilchrist an aggressive 53.

It wasn't enough. Michael Atherton made 113 (and won Man of the Match) and played particularly well after an early let-off. We had a good opportunity to run the English skipper out when he was on one, but missed the stumps narrowly. It was one of those games. We gave away four run-outs, and didn't pick up one from them.

Tonight in the wake of the match I have voted to leave myself out of the third one-dayer at Lord's. It's disappointing—I feel I'm hitting the ball okay now, but things aren't running for me. The hard fact is that my scores of 7 and 11 in the two internationals so far are not good enough. At the press conference after the match there was a pointed question from the *Australian*'s Malcolm Conn relating to our one-day defeats (in India and now in England) with me as captain. He obviously didn't include South Africa in that equation. I played two games in a winning series there, but that small fact obviously didn't suit the direction of his story. It was the first real sign over here that the press aren't going to miss me if they get the chance. Unfortunately, I'm giving them far too much ammunition at the moment, and I can't yet get them off my back. I know within myself that I'm playing better, but as they've said ... you've got to make runs—that's what it's all about. Anyhow, I'm out of the third game, and my focus now is the two three-day matches leading up to the Test series. That has to be my next goal—to make some runs there.

Why is this man laughing? Mike Atherton at Leeds during the one-day series, with England in the ascendancy. Alec Stewart is alongside.

To lose the Texaco Trophy is mildly disappointing, but no catastrophe. It would have been nice to win it, but the main task remains at hand. I'm sure there are people who will say that losing the one-dayers is the first step towards us losing the Ashes. I don't accept that theory. The interesting statistic is that Mike Atherton's England side have *never* lost the Texaco Trophy under his captaincy, yet their Test record is not so great. The one-dayers are a fine lead-in to the tour—but in the bigger picture they are relatively insignificant as a pointer to the six-Test series that lies ahead. We're going to be bloody hard to beat in that.

The One-Dayers: Match Three

The third game, at Lord's, turned out to be as disappointing as the first two. Leaving myself out was not too difficult. I was happy to give Matthew Elliott his chance to play in the side. But it was interesting after the pre-game warm ups that the press grabbed me—even though I wasn't playing. I think some of them see this as the beginning of the end of my career. I've got a pretty thick skin about that—they're entitled to their opinions, and I can live with that. What I've got to worry about is *me*—getting out there and doing the business for Australia. The County games and the Tests lie ahead. The chance is there.

In Game Three we lost our third toss straight and batted first. There was some loose stuff—and some lengthy periods of good stuff. Mark Waugh played particularly well for 90-odd. They bowled us out in the last over for a reasonable total of 269. Now, in Australia, 269 would be considered a very good total—but at Lord's on a good wicket and with a very, very slick outfield, it was certainly nowhere near out of reach for the England side.

We bowled pretty much the way we have been. We got Atherton early and applied some pressure, but then didn't sustain it. Alex Stewart made 70 and played very well and young Ben Hollioake, one of the two Aussie-born brothers in the side, came out and belted 60-odd in about 40 balls. We seem to be down a peg or two at the moment in the area of toughness. It's very unusual for an Australian side to allow guys in their first games to dominate—yet Adam and Ben Hollioake certainly managed that in the three one-dayers. Our fielding was average. We dropped a couple of tough catches and missed a couple of potential run-outs. We're still a fraction away from it ... not quite yet taking those half-chances. England have been much more wound up and on the pace so far. They deserved to win the series, and they deserved to win it three-nil.

They got the required runs four-down with an over and a half to spare. Really, we never had them in any sort of trouble chasing the total, and that's pretty disappointing when you have 270 to play with. I'm not reading too much into it, and I would caution other people not to. In my view the one-day series of recent times have become increasingly independent from the other side of the game. Our own one-day form has been inconsistent, despite our success in South Africa where the

South Africans were a touch below their best in the one-day game. What I'm saying is that in my view—which contrasts markedly with that of a now very optimistic English media—the one-day series just completed is no more than a very uncertain guide to the arena of Test cricket. The big value of the series is that it has created terrific interest in the Tests. It seems that all of England is buzzing in anticipation of what lies ahead.

We talked after the match about not turning a molehill into a mountain. We've been down this track before. In the West Indies in 1995 we lost the one-dayers 4–1 . . . then won the Test battle. In Australia's last summer we played fairly ordinary one-day cricket, only to beat the Windies again in the Tests. The thing now is for us to stick together, play some good solid cricket in these upcoming matches in Gloucester and Derby, and to get ready. We are, after all, the unofficial 'Test match champions'. My belief is that if we start to now build towards peak form and don't fall apart team-wise (which I'm sure won't happen), then we'll beat England in the Test series.

I'm looking at where we stand now as virtually the start of the tour. The prelims are over; the cobwebs lifting from the team. I don't think there's any doubt we came into the one-day series slightly under-prepared, and that's no excuse. The Poms played darned well, and deserve their victories and the praise they received. But we came out of that tough campaign in South Africa needing a break. It would be unrealistic to expect us to click straight into top gear the minute we stepped off the plane here. Maybe my own experience so far sort of sums it up. I've had a couple of little nibbles—a 70-odd in a one-dayer, a 40-odd. *Now* is crunch time—the opportunity to bat the way I like to bat, to accumulate, to stay out there for a long time, get the feet moving, and get some runs. The same applies to all the guys.

There may be critics back home who snipe away at the fact that we weren't ready for the one-day series and that's why we lost the Texaco Trophy. Very likely they'd be right. But I can't really see how we could have done it any differently. We had three weeks off after South Africa, and that was pretty close to the minimum. Cricket teams can't just go from tour to tour. There has to be a pause—a chance to freshen up, overcome niggling injuries and revitalise yourself mentally.

Now, in England's summer, we've had our wake-up call. England have shown they're going to be a better team than in the last few series. The alarm has sounded nice and early for us and we can now set about shaping up for the main task ahead.

CHAPTER 8

TRAVELLING FIRST CLASS

Gloucestershire

The start to the first class games on tour couldn't have been much worse. For me it was a misery—out to the fourth ball I faced, edging one to the 'keeper off Mike Smith. For the team as a whole, the news wasn't much better. We were sluggish, needing to find that elusive extra gear and failing to do so. Matthew Elliott and Justin Langer both departed early, also caught behind the wicket. Then the Waughs added some substance with a fine partnership, being the only two of our batsmen who looked to be in any sort of command out there. Then our tail got knocked over, and we were all out for 249, a decidedly below-par score. In reply they were 1-50 off 30 overs. Our bowlers improved as the afternoon session went on, which was about the only bright spot we could take from the day's play.

I'm going to retrieve the film of my own dismissal from one of the cameramen over here and see if I can learn anything from it. I doubt there'll be any great revelation, but I'll have a look anyway. The ball that got me was one that swung away, nipped off the seam and took the edge. It wasn't what I would have hoped. I'm told that back home the papers are in full cry. 'Dead Duck', screamed the Sydney *Daily Telegraph* back page. 'Failure puts Taylor at crisis point'.

These days I am going out into the middle decidedly nervous. Within myself I'm feeling good, and I know that generally I'm batting better than I was in South Africa (I had a net session after today's play and struck the ball well) but I'm not showing it on the scoreboard. Under the circumstances the nerves are natural enough, but hope springs eternal. I know there's an innings somewhere not far down the track that can turn it around for me. The top order hinges on me at the moment—and if that's putting pressure on myself, well ... it's simply the truth. Meanwhile I have to live with the reality that the loss of our debut first class game is only going to add fuel to the fire fanned with some enthusiasm by those who reckon I'm on the way out.

Day two was a tough grind, but not a bad one for us. We worked hard to bowl the Gloucestershire boys out and finally managed it an hour and a quarter before stumps. They're leading by 101, which is not so great for us on the face of it, but I'm not unhappy with the way we bowled. We plugged away on a slow wicket, and the bowling got sharper and better as the day unfolded. A good sign. Matthew Elliott and I batted through to stumps, gathering 20 or so each and giving us the chance to go on with it.

It was a very strange experience when I went in to bat in this second innings. I can't get over how nervous I am before going in to bat these days. It's a terrible thing being out of form. The pressure just builds and builds. The longer the bad run goes, the worse it gets. You start to think negatively, and it's hard to change that. Today I let a lot of balls go. I wasn't in any real trouble and managed a couple of reasonable shots. Basically, I'm hanging in there. It's a wicket that requires hard graft more than anything else. Its slowness does not encourage fluent stroke play.

After today I wondered how much easier it would be if I wasn't captain. Today I

'Keeper Jack Russell goes up—and the Australian skipper is out for 30, lbw to Martin Ball against Gloucestershire.

worked hard out there, juggling the bowlers and swapping fielding positions as we battled away to get them out. Then within ten minutes I was back in, needing to make runs to prove to everyone that I am rightly one of our two openers for at least the first two Tests. Both Matthew Elliott and I will be dreaming of big scores tonight. Matt hasn't made runs yet on tour and, like me, he'd love to have a long dig.

Today had its light side. Early on we took part in a charity promotion, raising money for a new children's hospital. It was a 'Wrong Trousers Day' in which everyone was asked to put in a quid and wear the wrong trousers for the day ahead. So, if you were wearing a suit and tie, the correct dress would be a pair of shorts, or perhaps trackie pants. In all, more than four million people got into the spirit ... and the wrong trousers. At today's warm-up before play started we were given various colourful pairs of pants which we wore with our training tops. It was a great photo opportunity for the local media, and I took a few snaps myself.

Day three of the match has done no more than heighten the tension which surrounds me. I had been there about half an hour and was starting to middle a few when I played back to an offspinner named Martin Ball and was given lbw for 30. A real 'nothing' score. I then watched Matthew Elliott and Justin Langer score a hundred each, both of them batting extra well. At the end of the day the score is 4–354, but irrelevant. We have come through strongly, but my own moderate performance has not helped the cause.

At the post-game media conference the main topic of conversation is me ... and whether I'll play in the first Test. It's a fair question, the way things are going. I know

I'm running out of time, and innings. I came over here telling everyone the truth—that I hadn't made enough runs and that I was gonna have to make some.

In today's press Ian Chappell is quoted as saying that I should give it away—sack myself from the team. Chappell is a bloke I respect a great deal for his achievements and his knowledge of the game. He is also a friend, a bloke I've known for a long time. I think that over the years he and I have shared a large number of theories on the game, and on the business of captaincy. Chappell today has offered the opinion that he has seen no change in my technique to suggest that I'm close to coming out of the form slump.

In truth, that's the *only* thing that is encouraging me to hang on—the feeling that I am hitting the ball better than I was, that my feet are moving better and there's a distant light at the end of the tunnel, albeit a faint one. I respect Chappell's opinion and know that he wouldn't have stepped forward with it if it wasn't what he believed. Back home his brother Greg has also had his say. 'Mark Taylor is in no fit state to be captain of the Australian cricket team,' he begins in the *Sunday Telegraph*.

I'll just say now to all my critics and inquisitors that there's *no way* I would jeopardise Australia's chances in the Ashes. There is no way I would put my career before my country's chances. I have never been a selfish player, and I don't plan to start now.

I believe that it now comes down to this: I have two more games, against Derbyshire, then the Test match at Edgbaston, to 'blow up the bridge'—a phrase once used by the great football coach Jack Gibson to his team when they had to make up some leeway fast. That's a maximum of four innings, and against top flight bowling attacks. The Derbyshire line-up includes Philip DeFreitas and Devon Malcolm and a guy named Harris who is apparently a very good swing bowler. After them comes England, with the best bowling attack the Poms can muster. If I can make runs in these next two, then the drought will have ended. The achievement will not have been against weak opposition. At 32 years of age I have to prove things to myself—and to my team. I have to prove that I am still the man to open the batting for Australia. The phrase 'the end is nigh' comes to my mind. One way or the other.

I awoke in good spirits that morning in Bristol to what I knew was going to be a day of opportunity. Downstairs a nasty surprise awaited me in the shape of representatives from the *Daily Mirror* newspaper who wanted to get a photo of me with a cricket bat three feet wide. It was a light hearted thing, they said. It wasn't light-hearted to me and I declined, firmly. Then at the ground as I made my way to the change room, a bloke jumped in front of me with the wide bat and there was a photographer right there who snapped a shot. Steve Waugh and our manager Alan Crompton intervened, and the film was reluctantly handed over. Alan later made an angry call of complaint to the newspaper. They still managed to run with a story the next morning headed 'Batman and Sobbin''.

It was pretty cheap and nasty stuff, and not a great start to the day for me. The pressure was extraordinary. When I walked out to bat (and remember this is

Australia v Derbyshire, not one of the world's most momentous cricket matches) there were a bunch of photographers halfway out to the wicket, taking photos of me. All of a sudden, as I told the assembled media later, the pressure seemed as great as any Test match, probably greater than anything I had ever experienced. If I get through this, I told them, I'm more than ready to continue playing Test cricket.

Derbyshire

It's the evening of day one v Derbyshire and I've just come off the golf course. We are staying at a place called Breadsall Priory, a truly lovely old manor which has been transformed into a hotel, and is surrounded by 27 holes of lush golf course. I used the chance of England's lingering twilight to get out and have a hit... to try and vent some frustration, I suppose.

We won the toss today, and batted on a good wicket. They left Devon Malcolm out of their side, apparently on late instructions from the England Cricket Board that he shouldn't play. I guess that's a tip that he's going to play the first Test.

Last night Judi and I talked for 45 minutes on the phone. She agrees that I should go out to be positive, play some shots, and get the Taylor feet working. Well, I went out today feeling very positive, got off the mark first ball, then knocked a couple of twos. At that point Phil 'Daffy' DeFreitas, a friend of mine over the years and a bloke on whom I have generally had the wood, bowled me a short ball, not

Matthew Elliott glides one away in his innings of 67 against Derbyshire.

terribly quick. I played a pull shot, hitting it straight to forward leg and was out for five. I was feeling positive—and got out playing positive.

That was about the only bad news all day. Greg Blewett made 120 (despite having to pass a fitness test on the morning of the match), Matthew Elliott got 60, Michael Bevan 50, and Steve Waugh 40. At 6-370, I declared and they were 1-70 at stumps. Everyone, bar me, looks in reasonable form. I hate to harp on it but again today I didn't feel at all bad out in the middle. I was looking forward to it, and far less nervous than I had been against Gloucestershire. The photographers are here in droves. I suppose the picture in everyone's mind in the current climate is the last one of Mark Taylor in an Australian cap. The last innings.

Today is the first time that I've really considered that I may be close to the end of my international career. Obviously I'm going to be here with the Australian side until the end of this tour in late August, but I suppose that right now is the first time I have seriously contemplated the possibility of standing down from the captaincy. The runs aren't coming. There can be no more excuses. It no longer matters how I get out—whether it's a sensational catch off a good shot, a run out, or whatever—the thing left for me is to make some runs. And very, very soon.

The perplexing thing is that there has been no consistency about my dismissals. I'm nicking the odd ball, I've been lbw to a spinner, run out, and, now, caught at forward leg. If there was a common thread, maybe it would be easier to work on. My problem is that I'm finding ways to get out and not finding ways to make runs. I guess I've got a chance here in the second innings at Derby. But it's not any real great lead-up to a Test. Derbyshire are below strength and the wicket is flat and fairly slow.

The consideration is now in my mind that I may not play the first Test. I haven't made a decision yet, and I do have a couple more days to think about it. I know that to stand down now probably means that I won't play the rest of the series, so it's a profound decision that I'm wrestling with. Effectively it will mean the end of my international career. As I've said to the media here, that wouldn't be the end of my life. But it would be an immensely disappointing end to my life in cricket—a game that has been so good to me.

I have achieved so much more in the game than I ever thought I would ... so much more that my hope is that when I do leave, it will be in the grandest of styles. But to stand down now has to be a consideration. It seems to me right now that all the guys in the side are doing the job—except me. Just about everyone else seems to be running into form coming up to the Test, and I'm still struggling. As I said before I won't put myself before the best interests of the Australian cricket team. We have to pick the best 11 guys we can put on the park for the first Test and if I don't fit that criterion, then I'm gonna have to leave myself out. And that's going to be very, very tough—but it's also something that is becoming more of a possibility each day.

Setting aside my own dilemma, there is some good and some not so good news in the lead-up to the Test. The good is that most of the batsmen—Elliott, Blewett, Langer, Waugh, Waugh, Bevan—have made some runs and look to be in reasonable nick. For this game at Derby we've got Brendon Julian and Andrew Bichel back on the park after both of them being sidelined in recent weeks with injuries. They both bowled today, and they were both very rusty. The fact that they're 1-70 after only 12 or 13 overs shows just how poorly we bowled. Both at least improved as their spells went on—and at least we're starting to get to a stage where we have 17 players to pick from, rather than 14 or 15.

But the *bad* news is that both Bichel and Julian are only just this moment back—and it's hard to imagine them being genuine contenders for the first Test unless they do something startling in these next couple of days. I'd certainly like to have more bowlers to choose from for the Test match. That's the ideal situation—to have everyone fit, in form, and pushing hard for selection. Jason Gillespie, our third bowler in this game, is going well and mustering good pace—hopefully he'll find a little more rhythm tomorrow.

The Test is fraught with some danger. The wickets for our last two games have been of the low and slow variety. From reports we are getting, Edgbaston will be a little different—a wicket with some more pace in it. With the likes of Devon Malcolm and Darren Gough certain to be in the England Test XI we're going to strike a couple of bowlers who are considerably brisker than we've faced so far. The bowling attacks in these couple of games have been largely medium paced, on slowish wickets.

I'm just back from the ground after day two of the Derbyshire match, and feeling a hell of a lot better. Their skipper Dean Jones declared at 9-250 today, 100 behind. Early in our second innings there came a crucial moment. Matthew Elliott departed early and I was batting there with Justin Langer, paddling around, not going all that well when I got a wide half volley from Phil DeFreitas. My drive was not quite to the ball and I nicked it, low and direct to Dean Jones at first slip ... who dropped me!

Justin Langer walked down the wicket to me and I said to him: 'Well, that's about it—I'm just about ready to give up.' I was starting to feel downright sorry for myself. (Justin has just left my room, and I had thanked him again here for the way he nursed me through the next few overs.) His reaction to my somewhat morose comment was fantastic. 'Just watch the ball,' he said. 'That's rubbish about giving up ... that's just rubbish!' And he was right of course. My defeatist talk was not the answer. Justin kept talking to me through the next few overs, and he helped me along until tea. 'Just watch the ball ... do the things you know you can do—watch the ball and you won't nick it any more,' he advised me. I put my head down and kept going. At tea, I was 9 not out.

Justin left in the second over after tea, out lbw in what was the second dubious call that had gone against him in the match. So he departed, and I stayed—and at the end of play I was 59 not out, and had struck some good meaty shots. All of a sudden my drive came back, as did my balance. All of a sudden the bat was no longer feeling like some sort of foreign object in my hands.

I got a bit angry out there today. I told a cameraman ... well, I can't say exactly what I told him. But he stuck a camera right in my face as I went out to bat, and I reacted. Probably the bloke was under instructions to get right up close and get the wrinkles under my eyes, but I wasn't happy with that and I told him so. I told Alan Crompton too, and he had a word with the bloke. Probably I'll cop some flak in the British press, but what the hell. Maybe I should have done it a few months ago—got angry with a few people ... maybe including myself. It's been too easy to think about life after cricket and the thought that when cricket stops for me, there are many things I'm looking forward to doing.

But I don't want it to end *now* and I don't want it to end badly. Thinking about that—the ending of my career—provided me with an easy option. Once Justin Langer pulled me into line today, I got angry with myself inside. I listened to Justin. He's right: that's not the way to go out of this game, I said to myself. You've got to give it bloody everything. All of a sudden after tea things started to click—the cover drive came back; the clip off the pads came back. I was watching the ball, hitting the gaps. Suddenly I was feeling like the Mark Taylor of two years ago.

When the clock ticked over to 6.30pm this afternoon, I didn't want to come off. I just wanted to keep batting—and I haven't felt that way in a long time. Today was only my second half century in first class cricket since I made 53 against Queensland at Bankstown Oval in October last year. Today it was not so much the runs, it was the way I *felt*.

Yet, all of it hinged on one thing. If Dean Jones hadn't dropped me at slip, maybe I'd be finished as an international cricketer tonight. I suppose that's how close it was. But Deano put it down and right now I'm back in there thinking that I can do this, that I'm the right man for the job.

It's an amazing game. A cricket career winding back almost a quarter of a century to the malthoid pitches of Wagga, in NSW—and here on a single day in an English summer it comes down to just one ball. If the world had been loaded against me as I had been starting to think, well, something happened today. My spirits were suddenly uplifted and I'm thinking that maybe it *is* meant to be. Maybe I am supposed to come out of this. Now deep inside there's hope—hope that I can get out there tomorrow, hit the ball around again, and that we can declare and win the match. Maybe ... dare I think it ... another 41 runs and a century.

Day three is over, and life is not a bed of roses after all. We've lost the match to Derbyshire—just—and my hope for another long stay in the middle did not become reality. I had hit the ball sweetly in the nets early morning, and strode out there ready to go when play began. But in about the third over of the morning I heard the chilling sound of leather flicking against willow and I was out caught behind. I had added just four more runs to my overnight 59. So there was no fairytale, no pre-Test century. But 63 is better than a smack in the mouth. The return to form that I have been seeking is just about there.

With some quick runs—a century from Michael Bevan, a rapid fire 60 off 50 balls from Brendon Julian—we set up the possibility of a result. The target for them was 370 in 68 overs. Then we stood around in the field, and turned in a fairly ordinary bowling performance. To be fair our bowling attack was hampered by the fact that Andrew Bichel didn't bowl a ball in the second innings. He's got back trouble again and is off to have a check-up. Jason Gillespie had problems too, with a foot injury. Aware that he was struggling, I delayed the declaration, realising that quick runs were very possible on the quick outfield at Derby.

Anyhow, Shane Warne got 7-100 and bowled well—but even that wasn't enough to stop them winning by a single wicket, with three balls to spare. That's about as close as you can get. The fact that we lost the game doesn't mean that much when you consider that we lost only 10 wickets in the game to their 19. But a loss is a loss. My major concern today was a feeling that we lacked the necessary drive. It wasn't until the last half hour when it suddenly became apparent that we might actually lose the game, that a real sense of urgency came into our play. We upped the ante, took three or four wickets and almost pulled a fast-disappearing match out of the fire. In fact if Greg Blewett had hit the stumps with a throw in the last over we would have won. The disappointing thing was that it took us such a long time to realise that we might lose the game. When it finally sank in, it was on the verge of being too late.

Injury worries are our other problem as the Test nears. Glenn McGrath was rested from this game with a troublesome knee, Jason Gillespie is limping and Greg Blewett's been living day to day with a knee injury. The preparation hasn't been anywhere near perfect … for me or the team.

CHAPTER 9
A TEST IN MORE WAYS THAN ONE

On the eve of the Ashes campaign of 1997, the people of Sydney and beyond awoke to the *Daily Telegraph*'s version of the cricket news. HE'S OUT screamed the front page headline alongside a picture of me, with the caption, 'After his latest failure yesterday ... ' Below, the sub-heading read: *Taylor drops himself from Test side.* The story began: 'Captain Mark Taylor has decided to step down from the Australian cricket team for the first Ashes Test, finally conceding defeat after 18 months of disastrous form'. The story went on to suggest that I had told 'only a close circle of friends' about my 'decision'. The story was wrong—and the newspaper knew that before it went to press. It brought urgent phone calls to me from both Judi and my manager John Fordham. Was it true? Obviously they wanted to know. I reassured them both that they were most certainly in my 'close circle of friends' and if the claims in the story had been true, they would have been the first to know. John Fordham, in fact, had been alerted on the Sunday night by a sympathetic journo on the paper to the thrust of the story the *Tele* was going to run. John promptly rang me to check—then the paper to inform them they were off the mark. It ran anyway.

Meanwhile, in England, I had completed my 63 against Derbyshire, and made my decision with Geoff Marsh and Steve Waugh, the other tour selector, to carry on as Australia's captain and Test opener. The truth is that the tour has become almost a game-by-game proposition for me. I didn't make the hundred I had hoped for against Derbyshire. In the circumstances this first Test becomes a selection trial for me. If I miss out this time, I will probably stand down. That's the reality of the situation.

On the eve of the Test I'm worried about the team. I don't believe my own personal struggle has anything to do with it, but the fact of life at the moment is that as a team we are not playing to our potential. I think it's a lot of things—one of them being that we've been playing in a lot of games that haven't meant much to us. I've just gotta hope deep down that we've been holding a bit back and that when the Test comes along, we'll click into gear. Come Thursday we're going to have to up the ante—and keep the standard up if we're to hang on to the Ashes. We've come over here as huge odds-on favourites, but we're certainly not playing that way at the moment.

As I found out (again) today, cricket is a very strange game and things can change dramatically within 24 hours. We need two very good practice sessions in these next 48 hours to get ourselves ready. I have no doubt at all we have the players for the job, but lately we've been a bit tired and lazy, just waiting for things to happen in matches. Cricket is all about getting out there and *making* it happen and we've been very, very good at that in recent years. It nags away at me that we seem to have lost that quality over the past three or four weeks.

One of the really special things for me over these past few days has been the support I have received from home. The report in the *Telegraph* seemed to spark off a wave of support for me and in these days leading up to the Test I have received close to 500 faxes from people back home offering their support, wishing me well

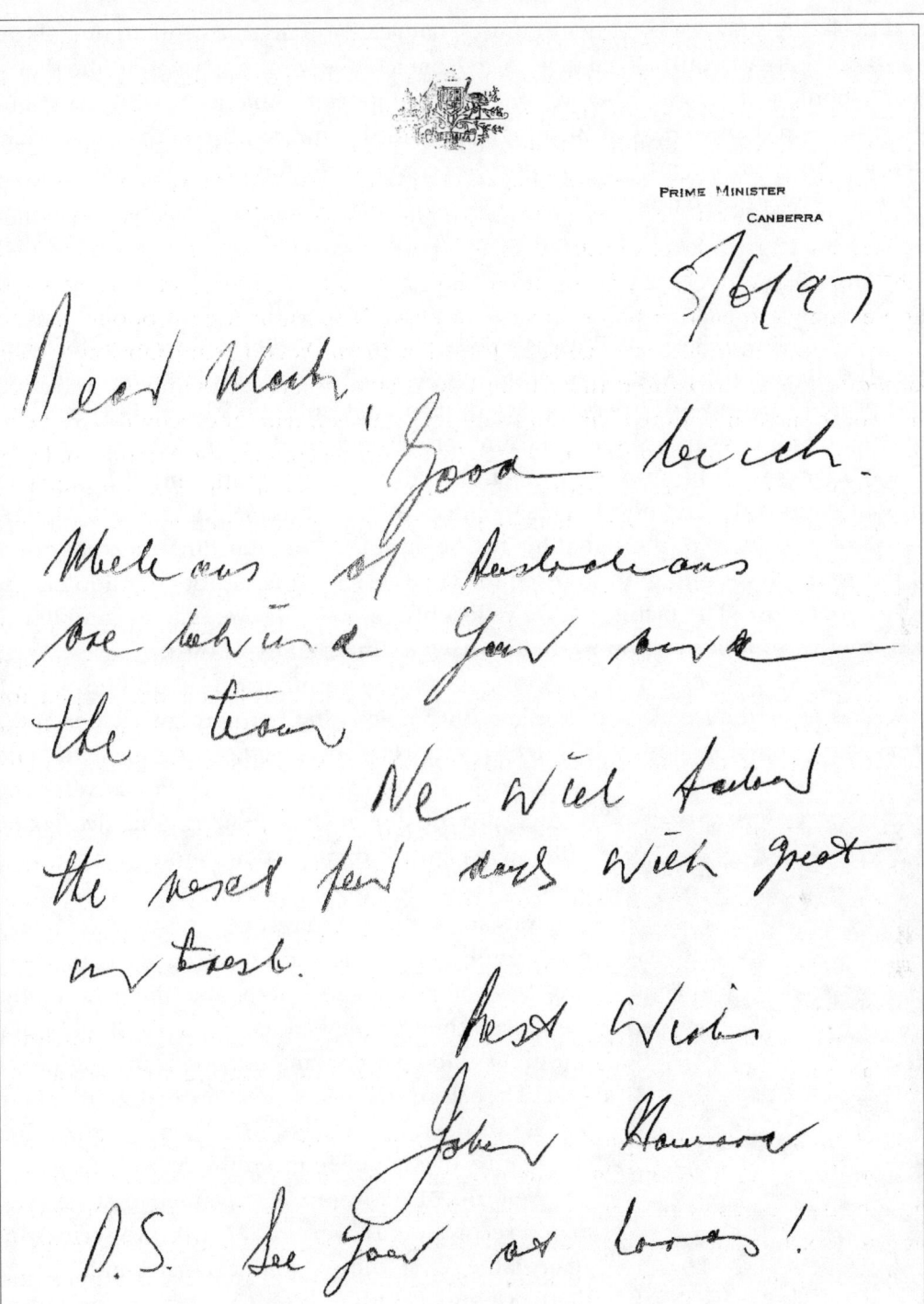

Prime Minister John Howard was a great supporter of Australia's cricket team during the summer battles in two hemispheres, sending regular messages of encouragement and congratulation.

and declaring they are right behind me. That really is fantastic. And among all the messages there was only alternative voice from a bloke who subscribed to the theory that I should give it away. The overwhelming support is immensely heartening, and I just hope in the five days of Birmingham's Test I can repay the faith that so many people have shown in me. The support has come all the way from PM John Howard through to working battlers.

JUNE 3

We're two days out, and the mood is serious. At today's training at Edgbaston, Geoff Marsh didn't hold back. He had some tough things to say on the score of attitude and professionalism—or worrying lack of it so far. Geoff and I had talked late into last night. Our concerns about the team were shared ones and we agreed that some tough talking from him was very much in order. I said my bit, reinforcing Geoff's message, and at the end of it Ian Healy chipped in. It's business time. Geoff Marsh's hard words today were the signal for the beginning of the fair dinkum component of this tour. Now it's up to us to respond. The one sure thing is that we didn't come over here to lose. The fact is that we've lost five of our last seven games (and drawn the other two), so it's right now that we have to find that extra yard.

I feel good, although my form in the nets today wasn't great. I didn't hit the ball as well as I would have liked at training. But I'm working hard on my balance at the crease and thinking positively. I feel pretty relaxed. The task for me is to play positively—not to get out there negatively and scratch around for an ugly-looking ten. I've got to pull my weight and play some shots. I'm looking forward to it.

I was hit with an interesting question at today's press conference. This was a traditional get-together two days before the game, to enable the print media guys to get their previews done. I fielded all the usual questions—about my form, and about playing in the Test. Then I got this one: 'Do you feel guilty about leaving yourself in the team when some of the other young guys haven't been given the opportunity?'

'Well, no,' I answered. I explained that my Test match record was 15 wins in 27 Tests; two series wins against the West Indies, wins against South Africa, England, and Pakistan. We've beaten all the best. I told them of my belief that I had played my part—even though I hadn't played my part in recent times as much as I should have with the bat. I admitted it was a hard way to survive, but that I was hoping for better times just ahead.

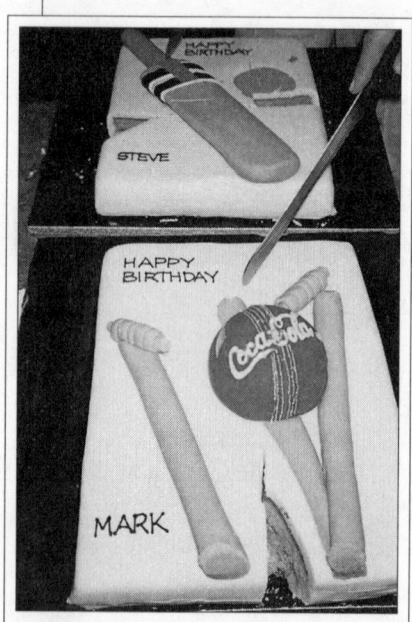

Birthday celebrations are part of the long tour and there was more than enough cake to go around when the twins Mark and Steve Waugh had their day.

Deep down, I know this: if I don't find my form very shortly—and especially if the team happens to be playing badly—then I'll have to go. I would have no option then, as the pressure would be too great. No, I don't feel guilty. Over the period of my tenure as captain, I have done the business. But I can't keep doing what I have been doing and see this side slip into an ordinary Test side when I know we've got the talent to be so much more than that.

During the day Warnie showed me a story from the (English) *Mirror*. He's doing some work for the paper over here, so keeps pretty close tabs on it. Ian Botham had written a piece headlined: 'This man is being stabbed in the back'. It was about me. Botham referred to things written and said about me by previous Australian captains such as Ian and Greg Chappell and even my predecessor Allan Border (although I hadn't seen any comments from AB). I know that Greg wrote I was mentally unfit to captain Australia—which I reckon was A-grade rubbish. Botham mentioned that the treatment I was getting was what used to be done regularly to the Pom Test players. The media would dig up ex-players and ex-captains, extract a juicy quote, and take great delight in digging in the knives. The strong theory is that this regular pastime has done a fair bit to undermine English cricket and confidence at the top level over the past 15 years or so. Botham suggested that he hoped the trend continued in my case—that it might at least benefit English cricket ... although that would be about all it would be good for. I just hope that any negative stuff involving the views of ex-players and focus on me doesn't affect us as a team. If so, I suppose you can say that some great players of the past have acquired the English trait of helping bring down a team.

After training we headed to the Belfry Golf Club where they play some of the Ryder Cup tournaments. We played the main course, and it was great fun. I shot 83, which was surprising considering that I haven't played much golf at all in the last year thanks to my back problems. This was probably my third game since I did my back, and to shoot 83 in a round in which I barely made a single putt was terrific fun.

We had a team dinner at the Golf Club, followed by a video of Kieren Perkins' 1500m swim in Atlanta, plus some film highlights and lowlights of our own performances since 1993. This was a great idea, reminding us of good days, and not so good. Not all the guys played in all those matches—and the film was both a reminder of what we had to do (and not do) and an education. Sitting there I just hoped that we would recapture the feeling that marked those big successes. It's been lacking in the team to this point although once we get it back we're going to be very, very hard to stop. This was a day well spent.

Tonight I'm thinking about the team breakfast tomorrow at which we'll announce the side. And I'm thinking about what I'm going to tell my team. I'm going to talk about the meaning of the Ashes—try and somehow tap us back into that elusive spirit that seems to have slipped away a little since our achievements against the West Indies, then South Africa this year. I'll remind them that the four-year cycle of Australian cricket starts with the Ashes, and that collectively and individually we are all at the crossroads.

My own inner feeling is of positive anticipation ... but a realisation too that it could be my last Test match as a cricket player if things don't go well. I'm thinking about Kieren Perkins in that 1500m race—how, against the odds, he gave it everything he had, and produced one of the greatest swims you could ever imagine.

The night before Edgbaston

I'm in my room—nervous, but okay. There is some sense of personal relief. I know that crunch time is here, that over the next five days of my life, my future as a cricketer will be decided. I have told Judi that if things don't go well for me in this match then I'll have no choice but to stand down from the captaincy. But I'm not thinking about that. I'm thinking about Mark Taylor and Australia playing some darned good cricket. If that happens, I can tell everyone to shoot through. Which is putting it politely.

Our net session this morning was very good. I hit the ball reasonably well, and I'm feeling pretty confident—although I'm well aware that the personal weight on my shoulders is about as heavy as I've ever carried. I'm feeling more or less the way I did eight and a half years ago before my first Test against the West Indies. The bowling lineup from memory was Ambrose, Marshall, Patterson and Walsh. I can't begin to explain how nervous I was when I walked out to bat against them that first Test day, wondering whether I was good enough ... wondering how long I'd stay in the side. Now here I am 81 Test matches later, once again nervous as a kitten. Who knows what the future holds. Maybe the tide will turn in Birmingham and I'll play for another eight and a half years!

About the only disappointing news came at the press conference today—that Bob Simpson had made some detrimental remarks about me and the captaincy and the Australian side. He suggested that I should no longer be skipper and that he could see things that he believed were wrong in the side. It was disappointing that the former coach had jumped on the bandwagon. People are entitled to their opinions, of course, but suffice to say they are not helpful on the eve of a Test match. Memories are short too. These negatives fly in the face of the sort of season we have had— notable series wins against tough opponents in the West Indies and South Africa. Certainly our start here has been ordinary, but the quality that lives in this side has been proven. It will emerge, for sure—and I just hope that it's here in Edgbaston.

In years ahead, when my cricket days are over, I'm going to do my darndest to remember some of these things. If it happens that I go into television commentary (and while I already have a current deal with Channel Nine, I have no idea what the future holds) I'll remember back to now, and how previous captains have added to the pressure on an Australian team. And I'll do my best not to fall into the same trap. I know I speak for Bob Simpson and the Chappells when I say that we all want to see Australia do well, and continue to do so. I question publicly whether their airing of negative theories, sometimes in sensational terms, is for the benefit of the Australian team or its players. I very much doubt it.

The team is picked, with Michael Kasprowicz winning the final spot over Brendon Julian for one significant reason: he's been bowling better than Brendon to this point. Brendon has had a neck complaint and is struggling to find consistency. We rate Michael more likely to take wickets at this stage.

A slow, quiet night coming up. Time seems to drag on the night before a Test, and especially so at the opening of a series. There'll be dinner with the guys in the hotel restaurant and as usual we'll be trying to avoid talking about tomorrow as much as we can. A good night's sleep is no certainty. I'm doing some self counselling by telling myself that it's just a game of cricket and tomorrow, as I've always done through my career as a Test player, I'm going to go out and give it my best effort for my country. For me it's black and white: to get out there, make runs and shut everyone up or in the event of my fruitless struggle continuing, to begin coming to terms with the reality than in five days time I will very likely no longer be Australia's Test captain. I'm going for option A. I admit some concerns for us as a team. We've been slow out of the blocks. There is no question we can do the job we came to do ... it's just a matter of us finding the go button.

First Test, Edgbaston

DAY 1

Well, I thought things could only get better. In fact they got a bloody darned sight worse. We had a day that was nothing short of a shocker. The only thing that went right was when the coin spun in the air and I called correctly. The choice was easy—to bat first on what looked like and I think *is* a reasonable Test wicket. I'm sure Mike Atherton would have batted if he'd won the toss, too. For reasons that will be speculated on for quite a while we went out and had one of those days. At one stage we were 8-54, and we eventually scrambled to 118, lasting only 32 overs. I made seven. Funnily enough I felt pretty comfortable; I hit a cover drive off Devon Malcolm which was as sweet a shot as I've hit for a long while. Then he bowled me exactly the same ball and I nicked it to second slip. So the personal news is not great, and nothing much else is either.

We played a few bad shots today, but only a few. I must say that the Pommies bowled and fielded very, very well. The match ran beautifully for them. Anything nicked seemed to go to hand, anything that got through picked up a wicket. Matthew Elliott and Mark Waugh were both bowled through the 'gate'. I nicked one and so did Steve Waugh, Greg Blewett and Ian Healy. At 8-54 things were absolutely desperate, and only a swashbuckling 47 by Shane Warne edged us up to anywhere near respectability at 118.

We then went out and had them 2-16 and 3-50. When Graham Thorpe came to the wicket at 3-50 I tossed up whether to have a bloke at fifth slip, or to put someone around the corner in a catching position at backward square leg. I opted for the latter. The second ball Thorpe received took the edge and flew straight to where the fifth slip would have been—and through to the boundary for four. Ha! As I contemplate the day, Thorpe is 80-odd not out and so is Nasser Hussain. They're already 80-odd in front, three down. As I said—an absolute shocker.

The explanation of what happened to Australia today is not easy to find. There's some uneven bounce in the wicket and some movement off the seam and in the air. But you expect that on the first morning of a Test match. We certainly can't blame the wicket. Adding to our woes, Jason Gillespie has slightly torn a hamstring. I have my own small problem, having felt my back 'catch' while running between wickets.

The bottom line of course is that we've got a hell of a lot to do. We've got to restrict them to something around 300, then begin the rescue operation. The one sure thing is that tomorrow is going to have to be a heck of a lot better than today if we're going to be any chance of winning the game or even saving it.

I've got some welcome visitors tonight—my mother and father, who arrived in Birmingham yesterday. They'll be round for dinner and it will be great to catch up and to talk about things other than cricket. Especially after a day like today.

FIRST TEST, EDGBASTON, DAY 2

We're in a terrible situation—simple as that. If I thought it couldn't get any worse after yesterday ... well, it has. We bowled all day apart from the last hour and a half

Shane Warne pleads for the umpire's verdict. First Test, Edgbaston.

Nasser Hussain (left) and Graham Thorpe, England's heroes in the first Test at Edgbaston. Hussain scored 207, Thorpe 138.

which was washed out. At the end of it the Poms are six for about 450, an overall lead of 330. Nasser Hussain played particularly well (better than I've ever seen him) for 207. Graham Thorpe made 138—very solidly, but not as impressively as Nasser. The pair of them put on a record fourth wicket partnership of 288. Just about the only good news is that there's some rain forecast for the weekend. Maybe the formula of some good batting and a drop of rain can still get us out of it.

My nagging fears about the way we're going have been realised in these two days. We're really struggling to bowl them out, which has never been a problem for us in the past. The fact is that in each of the three one-dayers we took only four wickets. Today we managed only three wickets all day on a pitch which, while certainly not a minefield, is not a freeway either. Warnie's not turning the ball as much as he has in the past and probably hasn't done so since his operation last year. Jason Gillespie's injury prevented him bowling today, and that hasn't helped.

But the real concern today is that in 70-odd overs we only created *three* chances. That's very unlike the Australian side of recent years. I was trying to figure out today as the scoreboard ticked over when it was that a side last made 400 against us, let alone in the first innings of a Test match. I was struggling. My memory goes back to my second game as skipper, against Pakistan when they made 500 against us in the second innings after we enforced the follow on. I was a contributor to that. I dropped Salim Malik on 20 and he went on to make 237! It's been a pretty rare occasion when a side has made 400 against us. Generally if we've been bowled out for a modest score, we've been able to hit back, bowl the opposition out and stay in the match. The

MEMO FROM THE OFFICE OF KIEREN PERKINS OAM.

Date: Thursday, 5 June 1997

To: MARK TAYLOR – Captain
Australian Cricket Team
Holiday Inn, BIRMINGHAM.

From: KIEREN

Mark,

I feel compelled to send you my best wishes for success.

It must be tempting to succumb to what I call the "FUD factor". I know because I've been there. The fear, uncertainty, and doubt is only put there by the detractors and critics who don't know anyway. You are there because you are the best and they are not, remember that.

I know you will <u>ignore the distractions</u>, FOCUS on the job at hand, and CONCENTRATE on yours and the Team's GOALS (in that order!) <u>You will succeed because you have what it takes.</u>

I am reminded of a little saying which used to be on my wall when I was younger -

NOTHING IN THE WORLD CAN TAKE THE PLACE OF PERSISTENCE

TALENT WILL NOT - NOTHING IS MORE COMMON THAN UNSUCCESSFUL MEN WITH TALENT

GENIUS WILL NOT - UNREWARDED GENIUS IS ALMOST A PROVERB

EDUCATION WILL NOT - THE WORLD IS FULL OF EDUCATED DERELICTS

PERSISTENCE AND DETERMINATION ALONE ARE OMNIPOTENT

You can do it, and I know you will.
Good luck to you and all the guys

Regards,

Before the first Test, the Australians watched film of Kieren Perkins' against-the-odds 1500 metres freestyle triumph in Atlanta. On the day the game began, Mark Taylor received this message of support from the Olympic champion.

report card so far on this Test is that we're gonna need some improvement in all areas. First thing is to try and weasel our way out of this game. Realistically, Mother Nature looms as the big hope. Rain would certainly crush English spirits when they're so well placed to win the Test and go one-up. That's out of our hands; all we can do is play as well as we can from now on.

I've been mulling over what it is that's wrong in the side. The team spirit seems fine. There's been talk in the papers from some ex-players and even from ex-coach Bob Simpson that there are signs of complacency in the team. I don't accept that theory. We have worked very hard on this tour so far, both physically, and technically on our skills. I'd say we have done more than on any other Ashes tour—and especially so now that we have a physical trainer in the ranks who works the guys every day. No, I don't think it's complacency. It may be a residue of tiredness after a long and draining campaign starting back in India last year. Maybe what drives us as a team is not quite at full throttle yet, and the edge that it takes to win Tests is not quite there yet.

FIRST TEST, EDGBASTON, DAY 3

I'm sitting here tonight tired and happy and just a little emotional. The drought has broken for me at last. That's about the only way I can think of putting it. I'm 108 not out, Greg Blewett is about 60 not out and we're one for around 250 and hanging in there. The Poms declared at 9-478, a lead of 360; we've got a long way to go yet before we drag ourselves out of the woods. But the day was a beauty for me, and for the team. No doubt about it. Maybe a little further down the track it will be seen as a turning point on the tour. We bowled well, putting some pressure back on them and picking up 3-30 odd in the morning. Then we came out to begin climbing the mountain in an effort to save this match …

I have all sorts of mixed feelings about my 100. It wasn't an absolute *classic*—I know that. But I gutsed it out. And along the way it occurred to me that during the wretched, dreadful run of form I've had in the past six months, I had forgotten the way that I *do* bat. Until today I've been going out there on a quest for the perfect innings—looking to hit every ball in the middle, play the beautiful cover drive, the square cut, the pull shot … all the shots I can play. I was looking to do all those things each time—and when it wasn't happening, the feeling that I was still out of form chipped away at me.

Today, really, was just about taking care of business. It was about graft and hard work and concentration … not a pretty hundred by any means—but then, not such an ugly one either. I had forgotten that a lot of times in Test cricket you just have to plain guts it out. Sometimes you've gotta get through the tough periods anyway you can. Get 'em off the inside edge … get 'em off the outside edge … wear a few on the body. Let's face it—I'm not a Viv Richards-type player who goes out there and strokes the ball to all parts of the boundary and is guaranteed to look a million dollars if he makes 100. The problem has been that recently I have been going out to play like Viv

Richards. Today I played like Mark Taylor. You know what I've realised? That I've thought of every possible way to get out of this slump in recent weeks except to be *myself*. I'd forgotten things that are important. I won't forget again. Now I can look forward to the rest of the series—as opening batsman and captain.

It's a funny old game. As a result of the product of one day in the middle, the monkey is off my back—and off the team's back. I hope that all of us—me, the team, the media—can settle down to getting on with the job at hand, notwithstanding the scratchy start here at Edgbaston. As the events of the last three days have shown, it won't be easy. We are facing an England team which is playing better cricket, and with more spirit than some of recent times. The cloud surrounding me has perhaps been destructive to an extent in the area of our own team focus. Today, it lifted ...

Tomorrow there'll be some positive press and maybe an apology or two. None of that matters too much. I certainly have no inclination to hit back at people who were howling for my head. I wouldn't be human if I wasn't disappointed and cut by some of the things said and written. But there are no vendettas.

There are many things going through my mind as I sit here. I feel very happy for all the people back home who have stuck with me, and the hundreds who have taken the trouble to send me those messages of support. Blokes like Alan Jones and John Laws at radio station 2UE in Sydney are high on that list; Alan has sent me a number of messages, reinforcing the positive.

Kieren Perkins played his part today, too. I mentioned that before the Test we had watched the video of Kieren's 1500 metres freestyle victory in Atlanta. On the second day here, a fax arrived from Kieren in Brisbane. In it, he talked of our similarities, how he felt before the final in Atlanta, how he doubted himself. 'Just get out there and do it...believe in yourself,' Australia's greatest swimmer advised me. 'And beware of the "Fud Factor" (fear, uncertainty and doubt),' Kieren advised. 'You are there because you are the best and they [the critics and detractors] are not,' he wrote. 'You can do it and I know you will.'

Today out in the middle I thought of Kieren, especially after I reached 100. No, I don't believe I've done a Kieren Perkins today. His effort in Atlanta, against the predictions and the odds, was genuinely great. I wouldn't rate my innings today alongside that. But I did think of him out there and the fax he sent me is something I'll treasure. It will be safely tucked in my bag when I come home in late August ... and I thank him for it.

The note from local cricket commentator Jack Bannister meant something to me too. Jack is a helluva nice guy, with a good knowledge of the game. Jack paraphrased Rudyard Kipling in the note and a newspaper cutting he sent me, and wrote of the need to keep your head while others are losing theirs.

A great thing about today was that my mother and father were here to watch me bat, and to share the good news, just as they were in 1989 at Headingley when I scored my first Test century. The meal with them tonight will be special. I tried to call Judi from the change rooms, but the number just continually dialled busy. I suspect that either the phone was running very hot, or it was running so hot that she took it off the hook for a while. No matter—she's been a fantastic support for me, even from 20,000 kilometres away. It's been a tough time for her, dealing with things back home in high pressure times, and looking after our two kids who I love and miss so much. I'm very happy for her—maybe life will get back to normal now for her too.

Anyhow, enough of me. That's over now (though I'm hoping for some more runs tomorrow). It's time to think about the game, and the fact is it's really on. This morning we were out of it—down and out. Gone. I suspect plenty of England supporters would have been chilling the champagne for tonight's celebrations. By stumps we were back in it, still well behind—but nowhere near as far behind as we were.

This has been a troubled Test for us though. Tonight we have Mark Waugh in hospital, initially diagnosed with suspected appendicitis. The latest report that he won't be having an operation gives us a little hope. If it happens that he can come out and bat for us tomorrow that would be a huge bonus.

FIRST TEST, EDGBASTON, DAY 4

We've lost the first Test, after a start today that was full of promise. Blewie and I got comfortably through the first hour and the second new ball and nudged the score along to 1-327. At that point I played a bloody terrible shot and was out, caught and bowled by Robert Croft for 129. We were two down, and 30 behind. Greg Blewett went for 125 (3-354) just before we passed their total—we got back on to the right side of the ledger three down and seemingly in reasonable shape. The wicket was getting a little bit variable in its bounce and they had to bat last. But we collapsed, losing our last eight wickets for about 120 runs. That's what they needed to win—and they got the runs surprisingly quickly in 21.3 overs.

That was nearly the worst thing that came out of the game—that we again bowled badly, just when we needed to apply pressure and make it tough for them. Over the last three years our bowling has been little short of sensational. Yet here at Edgbaston we've just finished a Test in which our opposition scored 9-478 then belted 119 off only 21 overs to win the game. In this game we just didn't apply the sort of pressure that we usually do. We were outplayed, no risk about that. We did fight reasonably well, although today's tumble of wickets in a match that looked salvageable was disappointing.

All is not lost. Not by a long way. As I told the media at today's post-game conference we now have a challenge on our hands. We've had a dream run in first Tests over the past few years, enabling us to set the pace in the series that followed. We've won five or six of those in a row. Now we're gonna have to come from behind—and the good news is that it's a six Test series, and many long miles ahead.

I was upbeat at today's conference even though we had just lost a Test. As I told the gathering you don't lose the talent in a single month. It doesn't go up in smoke. We've got things to work on—me too, despite the century. The shot I played against Croft to lose my wicket was a real shocker. There is some hard graft ahead.

The task at hand is to prove to ourselves and to all our supporters that we're not just 'front-runners'. And we're not. In Trinidad in '95 we lost the third Test, drawing the Windies level in the series. We bounced back and won again a week later. I know we're going to face a chorus of: 'He should go' and 'This should change', but that's not the answer. The answer is to get ourselves together, work a bit harder and uncover ways for each of us by which we can improve both our own games and the team's game. I *know* we have the talent to win the series.

The next day

I have a pile of faxes here you couldn't jump over, and that's very gratifying. It's a thrill for me to think that so many people have taken so much trouble to make contact. Relief has sort of washed over me these last 24 hours, although tempered with disappointment that the Ashes campaign started with a loss, and concern for the fact that we are battling injuries.

Geoff (Marsh) called a training session for this morning—back down at the scene of our defeat. It was an unusual step and I'll admit I had a few concerns. But it turned out to be a very worthwhile exercise. We didn't train too hard physically; most of what we did was just talk. The batsmen sat together in the nets and talked for half an hour or so. There was no chairman, no agenda. We just talked ... about our batting, and what we can do to improve it. There was some really good stuff that came out.

The bowlers did the same thing. Later on as they went through a light workout I went over and talked to them about basic things—line and length, working as a group together. At the end we all got together and had a little fitness drill. It added up to a very worthwhile exercise and if we do improve our cricket over the next week or so I'm sure we'll look back on the second half of this Test match and the training session the day after as significant turning points.

This afternoon, I lost again. Mark Waugh and I teamed up to take on Ricky Ponting and Michael Bevan at the Belfry course. Unfortunately the senior members got their bums kicked. We did our dough. I played okay actually, but Ricky Ponting is just a whiz. He was under par today—he plays off four, but he's better than that. We played the PGA national course off the white markers and he still managed a 71. I shot 80, seven over, which was the first time I've beaten my handicap (I play off eight) in about three years. Maybe I'm hitting form at cricket *and* golf!

CHAPTER 10

MOVING ON

The dogs bark and the caravan moves on. Today against Nottinghamshire at Trent Bridge (our first County match since the Test) we've struck some trouble—although for reasons pretty much beyond our control. I'm having a spell and when Steve Waugh spun and won the toss on a very greenish looking wicket, we sent them in. It was a promising start to a match that can help with the re-building process towards the second Test. But almost immediately large grey clouds rolled over the ground and the rain came. It didn't ease, and eventually the day's play was called off. So now it's down to a two-day game which is a shame. We're very keen to shove a foot in the door of this tour by winning a game of cricket right now. The last thing we wanted was for the rain to come and wash away a vital day's play.

The other bad news is that Andrew Bichel is going home. Andrew hasn't played on tour because he has a bone stress problem in his lower back. Finally after all types of examinations and scans, the specialists have recommended that he not bowl for three months. It's a darned shame that we're going to be losing him. Andrew is a great competitor and very good to have in and around the side. In his disappointment, I did my best today to re-assure him that he's young enough to make a full recovery. Hopefully, if things go well for him, he'll be back here in four years' time. Andrew must look for the positives now and I'm sure he'll do that after he gets over the initial disappointment of what has been a tough and frustrating month for him. I'm sure that today's weeping skies reflect exactly the way Andrew Bichel feels.

Leicester

The tour has rolled on a few days, and we're in Leicester, a couple of hours after the close of day two here. The Notts game is now no more than an entry in the records of the tour. It faded into a draw and was disappointing from that aspect, but it did provide some positives for us in other ways. Paul Reiffel, who has joined us on the tour and is happy to be here, took 3-15 off 10 overs, an excellent start to his English campaign. Steve Waugh (115) and Matthew Elliott (127) both made hundreds in our first and only innings of the match, spending valuable time in the middle. This will do them a power of good.

The rain chased us down to Leicester and washed out the first session of play. I then lost the toss and we were sent in to bat; at close of play we were 8-220. I got bowled for one by a ball that I just didn't pick up. The bloke who bowled me is not express pace, or anywhere near ... I just wasn't too tuned in and it sneaked through me. Later, in the nets, I hit the ball well. Ricky Ponting got 60-odd and Ian Healy 34. Generally, it was a struggle.

The rain was the main winner again today. I declared at our overnight score, but we only managed to get a couple of hours at them, thanks to the weather. There was good news however ... some really encouraging news. Today we bowled the best we

Touchdown England—a light training session at Lord's and a jog to iron out the kinks. The campaign begins.

The first net at Lord's—with skipper Taylor at the crease.

One of the joys of English cricket—a truly majestic setting for Australia v Worcestershire.

In South Africa it was silly shirts; in England Mark Taylor and his men joined four million others to take part in 'Wrong Trousers Day', helping to raise money for a new children's hospital.

Spectacular action from the first Test at Edgbaston as Darren Gough runs out a stranded Jason Gillespie for 0 in the second innings.

The 'real' Mark Taylor stood up at Edgbaston under the intense pressure of the first Test. Here, a slash to the boundary on his way to his acclaimed and oh-so-welcome second innings 129.

The gloomy scene at Lord's. Weeping skies and a sodden, covered field. Second Test.

Mark Taylor at Lord's with his friend and admirer, Prime Minister John Howard.

Andrew Caddick is out lbw and a jubilant Glenn McGrath (centre) has his eighth wicket in England's first innings at Lord's.

Shane Warne grabbed some headlines and photo space in the English press with his champagne-swigging performance after the Aussies had squared the series in the third Test triumph at Old Trafford.

Cricket was the main game ... but there was often variety in the training sessions on tour.

This one went straight to the skipper's head, as Australia celebrate victory in the third Test.

These days you find Swans' fans everywhere.

Classic balance, timing and command as Matthew Elliott heads relentlessly on to his 199 in the fourth Test at Leeds.

Please ... can you help me get a decision? Shane Warne, in appealing mood, fifth Test at Trent Bridge.

Shane Warne and Ian Healy celebrate the 264-run fifth Test win at Trent Bridge.

In Northern Ireland near the end there was time for some relaxation ... and even some fishing. Here, Matthew Elliott does his best to figure out the mystery of a good cast.

Mark Taylor and the spectacular backdrop of the famous Giant's Causeway in Northern Ireland.

Fabulous action from the sixth Test as Steve Waugh makes a stinging drive in the first innings.

Andrew Caddick, whose five second-innings wickets went a long way towards destroying Australia in the second innings of the sixth Test.

have in any game—and by a mile. Glenn McGrath didn't get a wicket, but he bowled particularly well. He found his rhythm and didn't bowl a loose ball, reversing the problem he has had recently with some wayward deliveries. Paul Reiffel bowled exceptionally well as his figures (3-12 off 10 overs) reflect. Already there's no doubt about the value he's going to be to us.

Probably the biggest signal of all was that Shane Warne is edging closer to the form he seeks. There's no doubt that Warnie has been below his best, but today I saw something from him that I haven't seen before on tour. The old *dip* was back—the ability to toss the ball up above the eye level of the batsman and then make it drop, just when the batsman figures he's got it worked out. Warnie bowled only five overs, but they were overs of real promise.

I'll probably have a yarn with Leicester captain James Whittaker tonight and see if we can work out the best thing we can do to make it interesting tomorrow for both players and spectators. I've never been a subscriber to the theory of 'contrived' results—and by that I mean captains working out a scenario which might help out a particular team in a structured competition—but this game is not part of any competition. It's just a one-off and I think it's quite legitimate to look at creating something as good as we can manage tomorrow. A quick declaration by them, 20 or 30 overs at the crease for us ... then a target for Leicester to chase. That would be useful for us—especially for the bowlers who would be operating under match conditions against batsmen determined to score off them. It would certainly be better for the crowd than some sort of glorified centre wicket practice session.

Meanwhile, the rest of the Taylor family—Judi, William and Jack—have touched down in London after the 24-hour flight from Sydney. We'll be catching up tomorrow night when the team travels down to London, which will be great. It's been five weeks since I last saw them and Judi tells me the boys are super keen to see their dad.

Getting there

The match at Leicester finished exactly the way I hoped it would. Their skipper James Whittaker and I had no problems about setting up a scenario which would produce some good cricket and, maybe, a result. It did both. And from our viewpoint everything went perfectly to plan. They declared, we knocked up 3-105—in which I managed a solid 50—and we set them 260 runs to get off 67–70 overs. Out we went—and knocked them over, with Shane Warne getting five wickets in another performance of considerable encouragement.

This was the pre-first Test Derbyshire match all over again—but with a significant difference. This time instead of getting beaten after setting a team an achievable target on the last day, we won. Was this a sign for the second Test coming up?

At the end of the two-hour bus trip back to London, my family awaited me at the Westbury. It was just great to see them.

In the lee of Lord's

There's a special buzz about, as there always is as the Lord's Test approaches. Many Australians are converging on London for this most special of cricket matches, and we're busy getting ready—thoroughly committed to the idea of squaring the series right here. There is much going on. After a nets session yesterday morning we were guests at a luncheon at the Cafe Royale, run by the British Sportsmen's Club. I had some official duties to perform, introducing the team and saying a few words as skipper. At night, another function at the Sports Cafe for Carlton & United Brewer's.

Today, the day before the Test, the focus sharpened noticeably. The morning nets session was good hard business. The spirit is good. I think we've lifted. The Lord's Test has always been a big one, but when you're one-down in the series it takes on added importance. It's reassuring to reflect on how good a ground it's been for Australian teams over long years. We've won the last three Lord's Test matches, and, remarkably, Australia has lost only once here this century! That was back in 1934. The knowledge of all that is a good psychological boost for me as captain and for the team.

The day felt good—relaxed and harmonious. With an afternoon off, I was down at the park kicking footballs with the kids and just mucking around. With the match and all that surrounds it parked firmly in the back of my mind, I can't think of a better way to pass the time.

One problem looms—the weather. The forecast for the next few days is a bit more than just worrying ... it's bloody terrible! They're talking rain for the next three or four days, which is quite possible in an English summer. Beaten fair and square by the cricketers of England in the first Test, I can only wonder if we are now to be frustrated by the country's fickle weather.

CHAPTER 11
THE HOME OF CRICKET

Mark Taylor leads his team onto hallowed turf. Second Test, Lords, June 23, 1997.

Second Test, Lord's

DAY 1

Things couldn't have looked any bleaker as we arrived at the most famous ground in cricket. There wasn't a blade of grass to be seen—the entire field was under covers—and overhead the sky was slate grey. The rain tumbled down. The first glimpse set the scene for the day that followed. The sun bravely struggled through for about an hour after lunch and a big mopping up session was instantly underway. But the clouds closed ranks shortly afterwards and the rain came sweeping back over the ground.

By mid-afternoon it was officially a wash-out—an immense disappointment considering the great expectation that exists when you are going to play a cricket match at Lord's. Worse still is the fact that the forecast is grim—more rain tomorrow and further rain periods during the weekend.

Prime Minister John Howard came to the change rooms to say g'day to the team, and that was appreciated. The PM is a keen sports fan and it was good to see him, and to know that he's there providing high-level support . . . if we can happen to get a game of cricket out of this match.

SECOND TEST, LORD'S, DAY 2

Things improved only marginally today, thanks to the stubborn reluctance of the rain to go away and leave us alone. But the ground was in reasonable shape when we arrived and I managed to win a toss for the second time in succession—very unusual for me considering that my tossing record is little short of terrible. I sent them in—something I've rarely done in my time as captain. I figured that our only chance of winning a rain-shortened match was to give ourselves the chance of bowling them out twice. Things went to plan. We headed out there and bowled very, very well. Glenn McGrath in particular was superb. We had them 3-30 at one stage—at which point occurred one of those touch and go moments on which games can sometimes swing.

The first ball he faced, Graham Thorpe edged one. Ian Healy dived low to catch it—and all of us in the slips, including Heals, were unsure whether or not the ball had bounced before Heals gloved it. Healy ran to the umpire and told him he was unsure, and the umpire did the only thing he could do—gave Thorpe not out.

I think it was the right call. I've subsequently seen the replay and it looks as though the ball touched the ground just a fraction short of Ian's gloves. It would have been a nice one to get, but justice was done, and that's as it should be. Instead of 4-30 it was 3-38 when the rain paid another visit around 12.30 and washed out play for the day.

The situation of disputed catches such as today's is currently on the agenda for discussion by the ICC (International Cricket Council). They're discussing whether to use the video replay facility to assist—and I must admit I was a bit of a fence-sitter until today. I'm not keen on too much electronic involvement in the game. Today I was standing right next to Heals at the moment it happened, and my inclination was that the ball probably *had* carried. The slow-motion TV replay proved me wrong, so after today I'd probably have to say yes if the ICC asked my view on the use of the video ump.

I reckon we're still in with some chance of winning this game, despite the time lost. At 3-38 they're in some trouble and the wicket is doing a helluva lot more than

British bulldogs—Nasser Hussain and friend.

I thought it would. The ball seamed around a bit today, and the bounce is variable. The odds are against a result, but if we keep bowling well and then back that up with some decisive batting, it's not impossible.

SECOND TEST, LORD'S, DAY 3

Despite the weather, we've had a great day at Lord's . . . and for Glenn McGrath, a day that he will never forget. Glenn skittled the Poms, taking a career best of 8-38— the best performance ever by a visiting player at Lord's. McGrath just destroyed England's batting and they were back in the pavilion for 77, the lowest England total for many years. In reply we're 2-131. Greg Blewett made a very nice 40 and Matthew Elliott reached his half century (55 not out). We have been nicely aided and abetted by some poor fielding by the Poms. They dropped about four catches and missed a couple of run-outs and a stumping. We've had a lucky day, but we've been making our own luck too, through good positive cricket.

My own involvement was disappointing. Hoping to build on what I achieved at Edgbaston, I was out for one. Trying to drive I chopped a ball from Darren Gough onto the stumps.

Glenn McGrath and Paul Reiffel bowled superbly today. Paul's figures were modest in comparison to Glenn's (2-25 off 16 overs), but he bowled beautifully and could have had more wickets. Glenn McGrath had a day that will go down in Lord's history. So . . . we're 54 in front with two days to go. All of a sudden a Test that looked as though it belonged to the weather is still there to be won. However, even as I sit here reflecting on the day's activities, the streets of London are gleaming outside as the rain tumbles down. All we can do is cross our fingers.

SECOND TEST, LORD'S, DAY 4

The word that comes to mind is 'frustrating'. A day spent waiting in the pavilion watching the skies. Not until 5.50pm this afternoon did we finally get on to the park, offering us just 20 overs of play. As it turned out we were off again for another 10 minutes, so the day's play in its entirety consisted of 17 overs.

My instruction to our batsmen was to be extremely positive and they sure took it on board. There were plenty of interesting shots played—Mark Waugh got caught down at third man, Shane Warne went out as a designated hitter and got caught trying to play a big pull shot, Steve Waugh got nought and Michael Bevan four— each of them trying to push it along. The highlight by far was Matthew Elliott's maiden Test century—his last 50 runs coming off about 40 balls. Matthew advanced from 55 to score 112 and played some tremendous shots—particularly off Darren Gough. There were cuts, pulls, drives . . . the whole lot. He played superbly. Near the end of the day he was the last man out and at stumps we were 7-217, having added 82 in those 17 overs. The fall of wickets was of little consequence. The job at hand was to get some quick runs, hope that we're going to get a full day's play tomorrow,

Ian Healy tells the umpires he is uncertain whether he has taken a fair catch of Graham Thorpe on Day 2 of the Lord's Test. Thorpe was subsequently declared 'not out'—and Healy's honesty was applauded by the British media.

and then have a real crack at them in their second innings. The weather forecast isn't great and it's in my mind that I'll be declaring overnight.

The odds are against a result. The wicket has settled down now and is playing well. The weather remains its usual threat. As I said, a frustrating day. It could have been a very different ball game if we'd had the full 90 overs today. Anyhow, we'll give it our best shot.

SECOND TEST, LORD'S, DAY 5

It's the aftermath of a disappointing Test. On a wicket that was playing true we never looked like bowling the Poms out today and at the close they were 4-250 and home safe for the draw. I didn't help matters when I dropped Mark Butcher in the first hour when he was two. He went on to make 87. It was the only chance we missed though and on a good wicket less than 100 overs old they batted solidly, with Mike Atherton getting 77.

About the only good point that came out of the day for us was Shane Warne's bowling performance. I thought he bowled a lot better today—turning a few balls and getting drop and drift as he does when he's at his best. It was a good sign.

We wanted a win here, but I can't be too disappointed. There were only 180 overs bowled—the equivalent of two full days out of five—and you can't really expect a result in that sort of time frame. As much as anything the disappointments here were personal ones, that it had to be the Lord's Test of all of them that was so badly messed around by the weather. Many of us had family and friends over here. I sure had my own little support team in Judi and William and Jack and my mother and father, Tony and Judy, plus my manager John Fordham—all of them hoping for something special at this special place.

We took some positives out of the match, though, no doubt about that. We bounced back strongly after the disappointment of the first Test—and the bowling of Glenn McGrath and Shane Warne were outstanding pointers to the fact that we are building momentum as a team day by day.

Tonight the thoughts in everyone's mind were probably bitter sweet—of having been at that famous ground, but experiencing such a frustrating match. I headed out for dinner with the family, plus my wife's brother John and his wife Rahni and a couple of pals from a beautiful place up on the NSW north coast, Brooms Head—Joe and Narelle Davis. I dropped the troops back at the hotel and then went for a beer at a pub in Piccadilly with the guys—a post-Test tradition. The spirit was great, despite the disappointments of the match. The feeling was there that we are turning the corner, and better days lie ahead.

The morning after

There were some sore heads this morning, and a big day stretching ahead. For some of the team, it's a day at Wimbledon, for others, a game of golf. For my own part I have some domestic matters to attend to—to put Judi and the boys on the train north, to Bury, where they're going to stay for the next couple of months with friends.

Mission safely accomplished I headed off to a restaurant in Covent Garden with John Fordham, a bloke who knows a thing or two about lunches. A nice piece of fish and a glass or two of Stonier's Chardonnay from the Mornington Peninsula—it was a good way to wind down ... and to start talking and thinking about revving up again ... The day moved on to an Ashes exhibition at Australia House, opened by John Howard—and then to a 90 minutes' drive north through England's long twilight to Oxford, to get ready for our next game, against Combined Universities.

It's now 11.30pm and we've reached our (new) home base. I'm playing tomorrow. I feel that the way I'm going and the way the side's starting to roll, it's important I play this game. I'm keen to try and keep a good thing going; my form was picking up, but I haven't had a decent bat for nearly a week now thanks to the weather. I'm very hopeful of getting a reasonable hit in this game to keep in some sort of touch for the Old Trafford Test which now looms as an especially crucial game. Shane Warne is playing tomorrow for exactly the same reasons. For the Aussies of '97 there's a lot to be gained from this game—even though it's generally considered one of the least important fixtures on tour. We have only one problem ... the weather forecast.

A new dad celebrates.

Rain and more rain

It's now four days since the end of the Lord's Test and we haven't played a single minute of cricket. The weather has taken charge and our match against Combined Universities was washed away. It's the only time in my career that I can remember a complete wash-out—not getting even one ball bowled. We have moved on to Southampton for the next game (against Hampshire) and we're desperate to get some cricket, but the grey, heavy clouds have trailed us.

Things are difficult for the other selectors and myself. Everyone is desperate for some cricket, but because of the intervention of the weather, I'm afraid guys like Michael Slater, Justin Langer, Ricky Ponting, Brendon Julian and Adam Gilchrist won't be playing in this game. We're forced—by circumstances outside our control—to play what we think is going to be the Test team. I really feel for the five blokes I've mentioned above. None of them have anything to prove to me and the other selectors; they can all play, we know that. And they're all as keen as mustard, yet they've had hardly any cricket at all in the last month. They'll accept it, I know—they're all professional cricketers. But they'll be disappointed, too.

Thanks to the weather, the cricket news is limited—but we've got a new father in the team, Shane Warne, who became a dad around 10am today when his wife Simone gave birth to Brooke. We were all standing around in the hotel waiting for the news and when it came through there were champagne and cigars all round. The cigar tasted bloody terrible ... I've never been a smoker. But it was a great moment for Warnie and his family. I know he would rather have been at the birth—but he had his parents here with him, and all the guys around him, so that was some sort of consolation. We're all thrilled for him, and I know it will be a day he'll remember for the rest of his life.

With the rain interrupting our momentum, this has been a marking time period in the campaign. In Oxford we kept active ... working out in a local gym and hitting a few golf balls at the Chip & Putt out the front of the Oxford Hotel Roadhouse where we stayed. Yesterday we had a quick net at Sommerfield Prep School at Oxford. I hit the ball very well and feel I'm still in pretty fair form. The problem now is actually getting a game here in Southampton, where the clouds continue to hang heavy.

Hampshire

The Ashes exhibition at Australia House was an off-the-field highlight for the Aussies on tour—acclaiming legends such as Bill O'Reilly (left) and Dr W.G. Grace.

At last the weather smiled just a little, and we were delighted to work out some cobwebs with a full day's play at Southampton. A good day it was, too— I lost the toss but they decided to bat (I was going to send them in anyway) and we bundled them out for 165. We had them 8-93 at one stage and everyone bowled well, with Michael Kasprowicz making the early breakthroughs, Paul Reiffel picking up a couple early and Shane Warne bowling the best he has on tour for 3-30. Near the end Jason Gillespie picked up a couple of wickets too, so everyone chipped in.

At stumps we were 2-157, with yours truly on 61 after a fairly scratchy innings. I don't think I played and missed all day, yet the timing wasn't quite there. My concentration was good though. On a slow and seaming wicket which wasn't the easiest to bat on, I was out there for 50-odd overs which was exactly what I needed. An uninspired innings? Yep, I'd go along with that, but I'm happy anyway and hoping for some more runs tomorrow.

Things are definitely coming together, and already I'm feeling confident about the approaching Test. I'm hoping that Steve and Mark Waugh will get runs tomorrow to fine tune them for the Test; Ian Healy's in excellent nick behind the stumps, Shane Warne's going better than at any stage on tour, and the quicks are really coming on. We've got 17 fit guys on tour to pick from, and that's a real plus. I think a strong win here will have us poised to click in the Test. We're going to be hard to beat from now on.

DAY 2

With the weather thankfully holding, it was another good day for us. Mark Waugh's 170 was a very sweet innings, and I went on to get 109—out trying to smash one of the medium pacers back over his head. The only disappointments from the team point of view were that Steve Waugh missed out, falling to an excellent catch, and Michael Bevan got a start (24) and no more. I was hoping Michael would have got amongst them. But it was pretty satisfactory all round, and we've got the home side 2-70 at stumps.

I know that Matthew Hayden will be very disappointed tonight. He missed selection for the Ashes series after being well in the running—and was obviously keen to do well here to make some sort of statement to the selectors and to the guys who beat him for the tour. He's been having an excellent summer with Hampshire. But he failed twice here—out to a very sharp bat-pad catch in the first innings, then bowled off stump by Jason Gillespie in the second when he didn't play a stroke. Matthew is a darned good player and he'll make plenty more runs over here.

There's a really good battle going on between Jason Gillespie and Michael Kasprowicz for the third fast-bowling spot in the Test side. That competition is going to be very healthy for us when we bid to wrap up this game tomorrow.

DAY 3

The result of that little personal duel is that Jason Gillespie has taken five wickets, Michael Kasprowicz three and we've knocked over Hampshire for 170 midway through the middle session. It was an ideal prelude to the Test match. Neither of the two quicks did themselves any harm—they were both very sharp at times, and reaped their just rewards. It was an emphatic victory, and one we needed.

Despite the 100 I scored here—which was no classic as I've freely admitted—the questioning continues about how I'm going ... and where I'm going. I can only shrug my shoulders and accept that this is going to be a never-ending story. Three Test hundreds in a row *might* shut things down—but I doubt even that. The questions were still coming after today's match. My only answer must be to score runs and keep the pack at bay.

Today's early finish was a real bonus. Ahead of us lay the longish haul from Southampton on the south coast all the way up to Manchester. A 6pm finish would have meant a very late arrival at the scene of the third Test. As it was we were there at a respectable 8pm—and the Taylor family were there waiting for me, having booked in earlier in the day. They all seemed happy to see me—especially my wife who has been cooped up with the boys in a house 20kms north of Manchester in pretty ordinary weather. Anyone who has ever had to contend with little kids indoors while the rain pours down outside will know what I'm talking about.

The crunch Test

The Manchester Test is seen as the pivotal event of the series. It's a big one for us . . . a must-win game. And it's to be played on a wicket that is pretty much under prepared, thanks to the weather. It's not as good as I'm sure everyone would wish it—especially the groundsmen and the players. I had a walk around the wicket today and there's a lot of moisture in it. There's some grass there, but it's bare at both ends and in all honesty looks pretty ordinary. What am I going to do tomorrow if I win the toss? I haven't got a clue. I probably won't make up my mind until about ten minutes before that happens. The groundsmen will have had another chance to roll and mow it by then and I'll have another look. It's certainly not a very appealing prospect from a batsman's point of view, but I think it's going to be pretty much the norm for the rest of this summer.

Jack and William Taylor, happy to be on tour with dad—and dressed to kill.

The word is obviously out about our side: that if we play on good hard, flat Test wickets we're going to win a lot of cricket matches. I'm sure the idea of wicket preparation for the games against us from now on will be to put something into the pitch for the bowlers and level things up. Obviously I've got pretty mixed feelings about that—but we've just got to play the cards we're dealt.

Apart from the wicket, our preparation is pretty close to ideal. The time we lost through rain was a negative—but the strong performance against Hampshire was a real confidence-booster. Right through the team we have players running into form. The only guys who aren't getting that chance are the blokes who aren't in the Test team, and it's been very hard on them. They've been severely disadvantaged by the weather, virtually robbed of their chances to press claims by the fickleness of England's summer weather.

Tonight at our team meeting I made special mention of them all. An Ashes series is always a tough time for the guys who don't make it into the Test team, but when the rain comes along and washes out the other games, that's when it gets really hard. The guys are here, keen and ready to go and they can't get a game of cricket. I understand their frustration and I applaud their attitude—the way they are showing enthusiasm towards the whole team, doing their job, and playing their part in the task at hand.

Tonight we made a very tough decision indeed—and left Michael Kasprowicz out of the third Test team. Jason Gillespie is back in. This was one of the toughest decisions I have been called on to make as a tour selector. Michael hasn't put a foot wrong on tour; he's bowled his heart out. He's not out of the side because of anything that he has or hasn't done. It's just that Jason Gillespie has done such a great job for the team in the recent past. After all, in South Africa he took more wickets in the series than Glenn McGrath and Allan Donald. There's always a bit of gut instinct in a decision like this too—and there's always that feeling with Jason that he can rip through a team, as he did against the South Africans in Port Elizabeth.

Just about the only bad news in the camp is that Adam Gilchrist has had an accident at training and torn the ligaments in his left knee. Chances are that he may be forced to go home. It's rotten luck. To lose anyone out of a touring side is a blow—but it's especially disappointing for someone like Adam who hasn't yet had the chance to show the people in England his undeniable talent. He'll be very down about this. The only consolation is that he'll be back.

Two of the three members of Mark's personal support team, Judi and William Taylor, enjoying an afternoon in the English sunshine.

CHAPTER 12
TEST OF CHARACTER

Third Test, Old Trafford

DAY 1

I'd call this a 50-50 day—right from the moment we stepped out on to the playing field this morning and strolled out to look at the wicket. To bat or to bowl on this rather patchy looking strip? That was the question—and opinion was split just about down the middle as we assessed the grass, the moisture that the wicket held, and the bare patches. My initial reaction was that we should bowl, and it remained that way until I had one last look after the groundsmen had rolled the wicket. I studied the bare patches and I thought back to 1993 when we were sent in on a similar surface—and ended up winning comfortably.

I changed my mind. It was one of those mornings when I would have been quite happy not to win the toss, not to have to make the decision. But the coin fell my way again. 'We'll bat,' I said. By lunch time I was starting to wonder if I'd made the right call . . .

By the end of a first session in which the ball had been doing *plenty*, we were 3-78. I nicked one to first slip and was out for two, Greg Blewett chopped on for eight and Mark Waugh edged one and was gone for 12. The ball was moving around quite a bit and we had played and missed a number of times. Matthew Elliott did a sterling job, batting through the session for 44. Under the circumstances, 3-78 at lunch didn't look too bad. But after lunch when Matthew was given out caught behind, and Michael Bevan met the same fate, I was starting to rue the decision I had made. We were 5-120.

On a day cut short by bad light, it came down to the last 14 overs. We had moved haltingly to 7-160 when the Manchester gloom forced a two-hour break. On resumption Steve Waugh and Paul Reiffel put on a further 64 runs without loss. At stumps we were 7-224, back at least to 50-50 and breathing a little easier. I think if someone had offered me a day's score of 224 at lunch time, I would have taken it. Steve Waugh was the foundation stone of the innings. Uncomfortable early, he dug in and batted superbly for 102 not out at stumps. Steve toughed it out, then unleashed his range of strokes when he got their measure. It was an innings that gave me a lot of pleasure. After a fairly nerve-racking day I'm now able to relax just a degree or two and not rue the fact that I made the decision for us to bat first on a questionable wicket. Without Steve Waugh plastering it together in the middle stages, it might have been a different story.

We keep getting wickets over here that have plenty in them for the bowlers. My theory is that there always should be a little bit in the wicket on the first day of a Test match, but it's certainly proving a tough year for the top order batsmen. When I see a great player like Mark Waugh struggling against medium pacers I wonder if this is really what people want to see from Test cricket. Maybe it is. These sort of wickets are guaranteed to produce results and I suppose that's what people like. But batting is no easy task when the ball is seaming all over the place.

Tonight, I'm just hoping that the wicket keeps doing tomorrow what it did today.

If it does we're in the area of a very respectable score and right in this game. If we can bowl as well as we did at Lords, they'll struggle to make 200.

THIRD TEST, DAYS 2 & 3

This has been real hard-fought Test cricket—and three days in to it we're looking good. Our first innings of 235, modest by many standards, was always going to be pretty competitive. And especially so when Shane Warne came out on day two and bowled the spell he's been waiting for, taking 5-19 at one stage in their first innings. At stumps they were 8-161, with only Butcher (51), Stewart (30) and Ealham (24 not out) providing much resistance.

The third day has swung the match comprehensively to us. The Poms were quickly out this morning (for 162), leaving us with a handy lead of 73. Again we struggled early in our innings in the second dig. I went cheaply again (11)—to Dean Headley in a mirror-image of my first innings dismissal. Headley is bowling particularly well to the left-handers. He got Matthew Elliott and Michael Bevan again, so of his seven wickets (so far) in the match six of them are Taylor-Elliott-Bevan. He's engineering late movement away from the left handers, and we're going to have to do something about it for the next Test.

It wouldn't be a Test series without a streaker or two. Here's Manchester's contribution to the phenomenon (third Test).

At the end of day three we're 335 runs in front—still with four second innings wickets in hand—with Steve Waugh 80-odd not out and Shane Warne 33 not out. It's looking good. We're 6-260. Greg Blewett was the unlucky man of the day. He was given out caught at slip by Nasser Hussain off Robert Croft, but it was a bad call. Nasser Hussain said to Greg that he thought he'd caught it...the umpires conferred ...and eventually Blewie was on his way. Later, the replay showed that the ball had hit the ground before Hussain caught it. It was one of those things that can happen in cricket—I'm sure that Nasser genuinely believed he had taken the catch. Probably he'll cop some flak from the press over the incident. But it won't be from us—we won't be holding any grudge. Although we will use it against him when he comes out to bat in the second innings. Things can happen in the blink of an eye in the game of cricket—and this was one of them. Added to the Ian Healy incident at Lord's, it adds weight to the case for using slow-mo replays to help get the touchy decisions right. After all, the umpires are using the replays to decide whether a ball has reached the boundary or not...yet *not* using them to assist in making decisions on catches that can alter the entire direction of a match.

So, we're well in front here in Manchester, but still with plenty to do. I'll be reminding the guys of that in the morning. We're going to push on and get as many runs as we can, then set about knocking them over. I think the highest fourth innings score to win a Test at Old Trafford is 147, so we're way in front. But history, of course, doesn't mean a thing when you're out there doing it. We've still got to get the ten wickets. If Warnie can bowl the way he did in the first innings (6-48) and Michael Bevan can land the ball the way he did when he took the vital wicket of Butcher, then we're placed to win the match...and square the series.

THIRD TEST, OLD TRAFFORD, DAY 4

A day to play. A Test match to be won. I guess you could say that we're sitting pretty. Today our batting was so resilient that I eventually closed our innings—something I never expected to have to do. Steve Waugh was again the rock, batting superbly for his second hundred of the game (116), and joining Warren Bardsley and Arthur Morris as the only Aussies to achieve that rarest of feats in Test cricket against England. Shane Warne (53), Paul Reiffel (45 not out) and Jason Gillespie (28 not out) chipped in with their own excellent contributions. I declared 20 minutes after lunch, setting them around 480 to win.

I understand my 'late' declaration was the subject of some conjecture in the press box, criticised by some. However, I think a day and a half is always plenty of time to bowl a side out and if you can't do it in a day and a half you're not going to do it in a day and two-thirds.

Anyhow, the bottom line tonight is that we've got them 5-131, still some 340 behind, and with a day to go. Jason Gillespie has three wickets and Shane Warne two—and the ball is turning quite a bit on a wearing wicket. The declaration is looking okay.

Jason Gillespie bowled superbly, generating real pace and picking up the prize wickets of Atherton, Hussain and Mark Butcher. John Crawley's still there on 50-something and has played well—but Warnie is troubling the batsmen a good deal with the amount of turn he's getting. It's the sort of wicket that if we can get one early tomorrow, I think the rest of them will fall over. The thing is that it's terribly difficult when you first come in on this type of wicket. In the fair dinkum department I think it's only the weather that can stop an Australian victory tomorrow—and the forecast is promising.

This is a Test in which we've won the big moments. England's last chance was to knock us over quickly this morning and chase something around 350. They didn't manage it...and it's been pretty much the way of things this Test.

It was interesting in this morning's papers how little mention there was of Nasser Hussain's disputed catch yesterday. It rated a passing reference—and that's about all. In itself, that's a good thing—there was no thought in our minds that Hussain was cheating. He believed he caught the ball, the umpires agreed and that was that. It was just something that happened. But I wonder what the reaction of the British press would have been if it had been Shane Warne or Ian Healy who had been involved. Slightly bigger headlines, I would suggest.

In this morning's *Mirror* there is a story by Alistair Ross on the fact that Shane is flying home after the Test to see his wife and new baby daughter, Brooke. The Australian team management have given him the nod for that. I recall that it was Ross who wrote the story, with photos, of Steve Waugh's disputed catch of Brian Lara in Barbados two years ago. The headline was something of the order of: *This proves that the Australians are cheats.* Today the inconsistency is apparent. A similar event takes place in a match Australia v England, and Ross makes no mention of it. Steve Waugh took a catch which *he* believed was fair, Nasser Hussain took a catch which he believed was fair—yet a newspaper like the *Mirror* chooses to take a completely different approach. I think if a commentator or journalist is going to write a story about something that he perceives as cheating on the cricket field then at the very least he should be consistent.

THIRD TEST, OLD TRAFFORD, DAY 5

The job is done and the series is all square. All the worst scenario possibilities that galloped through my mind in the wee small hours last night were blown away today as we wrapped up the Test. As a captain poised to win a vital Test you think of all sorts of grim possibilities: awaking to the sound of rain on the window, the English tail showing bulldog spirit and battling through the day...or at least until the rain comes. You *know* who's going to win...but still you worry.

The good news for us was that the five wickets came fairly quickly for us on the final morning. Greg Blewett at bat pad dropped a sharp chance off Shane Warne early (John Crawley) and the old nightmares started stirring somewhere deep down in my mind. But once Ealham was removed (caught Healy, bowled McGrath) and then John Crawley trod on his stumps at 83—a very good innings—the outcome was never in doubt.

I couldn't get the ball off Glenn McGrath. He was ready for the kill and took four of the five wickets to fall this morning. Warnie was the same. So I just left 'em to it and they bowled through the 90 minutes or so it took to wrap up the Test match. No doubt Jason Gillespie would have loved to get the ball in his hands too after his three early wickets, but McGrath and Warne were so much in the groove that it made sense to let them complete the job.

It wasn't an easy Test by any means. I don't believe we had the best of the conditions—even though that came down to a question of my choice. I still don't know if I made the right decision in batting first—I doubt that many other skippers would have chosen that option. I honestly think that if we had bowled first, the result would have been the same. We won because we played the better cricket. We found a way of making 235 in difficult conditions on the first day, with Steve Waugh and Paul Reiffel performing great deeds, then Warnie putting his hand up to bundle them out for 162. We were never going to lose from there.

Unfortunately the match has rebuilt some more personal pressure on me, and I'll be feeling a bit nervous when I go out for the fourth Test. The critics have me in their sights again after my failures here. I'm less worried this time around. The century at Edgbaston has given me a slab of confidence which had ebbed away before that game and a basis for some more good scores coming up, I hope. Here at Old Trafford I got a couple of pretty good balls, and nicked them both. As an opening batsman you're always vulnerable to that happening, especially if you bat first on a wicket that's green. Then you're always gonna need a little bit of luck to get you through—although I am a subscriber to the belief that, largely, you make your own luck—and this time I don't think the luck went my way. I'm feeling good, and looking forward to the next dig.

Mark Waugh's second innings 50 here was a good sign, as he's been struggling a bit. Steve was just superb. Add those positives to the quality of the bowling here in Manchester—which was exceptional—and the signs are there that the tide has turned. Looking ahead to the next three Tests I'm sure now that we've got the advantage. In saying that I am in no way under-estimating this England side. They're not the side we've beaten here in the last two series—they've got more in them than that and there's some fight left yet. But the bad news for them is that we found the groove in this Test. We stuck at it for five solid days and every time England got a sniff of getting back into the game we found a way of answering the challenge.

Tennis players talk about the 'big points'—and how winning them separates the world's Top Ten from the rest. It's exactly the same in Test cricket. There are turning points in every game. In recent years we've become very good at winning those when the pressure was on. As I read the signs here, we are right on track. It's a darned good series, though—three Tests and still very much alive and well, exactly as the organisers would have wished. In the last four series at this stage we've been 2-nil up, with the series virtually gone. This time it's different; England have a much

Australia whipped England by 268 in the third Test at Old Trafford, leaving Mike Atherton deep in thought, pondering the challenge ahead.

more relaxed Mike Atherton as captain than he was in Australia in 1994–95. They're going to be trying to bounce back—but we're ready now.

The feeling in the change rooms after this Test was fantastic. After all, it was our first win over England on tour, considering the three one-dayers, the loss in Birmingham and the draw at Lord's. There was just a great feeling in the air. We were back on track—and the celebrations were very real, not forced. Sadly, I'm just about to part company with my team, just when we're all on a roll. The rest of the guys are off to Newcastle to play Minor Counties en route to Edinburgh for a game against Scotland, while I'm heading down to London in a couple of days for a meeting with all the Test captains from around the world on the subject of the future directions of the game. So I'm a scratching from the post-game celebrations, which is a shame. There was a real buzz in the room after we won this Test. Warnie's gonna be missing too, flying home to see his baby daughter. I think we've made the right decision in giving him the green light to go. The chance for him to be at home with the family for just a day or two at this time will be great for him—and I can only see him coming back even more relaxed and hopefully able to pick up exactly where he left off in this Test.

Holidays

It's now five days on from the Test and the captain has been taking a break. I haven't exactly had my feet up, however. While the team has been campaigning in the north, and playing some golf at St Andrews (I would have enjoyed that) I've been busy enough. After the Test I joined the family at Bury, the home of our friends, the Nevilles—a great bunch of people. It was great to catch up with them all and relax and go out to dinner for a yarn.

Along the way I spent a day with a crew from *Sixty Minutes* headed up by Jeff McMullen. Before I left Australia I had promised I would do a story with them along the way on tour when my schedule allowed. They trailed me around—to the local markets, to backyard cricket games with the boys. I hope they got what they wanted.

Then we packed and moved on—again—to London, where I attended the Captains' Meeting at Lord's. I think it's a fantastic idea, to get the skippers together to discuss the game. We talked about everything from the standard of wickets, to some of the rules, to umpiring standards and to broadening the use of the 'third umpire'. Recommendations will go to the International Cricket Council for their assessment and action. I really think it's a great thing that the players, represented by the national team captains, are getting this sort of input into shaping the game for the future.

In London on a day off, I did all the things I'd been promising William and Jack we'd do. We went to the Natural History Museum which William just loved, then we took the tube to the Tower of London and joined the queues there to see as much as we could. Then it was on to Trafalgar Square by taxi to feed the pigeons. This was young Jack's *real* favourite. He sat on the ground and fed nearly *all* the pigeons. It was a long day, a great day—a terrific interlude in the tour for me. I'm refreshed and ready to get on with it. On July 13 there was another parting, and we're all getting used to those. I put Judi and the boys on the train to Manchester and headed in the opposite direction, to the Excelsior Hotel at Heathrow where I'm linking up with the team again when they fly in from Scotland. It's great having the family in the country—even though they're often *there* and I'm *here*. Seeing the family, who mean so much to me, provides some balance on tour. It's great just now and then to get away from all the cricket talk and cricket thinking you do as captain. We were a bit sad saying goodbye at the train station, but I'll see them all again in a week's time at the fourth Test, at Headingley, Leeds.

Games against Glamorgan and Middlesex provide the path to that match for us. I'd love to pick up a hundred in one of those games (or both!) as I did in the run-up to the third Test. Before the County matches we've got a social game tomorrow against the XI of the very famous and wealthy John Paul Getty. It will be very much a carnival-type day and our coach Geoff Marsh is even thinking of donning the whites again and opening the batting with me. Talk about a blast from the past.

CHAPTER 13
HEADING TO HEADINGLEY

The good fun has ended. The serious business is about to re-start. Today's match at JP Getty's personal ground—on which he's spent some 800,000 pounds—was hugely enjoyable. They had a very reasonable side including the likes of Martin Crowe, Graeme Hick and Ben Hollioake. It ended in an honourable draw, the way such matches should. Matthew Elliott got 95 for us, Michael Bevan 50 and I got 30-odd at the end, just having a whack at some pretty ordinary bowling (although Geoff Marsh didn't end up playing). They fell about 40 short of our 270, with four down ... Martin Crowe scoring a very good hundred.

It was a very relaxed day—the highlight for me coming after tea when I left the field for an hour or so and visited JP Getty's wonderful library, which contains some extraordinary old books. He has manuscripts which date back to 1164AD, the first and fourth dated copies of the Bible from the 15th century, and the one that really caught my eye, an atlas produced by an astronomer back in 1482 which is claimed to be almost certainly the world's oldest existing atlas. The book is obviously minus a fair bit of the then-undiscovered world, but the countries of the known world, around the Mediterranean, etc, are easily recognisable—remarkable, really, considering the limited techniques and resources available way back then. I'm not a great reader, but I was fascinated with what I saw today.

Tonight, the re-focusing begins—on the County games that will tune us up, and then the Test.

Glamorgan, at Cardiff

A bit of a dull affair—I think that's a reasonable summing up. Glamorgan chose to leave out their three best bowlers—Waqar Younis, Steve Watkins and Robert Croft, who's in the Test side at the moment. They won the toss and sent us in on a good batting wicket, no doubt their reasoning being that we'd bat, they'd bat, then we might set them a target on the last day to make a game of it. Frankly I wasn't too delighted with the whole thing—firstly with the fact that they decided not to play their best side against us, and secondly, I'm getting a bit sick of these county matches in which they seem to expect us to cook up a result.

We batted well. Ricky Ponting scored 126 not out and I managed 71, hitting the ball as well as I've hit it for a long time. I went out there a bit angry about the toss and the way they were trying to direct the game, and my mood probably helped me. My runs came off about 90 balls, and I was eventually caught on the fence off their spinner while trying to hit him over it. I declared at 4-369, and we knocked them over for 254, with Michael Bevan getting the first three wickets and Paul Reiffel the last four. Unfortunately none of the guys who haven't been playing much (Michael Bevan, Justin Langer, Brendon Julian and Michael Slater) managed to get among the runs in our second dig and at one stage we were 5-42. Then Reiffel, Elliott, Blewett and Ponting rescued things and we declared at 7-217, setting them the extremely tall order of scoring 340 off 60 overs. They were never in the hunt and the game fizzled into a tame and early draw. I was down to bat at number 11 in the second innings, but didn't get a hit. So, a disappointing match—although with a highlight or two: Ricky Ponting's batting, Paul Reiffel's five first innings wickets, and my own solid form. Overall, though, it was no classic.

Middlesex, at Lord's

This match was preceded by the longish drive from Cardiff to London and a late arrival at the Westbury, followed by an early rise to assemble on Tower Bridge for what should be an exceptional team photo.

I lost the toss (again) on a good batting wicket, and we played like a tired side, although not too badly. The problem with the County games at this stage is that Test fever is rampant within any touring team, and it gets tougher to lift for these games, even though they're an important part of the tour. That's the way it was on the first day, when we were no more than solid and they batted through the day, the last wicket falling in the last over of the day, at 305.

From that point the match proved to be as good a lead-up game as we could have had. We batted right through the next four sessions of play on a fine wicket, mustering 7-432. Most of us got amongst the runs to some extent, with Mark Waugh's 142 not out certainly the highlight. Matthew Elliott scored 83, Steve Waugh 57, Greg Blewett 40, and Shane Warne 39. I got 27, at which point I was bowled around my legs trying to sweep the off-spinner, Dutch.

We then had a pretty fair whack at trying to bowl them out in two sessions—and weren't that far off it at the end. At one stage we had them 6-150, but they held on to be 6-201 at stumps. A result would have been nice, but it wasn't the major thing we wanted to get out of this game.

Overall, it was an excellent warm-up. I'm very happy with the way Warnie's going. He picked up three wickets in the Middlesex second innings, bowling as well as he has done at any stage since his operation. He's spinning the ball on nearly any sort of wicket at the moment. Here he was landing the ball just about right, bowling very few bad balls and putting a tonne of pressure on the batsmen. Mark Waugh was named man of the match. But Mark was not as happy as he could have been, having placed 30 quid each way on Jesper Parnevik to win the British Open at 66-1. Mark walked off the ground after his unbeaten 142 to the news that Parnevik had led by two shots at one stage in the final round, but had finally lost it to Justin Leonard. So Mark picked up a few quid to go with his hundred, but not the 2000 that looked in his grasp at one stage.

For me there was personal sadness on the final day—at the thought that this would very likely be the last time I would play for Australia on this famous ground. The chances of me being back are pretty thin, I guess—although the lure of the World Cup in 1999 is there, tantalisingly, in the distance. Today, I walked off slowly—looking around, and soaking it up. Lord's, after all, is the home of this game I play.

I've been here three times for Test matches, scored a hundred here, won two and drawn one—and had the honour of captaining my country here. Lord's is a special place, and I've loved playing there. It hit me pretty hard as I walked off on that last afternoon against Middlesex, July 1997.

Dark Deeds at Headingley

Something's cooking. The papers are full of news about the wicket at Headingley. The story is that David Graveney, England's chairman of selectors, visited Leeds and asked the groundsman to shift from his (the groundsman's) preferred Test wicket to the one next door. I can't agree with that happening. I said at the captains' meeting in London the other day that I believed the groundsman at the designated Test ground should just put out the best wicket he can for Test matches—and that should be that.

For the groundsman involved, it's the major game of any summer and he should just be left alone to prepare what he believes to be the best wicket. No-one else should have a say. In a way the suggestion of outside interference—by someone like David Graveney—is flattering. I suppose it's a compliment to us to think that a particular type of wicket needs to be produced to heighten their chances of beating us. But I'm not happy about it. I don't think there's any doubt we'll get a green, seaming wicket come Thursday. But no matter—we're going to be very, very hard to beat.

A Brush with Royalty

It's been a long time in my life since I felt as nervous as I was on the morning we went to Buckingham Palace to meet the Queen. As I paced the large, luxurious room where we were deposited before she arrived, the butterflies were galloping, I can tell you, and I had to keep drying sweaty palms. The worry was that I would forget someone's name when I was conducting the introductions. That might sound a bit strange, but the fact is that when you're playing cricket with guys day in and day out, real names don't come into it much. It's always nicknames. My worry at the Palace was that when I got round to introducing Jason Gillespie for example, I might say: 'And this is Dizzy, Ma'am'. Or for Steve Waugh, I might say: 'This is Tugga'. Fortunately I got through okay—although I did get stuck at Brendon Julian for some reason. I probably threw myself tactically on that; Brendon was next in line to Shane Warne and I had it in my head that I might tell the Queen a little story about Warnie as I figured he would be the most recognisable to her of all of us. I finally ditched the idea—but still had this little memory pause when I got to Brendon.

Anyhow, after the introductions, Steve Waugh and I had a good yarn with Her Majesty. She talked about horseracing—her favourite sporting pastime—and we mentioned about her not being at Lord's this series (her presence at that match being something of a tradition), and that we figured her not being there might have brought the rain.

Prince Andrew, the Duke of York, was also on hand to meet the team. I had seen him a few days before on TV, playing in a celebrity golf tournament, and I told him I reckoned his swing looked alright, and joked that we'd be looking for him at Royal Birkdale next year (venue for the British Open). He told me that, well ... yes he might get a run ... because he looks like Justin Leonard. The newspapers had made something of that fact after the Open this year. We spent an hour or so at the Palace, and it was a special time—very much the topic of conversation as we motored north to Leeds for the next big challenge of the tour.

Touchdown Leeds

Arriving in this fine old Yorkshire city, we trained late, brushing away some cobwebs for the Test. The controversy about the wicket—and the fact that a late decision was made to change the one to be used for the Test—is still very much in the news. The reported belief of the people who made the decision—David Graveney, plus the CEO up here at Headingley and the groundsman—is that there wasn't enough grass on the strip first chosen, and that the move was in the interests of the upcoming game. Now, I'm not against a Test wicket being changed if there is a belief that the alternative will provide a better all-round Test surface. But I do believe strongly that the chairman of the English selection panel should *not* be part of the process. My fundamental belief is that the groundsman should be left alone without outside interference to prepare the most important wicket he's going to prepare all summer.

Setting aside the wicket controversy, our preparation has been pretty close to ideal. We've been playing good cricket over the last month, with everyone running into some strong form. I fully understand the disappointment of the guys who aren't getting a run, but their contribution has been first class. They're in there playing important roles as part of the overall squad.

This is a big Test match. If we win here, I am confident we will win the Ashes—I can't see England possibly being able to pick themselves up to win the next two Tests if we beat them here. I also feel very confident that if we win here we'll go on and win at least one—if not both—of the remaining Tests. It's a 'must win' game for England—but we're as ready as we can be ... and that's great.

Test Eve

It's late evening on the night before the big game, and a chance for a little reflection. We went out as a team tonight to a Japanese restaurant—a nice relaxing meal at which the spirit and the feeling couldn't have been better. I know we're ready. The worry is a spit of rain on the night air outside. The chosen wicket is a little under-prepared and I'd like to see five uninterrupted days, with as little cloud cover as possible.

Fourth Test, Headingley

DAY 1

The words that come easiest to mind tonight are 'frustrating' and 'disappointing'. After all the kerfuffle about the wicket there were still mixed messages in my mind when I walked out to toss. Frankly, I had no clearly defined view—and the only thing to do was to let it come down to gut instinct. And that I did when the coin fell my way for the fourth successive time this series. 'We'll bowl,' I said. I'm sure that raised a few eyebrows; people who know me well realise that that's a very rare call from me.

The theory was this: the Poms aren't batting that well, and there's a little bit of mystery in this wicket. It'll give us something, I thought. Well, the story tonight is that not much was proven... one way or the other. Inclement weather cut the heart out of the day. We only got 35 overs at them, and at stumps they were 3-106. We didn't bowl with much luck—but we didn't bowl all that well, either. A lot of ball went past a lot of outside edges, but we bowled some loose stuff too. Five wickets on such a day would have been a very good return... four would have left it about even. Three? Well, if I was in their shoes I wouldn't be too unhappy about that after being sent in to bat on a chancy wicket in overcast conditions. One positive for us is that we're bowling first in what now is a rain-shortened Test match. That's always an advantage—the chance, at least, to bowl the other side out twice and give yourself a chance of winning.

FOURTH TEST, HEADINGLEY, DAY 2

This was a very, very good day. Jason Gillespie was on fire this morning and from 3-106, we knocked them over for 172 on an improving wicket. They played some not-so-great shots, we took some good catches and Diz bowled very fast indeed for his outstanding figures of 7-37.

In reply, after being 4-50 at one stage, we're now 4-258 and looking good. After being dropped at 29—a simple chance at first slip—Matthew Elliott has carved out a great century (134 not out). Ricky Ponting, in his first Test back (for Michael Bevan, this time) is 86 not out. Both played superbly, driving, pulling and hooking sweetly, and took the attack to the England bowlers who looked increasingly flat today after some early life. I have my doubts that Darren Gough is 100 per cent fit. His first spell was lively, but he fell away. Dean Headley was a bit the same. We're 80-odd in front, six wickets in hand, with three days to go. I'm feeling good about having sent them in.

On the personal front, a duck—only my fourth in 85 Test matches. It's an unwanted event that I've been able to dodge pretty successfully through my career. But today I got a short one from Darren Gough which I tried to avoid. It didn't bounce as high as I thought, and just grazed my glove. Umpire Mitchley took a long time before raising the finger. Unfortunately for me, he got it right. When Greg

Blewett went for one, Mark Waugh for eight and Steve for four, we were looking down a rather deep hole. But the young guns dug us out, and we're now in great shape to win this game.

The key wicket for us this morning was that of Mike Atherton. He batted for the best part of 50 overs for his 41, very much the backbone of the England innings. But we got him (caught Gillespie, bowled McGrath) as he tried to hook and it was all downhill for them from there.

There are similarities between Atherton and myself. Both of us, I guess, are feeling the pressure. Mine is from not having played well over the last six months, managing to drag myself out of it at Edgbaston—now backpedalling with Test scores of one, two, one and zero since the 100 in Birmingham. For Michael's part, he's not so much struggling for form, but struggling to dominate *us*. He's batting for a long time for his runs without ever really getting on top of the bowling.

My own struggle puts pressure on our middle order. Atherton's battle applies pressure on the England batters too. They see him as their number one batsman—and with him finding the going tough, the rest of them seem to be following suit. He has a few more runs than I have at this stage but I don't think he's been any more effective, really. The captains are pretty close to all-square. Being positive is probably the answer for both of us. The one sure thing is that we're both trying ...

Jason Gillespie reaches for the stars, and Alec Stewart is on his way (7). First innings, fourth Test, Leeds.

FOURTH TEST, HEADINGLEY, DAY 3

It's been another frustrating day, with the clouds gathering over the ground in the morning session, then opening up to wash out the rest of the day. The good news is that with Matthew Elliott pushing on (164 not out), Ricky Ponting celebrating his first Test century (127) and Heals chipping in with a brisk 27 not out we managed to add 115 runs before the rain came. We're 201 in front. We've lost some cricket time, but (weather permitting!) we've still got two full days at the Poms. The task at hand is to try and build a lead of 300 plus, then bowl 'em out and win by an innings.

England's fight will be to save the Test. They've got no hope of winning it now. They'll be trying to dig in and graft out a draw.

FOURTH TEST, HEADINGLEY, DAY 4

It's been a good day of fighting cricket, with our aggression in the morning session providing great entertainment for the fans. We put on 140 or so in the morning session. For Matthew Elliott it was a bitter-sweet experience. On 199, he got a good one from Darren Gough and was bowled. The disappointment in that was quickly submerged in the acceptance of a magnificent innings—one that he'll remember all his life. With Paul Reiffel (54 not out) and Glenn McGrath (20 not out) we mustered 9-501 off 123 overs (after being 4-50!). At that point, I declared, leaving us 329 ahead, and with five full sessions to knock them over.

After lunch, things went even better for us. We had them 4-100 at tea, with a quartet of their top men gone. But then came the fightback from John Crawley and Nasser Hussain, still together at stumps after putting on 120 for the fifth wicket. So that's where it stands—they're 117 behind with six wickets in hand and a day to go. I fancy our chances.

The key to it tomorrow is us getting rid of Nasser Hussain. Today he scored quickly, putting pressure back on our bowling. In the final session both Hussain and Crawley played very positively, scoring at four runs an over and knocking us around a bit. We'll be looking to strike quickly against them in the morning.

A big highlight today was the batting of our tail. It's a very secure feeling that someone down there—from Heals onwards—is going to get runs, whether it's Warne, Reiffel or Gillespie. Even Glenn chipped in with a nice 20 today, and won me ten quid in the process. I bet Ian Healy that he'd make at least 11, and Heals gave me odds of 10/1.

When it comes to the tail we've had the edge over the Poms for the last few tours. We've almost inevitably been able to knock over their tail fairly cheaply whereas ours more often than not chips in with some valuable runs.

In recent times, Headingley has proved to be something of a batting haven for us. This famous ground has the reputation of being a seamer's paradise, but it's the third tour in a row on which we've made more than 500 and we're yet to be bowled out here since 1985. If memory serves me correctly, we made 7-601 declared in our first innings here in 1989, after being sent in to bat. Then, in 1993, we scored 4-653, with Allan Border getting 200 and Steve Waugh 150. This time, on this controversial wicket, there's been a little bit in it for the bowlers, particularly with the new ball. But it's also a ground on which you can score very quickly, as we did for a substantial part of our innings.

And so to bed—with a Test match sitting there, waiting to be won.

FOURTH TEST, HEADINGLEY, DAY 5

It's done. We're in front in the series. The last day of the Test couldn't have gone any better. We got the wicket we needed early when Warnie tossed one up to Nasser Hussain (on 105). The ball dipped late on him and he didn't quite get to the pitch of it, lofting a drive to mid-off where Jason Gillespie took the catch. Mark Ealham then dug in for about an hour with John Crawley, although there were very few runs. On the introduction of the second new ball we got Ealham, caught in slips by Mark Waugh off Reiffel. Headley was soon gone to Reiffel who then removed Crawley with a spectacular off-cutter which took the off stump. When Mark Waugh caught Darren Gough first ball off Gillespie, it was as good as over. At lunch, they were 9-260.

With a wicket to go, the break was a blessing in disguise—a chance to relax, pack our bags in the shed and start to think about the celebrations which were to follow. It was also a chance to take on board some wholesome sustenance before the celebrations began.

After lunch, it was over in a single ball. Paul Reiffel, the late destroyer in this game (5-49), caught the edge of Robert Croft's bat, Heals took the catch ... and that was that. We had won the Test by an innings and 61 runs—a very, very comprehensive victory.

Yet, when I look back—and this may sound funny—it could have been a very different game. If Graham Thorpe had accepted that simple second-day chance off Matthew Elliott at 29, we would have been 5-50. This was a big moment. It was a classic example—and for Thorpe a cruel one—of how Test cricket can turn on a single ball. We seem to be winning the big moments now, and that's a great sign on this journey we are making towards (I hope) retaining the Ashes.

Again today, we knocked over the England tail very cheaply. They were 4-222; all out 268. Their last six wickets put on 40-odd runs; our last six wickets put on 460. The signs are great as we set about raising our sights to Nottingham—and the fifth Test ...

Aftermath

It was quite a party. Going back to the change rooms when you win a pivotal Test match like this one is a fantastic feeling. And we had some Aussie company too. Members of the Canberra Raiders rugby league side joined us; they had played Halifax the previous day in Super League's World Club Challenge, and won by plenty. To have fellow Aussies along—and especially respected fellow Aussie sportsmen—seemed to heighten the celebrations, making them even more special.

Jason Gillespie took man of the match, as he should have. His 7-37 in the first innings was a wonderful performance and I know that if he and Glenn McGrath can stay healthy they're going to be a wonderful fast-bowling combination for Australia for many years to come.

We lingered in the change rooms for three hours or more after the game, just soaking up the feeling and enjoying ourselves. Eventually we headed back to the hotel where wives and families and fellow revellers were waiting. It was a fantastic night. A Test match won, an experience shared—and a night of good spirit and good fun to celebrate what had been achieved.

The press conference after the Test was a novel experience. This time the media weren't asking so much about my captaincy and position in the team ... they were asking about Mike Atherton's. There was more than a little irony in that considering recent history—and the fact that I was walking into a press conference after making a duck in a Test match. I've made four low scores in the last three Tests—consistently poor. But I told them after the match that my aim was to finish off the series strongly, and that I felt I would do that.

My thoughts on Mike Atherton at this time are that he's doing a good job as England captain. I think a captain can make a huge difference in any team—but I'm not sure he can make *all* the difference. Great teams need the contribution of brilliant individuals and individual will ... qualities that no single man can instil. I suppose Mike's record as a captain is not too hot. But I don't think you can look at just him either. I think you have to look at the players around him, and how badly each one of them wants to play for his country and whether he'd give everything he had for that honour. I agree to a fair extent with Ian Chappell's theory that a captain must live or die by his record. But I'm not so sure that all the blame should be heaped on a bloke like Atherton, and especially considering that Australia has consistently beaten England for the last ten years. There are other reasons, of course—and England must look to them, rather than point the bone at a single person.

CHAPTER 14

ONE UP...
TWO TO PLAY

The days that follow Test matches on tours to England are quiet ones—a chance to relax, take a break, then gradually re-focus. After the win at Headingley we had three days off before the four-dayer against Somerset, at Taunton—the only lead-up match to the next Test at Trent Bridge. I decided to skip the County game, even though there were probably people saying that I should be out there working at it, considering my continuing personal struggle in these last three Tests. But I knew I was seeing the ball okay. The Somerset game was a chance for some of the guys who haven't been getting much cricket. For me it was a chance to rest body and mind ...

So I went again to Bury, to join family and friends. I learned that there had been a great deal of speculation in the press back home about my ongoing back problem. Some of it was true, some exaggerated. Yes, the back has been troubling me a bit. No, it wasn't the reason I took the Somerset match off. Fact was I hadn't had a game off since the Nottingham match which followed the first Test. It was always the plan that I would miss the game at Taunton.

Apparently my back is becoming quite notorious, and the subject of much speculation. There are hints that my career is close to over because of it. The fact is that I do have a problem—and I know it's going to be an ongoing problem, something that I'm going to have to live with. But it's not too much more than the myriad of injuries sportsmen carry regularly into battle. You put up with 'niggles'—that's how it is in sport. With me, some days my back is fine, sometimes it's bloody sore. After the fourth Test, I pulled up fairly sore, but not too bad. Bury did me the world of good. Nothing extraordinary; just family stuff, and friendship. It was what I needed.

Nottingham

Two days out from the Test and we've had a training session, a team meeting and a darned good feed at a Chinese restaurant. The Somerset game provided two days of cricket then two days of rain, so a little disappointing, although not overly worrying. I know we are in the groove now. The games away from the Test arena are paling into insignificance by this time on any tour—although part of the programme and there to be played as well as we can play them.

The mathematical equation for us now is simple: we need a single draw from two Tests to retain the Ashes. I understand this team well enough, though, to know that we won't be thinking 'draw' in our approach. The statistic is that of the last 21 Test matches we have played, we have won or lost 20 of them. Just one draw, brought about by the rain which dampened this season's Lord's Test.

England have made some changes. I would refrain from using the word 'panic'—although perhaps it's fair to say there's a good bit of optimism in their selections. Adam and Ben, the Hollioake boys are in, and good luck to them. They are exciting prospects for England, but their county form this season hasn't exactly demanded selection for them. I think the England selectors have picked two guys who they think are going to give the side a lift—more in attitude than in technique or skill alone. The brothers are a couple of 'goers' who have belief in their own ability. It will be interesting to see how they go over the five days of a Test match when the pressure's right on, and temperament and technique are tested in equal measure at the highest level.

The Poms have left out Mark Butcher, and that's something of a surprise. I think he's a player who has improved on this tour. I remember dropping him on two in the Lord's Test and he went on and made 87. I thought then: I've probably saved this bloke's career. They stuck with him after that, and I believe he has steadily improved, even though he hasn't made a lot of runs. He's been called on to bat on fairly tough wickets, at Old Trafford and Headingley, where the pitches did a fair bit under the new ball. He has played without much luck, and I reckon he's been rather harshly treated. I think he's played as well as any of the openers—except Matthew Elliott, who has played superbly.

The switch of Alec Stewart to open is an interesting one. Stewart has been batting first drop, and has been one guy who has struggled. I thought they'd move Alec around, but not to opener. I was guessing they'd shift him down the list to bat five or six. It's interesting to talk to Ian Healy about Stewart. Heals has more than a little sympathy for him, knowing so well the concentration and physical effort that goes into keeping wickets day in and day out. Heals has always said that he'd hate to bat any higher than seven, because of the need to recharge his physical and mental energies after a day or two behind the stumps. My view is that they've put a heavy load on Alec Stewart, and it's going to be hard work for him. If he can rise to the challenge, well, good luck to him. For our part we're hoping his batting slump continues, as he's been a key man for them in recent summers.

We'll be going in with the same XI. No reason to change. We're a team in good form—and individually we're in pretty sound shape, physically and mentally. I'm very confident about these five days ahead. We've got quality fast bowlers who are having a good series, the best spinner in the world and a very tidy batting lineup. I suppose the only downside so far is that a couple of the senior blokes in Mark Waugh and myself haven't been making as many runs as we'd like to. We're both hoping that's going to change here in Nottingham.

I'm here alone this time. Judi and the boys aren't coming down for the Test, although no doubt the TV at Bury will be getting a bit of a workout. I'll be concentrating hard, and working to get among the runs, because I know how good that will be for the rest of the team—especially if I can do it in the first innings. I'm looking forward to it.

At the press conference today I got the questions I expected, concerning my back, my form, and the fact that we stand on the brink of history. If we win this Test match we'll bring off the unprecedented feat of winning the Ashes five series in a row for Australia. Three of us—Steve Waugh, Ian Healy and me—have been involved in all five of those campaigns. I'd love to be part of that place in cricket history—I know all the guys would. The media also conveyed the news today that if we can win, it will be the first time since 1938 that an Australian side has come from behind to win a series. It's been noted now and then that we're generally front-runners—that we like to hop out fast, win the first couple of Tests and cruise in from there. Over here, we were caught on the hop early and have had to graft our way back—which we've done very well. Now, a date with history awaits us, adding spice to what should be quite a game.

Test Eve

We're fit and ready to play. I'm sure the week off has done me the world of good. I was a bit scratchy at training yesterday, and finished up having two net sessions, which is unusual for me. The second one was designed just to get my feet moving faster. Today I hit the ball really well—facing Glenn McGrath and Shane Warne, which is about as good a test as you can get. The feet were fine—now the trick is to get the mind right when I go out and bat. I'm aiming to enjoy this Test.

The wicket is the best I've seen on tour so far. It has a light, consistent covering of grass and it's flat and even. As I told the media today, the Trent Bridge groundsman has worked hard to put out the best possible wicket he can. He's done the job well.

The big news of the day is of trouble in the England camp. Darren Gough is out of the Test with injury, and that's a huge blow for them. It also means a chance for someone else, of course, and we're mindful of that. All the indicators are pointing our way, especially now that the Poms' best bowler is missing. We've won the last two Tests, had the better of things in the last three—we're fit, in form and at full strength. On form and ability we should win—and I'm confident we will if we keep the roll going and play the way we did in the last two Tests.

Fifth Test, Trent Bridge

DAY 1

Can you believe it? I won my fifth Test toss in succession and at the end of a day batting on this even-paced, well-prepared wicket, we're in good shape. No risk whatsoever that Mike Atherton would have batted if the coin had fallen his way. Our top order all got among the runs: Elliott 69, Taylor 76, Blewett 59—with Mark Waugh 60-odd not out and Steve 40-odd not out. We're 3-302 on this very good wicket—a wicket in which there's a *little* bit for the bowlers if they really bend their backs and hit a length.

No doubt the morning papers will be saying that the Ashes are now secure. But I'll be drumming it into the players in the morning that such certainty is definitely not yet the case, that there are four days to go and there is much to be done. The job is not done until the moment at which the Test is won ... or at the very least, drawn. I don't think I'm going to have to do much talking. All of us are pretty much in tune with what needs to be done. Tonight is quiet at the hotel. Most of the guys left the ground early, headed straight for the hotel and their usual gym session or a swim. It'll be early to bed for all of us, dreaming dreams of another big day tomorrow. It's opportunity day for sure—if we can score 500 runs we're obviously a great chance of winning the game.

I was about the only bloke who stayed back at the ground after the day's play. In the course of my innings today I passed 6000 Test runs, and the press guys were keen to have a talk about that. I didn't bat my best, but it sure was nice to get among the runs. I'm not relying on the square of the wicket shots, and that's a good sign. Today the feet were in position for some crisp drives, and they felt especially good. So, 6000 runs. I think I'm only the sixth Australian to get there. It's a nice milestone and an honour to be up in the rarefied atmosphere of the sort of company I have joined. A nice thought too that the passing of a milestone will perhaps help the team towards our goal.

I also waited back to have a beer with Mark Bosnich, the Aston Villa and Australian soccer goalie. Mark's up for the game, and I left him a ticket this morning. His delight at the fact that we're doing well really shone through. I think he's planning to hand out a fair bit of stick to his Villa team-mates if we go on and win the Test.

Mark Taylor blazes away in his innings of 76. Day 1, fifth Test, Trent Bridge.

Ricky Ponting, one his way to 45—second innings, fifth Test, Trent Bridge.

FIFTH TEST, TRENT BRIDGE, DAYS 2 & 3

This is turning into a very good contest of a high standard. The pendulum swung this way and that on day two, with their bowlers getting into our tail and restricting us to 427. They must have been happy with that considering we were sitting on 3-311 at one stage early on that second day. Alec Stewart (87) and Mike Atherton (27) then put on a hundred for the first English wicket, and at 0-106 they must have been feeling pretty good. But the last session of play belonged to us as Atherton, Stewart, Hussain and Crawley fell, with Warnie getting three of them and McGrath the other (Crawley). At 4-188 when stumps were drawn it was nicely poised.

Today's third day was extremely hard fought. We worked hard to pick up three wickets in the morning session, then eventually cleaned them up for 313, giving us a very handy lead of 114. Matthew Elliott and I then managed to settle back into the groove with an opening partnership of 51. Matthew scored 37 before he was out hooking, caught on the boundary, and I went on to make 45 before being caught by Nasser Hussain off Ben Hollioake. Greg Blewett chipped in with a very impressive 60 before he too was out attempting to hook. At stumps we're 4-167, 281 in front, and still very much in the driving seat. I take my hat off to the Poms; they're in there fighting hard—much harder than they have in some recent series. Against some English sides it would have been just about over on the first day when we amassed 3-302. We would have made 500 for sure, bowled them out fairly cheaply and won the game pretty much in the comfort zone. But this time the struggle has been intense—I'm just happy it's our way. A lead of 281 with six wickets in hand is a mighty healthy situation.

The question is: how much fight have they got left in them? I figure that if we can make another 120, giving us a lead of 400 overall—a very tough target to chase in the last innings of a Test match—then we'll be sweet.

FIFTH TEST, TRENT BRIDGE, DAY 4

The mission has been accomplished—after a day not without its nerve-racking moments. The Poms got a tremendous lift early; Steve Waugh hit the first ball he faced for four... and then was out to the next. At that stage Mike Atherton and his men might have been thinking that the target could be as low as 330 or 350. But such thinking reckoned without Ian Healy. Heals strode out there and whacked 63 invaluable runs off 78 balls. It was an innings containing a message: we're going to win this Test, and we're going to take the Ashes urn.

By the time the tail wagged a bit we had mustered 336, and the target for them was a big 'un—450 runs in about 130 overs. Well, they didn't shirk it. The Poms weren't going to die wondering, and went out there and played their shots...or tried to. But living dangerously has its inherent problems of course—and despite Graham Thorpe's stout-hearted, unbeaten 82 off 93 balls, we cut through them, with the

We've done it! Jason Gillespie and Matthew Elliott holler their approval after Australia wrapped up the Ashes.

Shane Warne clowns it up, keeping the cameramen happy and the celebrations are underway after Australia's 264 run victory in the fifth Test.

bowlers sharing the load in a real team effort. McGrath, Warne and Gillespie all finished with three and Paul Reiffel with the prize wicket of first innings' top-scorer Alec Stewart. We held our catches, gained a couple of lucky breaks...and that was the ball game.

The Poms died with their boots on, fighting. But I think in this match, they were outskilled by a few of our blokes. There is a gap between some of their batting at the top and ours—headed by Matthew Elliott and the Waugh boys. Between their spinner (Robert Croft) and ours (Shane Warne) there is a huge gulf. They are the sort of areas in which we won this Test match—and clinched the Ashes—on Trent Bridge's very fine Test wicket.

This has been a tremendous day for me, and for the Australian cricket team. I'm so proud that I've been able to contribute so positively as an individual to what we achieved in this critical game which has secured the Ashes. But in reality it has been a victory that sums up the true team qualities of this Aussie side of 1997. Every single bloke in the side pitched in and did the job. I'm thrilled by the performance—for us to have come storming back, so focused and determined after the slow start to the tour, and the jolt of losing the first Test. That's five winning Ashes series in a row—a record. No wonder I'm standing here in the room, thinking that I'm going to go right out that door very soon and downstairs for some celebrating . . .

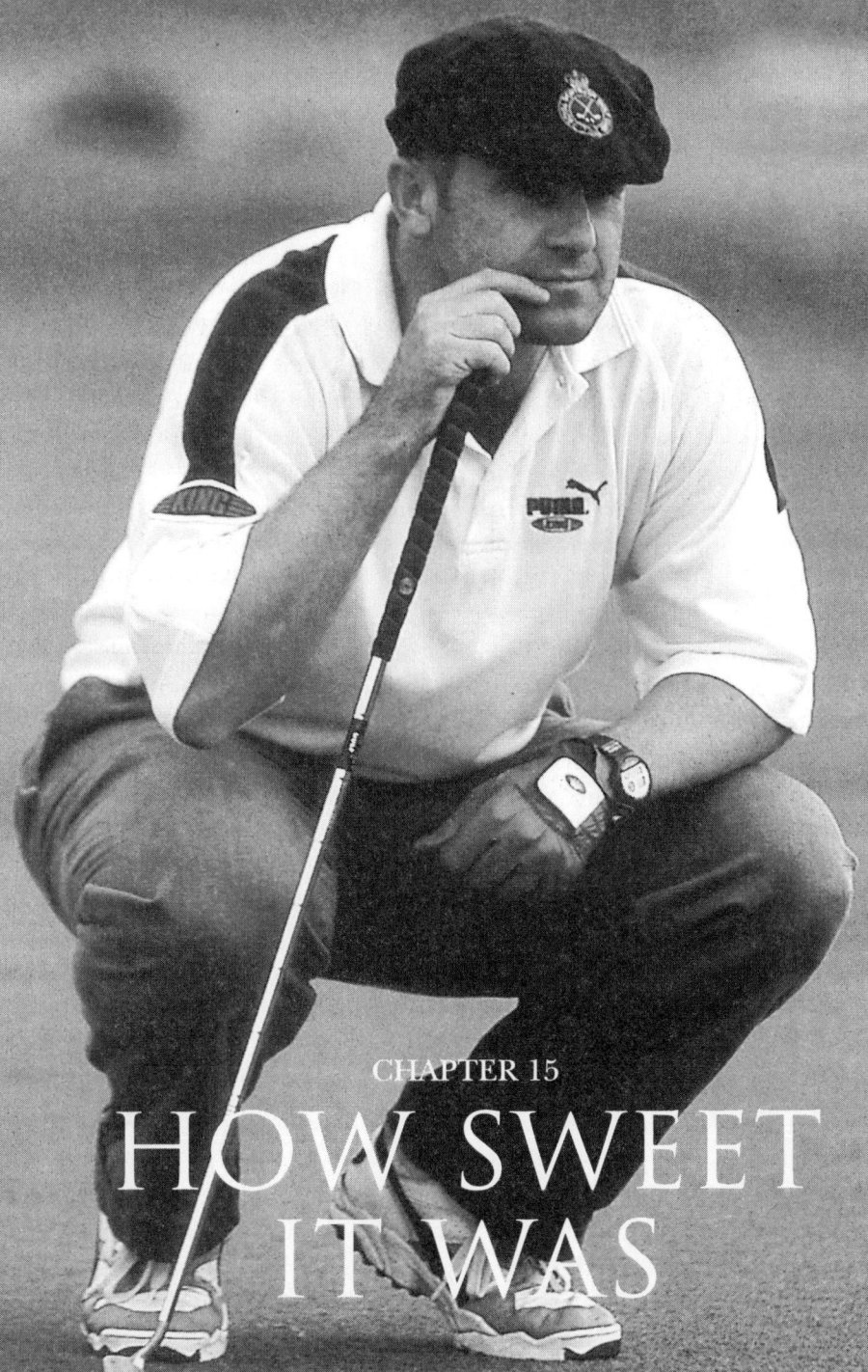

CHAPTER 15

HOW SWEET IT WAS

We got what we came for, and I'm sure now that the only things that could halt continuing success for this team in the seasons ahead would be complacency or laziness. In two years' time the Poms will fly to the southern hemisphere to try and stop the rot to reverse the trend of five successive losing Ashes series. Everything points to that being very tough indeed for them. Looking at the side we've got now, there are ready-made replacements in just about all areas, except for the unique place held by Shane Warne. It goes without saying that whenever it is that Warnie finishes in the years ahead, he's going to be terribly hard to replace.

Right at the moment we haven't got a Steve Waugh for the middle order—a bloke who's going to average 50. But I can see players in the future doing that. Matthew Elliott is averaging 50-plus in Test cricket, Michael Slater, who's not even in the side at the moment, averages 47 and Ricky Ponting has thoroughly proven his worth over here. Australian cricket is in good shape. I think the chances of complacency or laziness overtaking the team are remote; this is a team that is definitely enjoying its cricket. The feeling of coming back from one-nil down to take this series has drawn us all closer together.

When the Poms come over they'll bring some fresh faces and fresh ideas. But I really think if we can maintain our work ethic, and maintain the balance between the senior players and the gradual injection of younger players into the side, then we can keep a good thing going. We've got the talent, no doubt about that. We've just got to handle it the right way and keep working at it. If we do that, we'll hang onto the Ashes for the sixth straight series.

As for the captain's future? Well, I don't really know what the answer is at this stage. I feel I have the ability to play on for another year or so yet, but I also want to make sure that the selectors, the ACB and the players still want me as captain. My feeling on the latter is that yes, they do. Really, it's pretty much out of my hands; the selectors and the Board will make the ultimate decision. But if they give me the nod, chances are I'll keep playing. Our success, and my own contribution in this fifth Test, has buoyed me considerably. Winning is a very enjoyable pastime, and this Test one of the most pleasing I've ever played in ... in a thoroughly enjoyable Ashes series.

The Morning After

I'm wondering what I wrote last night. I hope it made good sense. I had a couple of drinks after our win ... but not too many. I think all of us were far more intoxicated on the feeling of sheer enjoyment and relief—of coming to terms with the reality that after a long haul through England's summer, we had achieved what we set out to achieve. This morning I feel as if the weight of the world is off my shoulders.

The headlines this morning look vaguely familiar, except that this time it's Mike Atherton's name up there in large type instead of mine. There's all the expected stuff: English cricket is in trouble ... Atherton's era should be at an end ... he should resign, etc. I feel for Mike. I've been down that road. But today, at least, I can enjoy the other side of the coin—the praise of the 1997 Australians, and how powerfully we rebounded after that first Test loss. Things can change so quickly in cricket ... and now and then it can get nasty.

The *Daily Telegraph* over here has just about got it right. Their theme is a simple one: that England were outplayed by a stronger team. That's about it—far closer to the mark than the papers that want to heap the blame on Atherton as skipper. The fact of it is that at the moment we've got the better team. We have more match winners than England have. I am of the firm opinion that this English team have improved a good deal in the eight years I've been playing against them. But so have we, and the gap remains. But they've pushed us hard in the series, and no doubt will do so again when we face up in the sixth Test.

I believe that changes are needed over here. I read that there are ideas being put forward to make their cricket more competitive, less repetitive, and to make their junior cricket more of the two-day variety than one-day hit 'n' miss stuff.

England's Test team is a tougher outfit now than in the last three or four series. I just don't think they had the necessary match winners in the side, and they didn't win enough of the vital moments. Most of the time when something had to happen to turn a match in this series, it was the Aussies who made it happen.

We've got a few mixed emotions in the team at the moment. Paul Reiffel is going home tomorrow, and will miss the sixth Test. He's going to join his wife who is due to have their first baby in September. Things have been a bit difficult during the pregnancy and the days of this Test were tough and emotional ones for Paul. We decided on the second night of the Test that regardless of the result, we'd put him on the plane straight after the match to be with his wife and family. In one way Paul will be devastated to leave the tour, after joining us late—but I also know he'll be very relieved to be on his way home to Janet. The best wishes of the team go with him.

Another 'quick' is in a spot of injury trouble. Jason Gillespie has been worried by a back strain for a week or two now and faces some tests which will decide his immediate future. If there are risks of further damage we certainly won't be playing him in the sixth Test which is now a dead rubber game. Diz is only 22, and the last thing I would want to do would be to jeopardise his cricketing future in any way. If he's got a problem that demands rest, then he'll be getting rest straight away. We've got a Test to play here, but already thoughts are drifting further down the track to the upcoming home series against New Zealand and South Africa.

The faxes and messages of support have really rolled in from home this time. There's one from John Howard—such a great supporter of the Australian team—and one from Kim Beazley. The support from back home—both on a personal level and a team level—has been really terrific this series. And so too the support of the small army of fans who made their way over here to watch us battle for the Ashes. It was a wonderful feeling to be on the balcony yesterday, receiving the winning cheque, to look out on the waving Australian flags, and to hear the cheering and singing. Many of the fans came back to the pub last night to join the celebration party.

Enjoying the Afterglow

Three days on, and the celebrations are pretty much behind us. We had a couple of tremendous days in Nottingham after the Test, including a team dinner at a place called Sawyers during which the harmony was about as good as it can be within a sporting team. We sat for hours talking about the Test, about cricket in general ... and just enjoying each other's company.

Now we're in Northern Ireland. It had been decided that if we secured the Ashes we'd trek over here as a sort of reward. So we flew to Belfast, then took an hour and a quarter trip to a place called Limavady. There's been salmon fishing in the river, and more than a little golf. Today we've been to Royal Portrush, which we're told is one of the top two or three courses in Ireland. It's indeed magnificent—a coastal, links-type course. I didn't play too well, but I enjoyed the experience of being there. Afterwards we headed to a place claiming to be the oldest whiskey distillery in the world, its licence going back to 1608. We were given a tour and I was lucky enough to be presented with a personalised bottle of their very best.

From there we headed on to the Giant's Causeway, one of the natural wonders of the world. There are various legends that surround this remarkable rock formation with its seemingly man-made 'steps'. One of them claims construction by an Irishman aeons ago, apparently trying to entice a Scot to come across the waters to fight him. If you'd been there this day you would have seen the Australian cricket team cavorting around, posing for photos ... just a happy bunch of tourists.

Cricket in Ireland

Our one-day match went pretty much as expected. We batted first and made 303 with Ricky Ponting getting a century. I batted at eight. In reply we had them 7-70, at which point we eased the reins just a little. They finished with about 160, so it was a game that provided some entertainment and enjoyment, if nothing too extraordinary—except for my first bowl on tour. I bowled three balls and took 1-1.

Brendon Julian has had some rotten luck. He got hit on the wrist in a net session before the fifth Test, and has been pretty sore. Before the game against Ireland he was still sore when he rolled his arm over, so we sent him off to hospital for some X-rays. The bad news is that Brendon has a cracked bone in the wrist, and will take no further part in the tour. It's a cruel blow for him—with Paul Reiffel and Jason Gillespie out of the sixth Test, he was poised along with Michael Kasprowicz to come into the team.

We've now lost four bowlers in total from the tour and, with matches still to play, we've had to do some improvising. We've conscripted Tasmanian all-rounder Shaun Young (from Gloucestershire) and NSW all-rounder Shane Lee (who's playing league cricket over here) to join the squad for the last week or two. Chances are that one of them—probably Shaun Young—will play in the sixth Test. It's a great break

Days away from the playing field can provide the necessary 'R & R' for the players during an arduous Ashes campaign. For the Aussies of 1997 one of the special ones was a visit to Ireland's Giant's Causeway.

for these young players, and good luck to them, but it would have been nice to finish off the tour with the team that has done the job in the last four Tests. Anyhow, we're fortunate we've got blokes we can call on, and comfortable too in the knowledge that the Ashes are safe and sound before a ball is bowled at The Oval.

Test Eve

We've come very strongly through the match against Kent at Canterbury. Now we face the last hurdle of a marathon campaign. The game at Canterbury produced a comprehensive win, with our blokes chasing 230 under some pressure on the last day—and getting them quickly and positively. I didn't play and will complete my own personal journey back here in London, at The Oval.

Wouldn't you know it? The focus has drifted away from the Ashes and the game ... and back to me. Everyone and his brother seems to want to know about my future as a player and captain. Will I be captain in Australia in the upcoming summer? The question has been asked dozens of times. I can only repeat that I don't know—that it's out of my hands and in the hands of the selectors and the Australian Cricket Board. Talks I will have at some stage down the track with Trevor Hohns, the chairman of selectors, will have some bearing on all that. From the reports we're getting over here it seems that the selectors and the ACB are keen on the idea of there being two sides next season—a one-day side and a Test side. Reading between the lines I think the

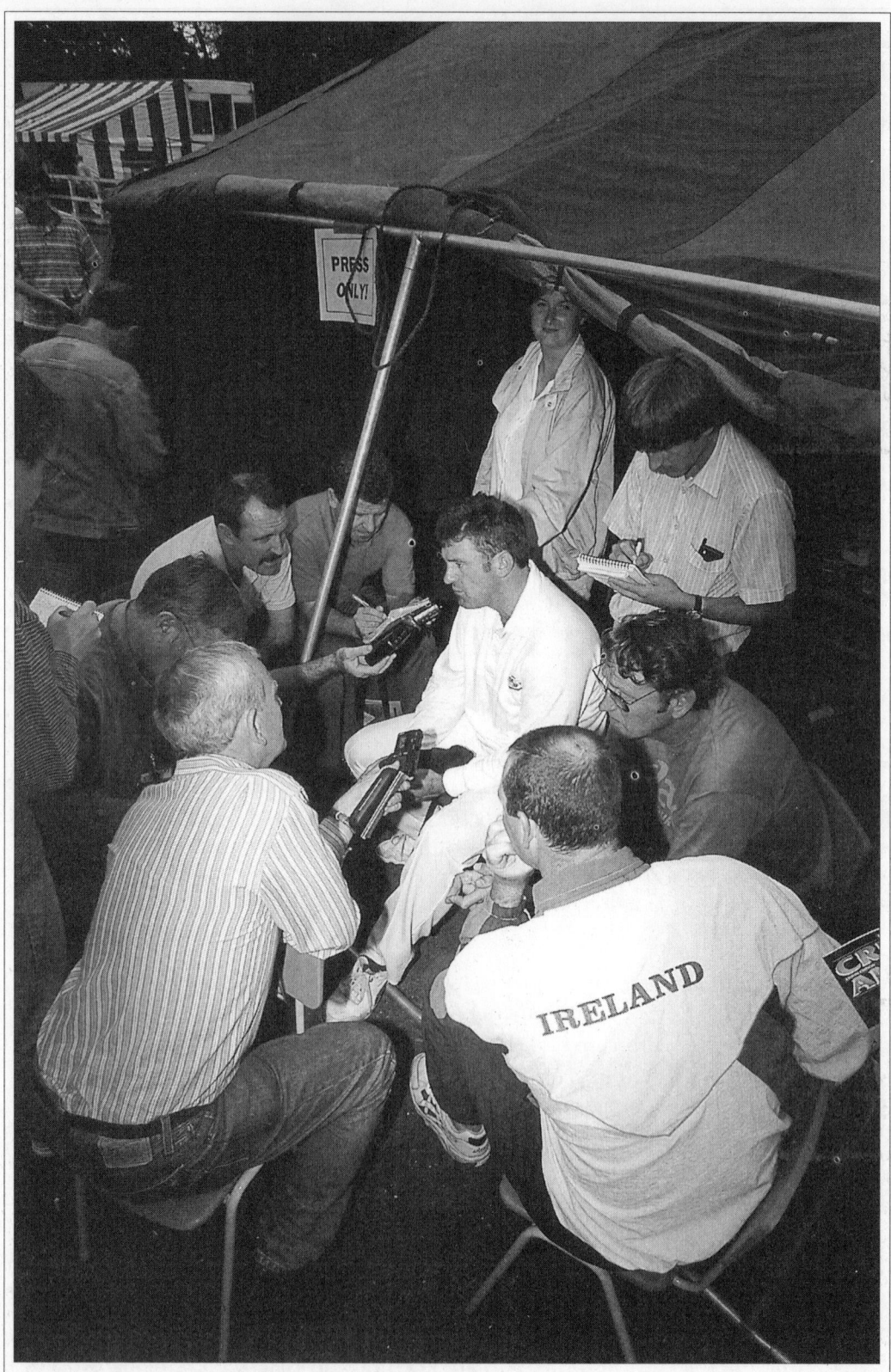

A regular scene on tour—Mark Taylor, grilled by the media.

plan is that I won't be part of the one-day outfit. Obviously I will be talking to the powers that be when I get home.

If it happens that I don't captain the Australian side in the 1997–98 summer, it won't be the end of the world. Life will go on. But I have certainly enjoyed it a great deal and I'm proud of the record that the team has built up under my leadership.

If it happens that it all ends with the last ball in this Test match in London, well, I'll still leave with tremendously happy memories of the time I've had at the game's top level. And whatever happens here I'm assured of going out on a winning note, with the Ashes safe again. If it's the wish of the Board and the selectors for me to keep going, then I'll talk it through with the family—and also sit down and do some quiet thinking myself. I'll have to ask myself the question—do I want to keep putting in all the hours you have to as Australian captain? It's a fact that there's a lot more to the job of Australian cricket captain than just calling heads or tails at the toss and putting the batting order into place. These days there are considerable demands away from the playing field. It's a full-time job and something that you've really got to want to do. It's something you've got to keep positive and enthusiastic about; if I started to get negative and grumpy at press conferences, that would be the time to give it away. There'll be some thinking to do over the next month or so . . .

CHAPTER 16
THE ONE THAT GOT AWAY

History is not on our side. Notwithstanding our keenness to win them, dead rubber games seem to slip with some consistency through our fingers. This time we've got a couple of fresh faces in the side in Shaun Young and Michael Kasprowicz. Their enthusiasm to do well should be a positive for us. Shaun is the 372nd player to represent Australia, and I know that he's absolutely delighted.

As I said to the players last night, the hardest thing about dead rubber games is finding that extra bit of fight in the really tough moments. We've had that sort of fight in us right through this series ... Steve Waugh's hundred on a tough wicket on the first day at Old Trafford, Shane Warne's six wickets at Manchester and Jason Gillespie's seven wickets at Headingley, Matthew Elliott making 199 and Ricky Ponting 127 at Headingley. The challenge is to retain that quality here at The Oval. When the going gets tough in a dead rubber, you can lose that edge and be prepared to accept something of lesser standard in your own play. We've got to really put our hands up if we want to win this Test match, and dig deep individually. The tough moments will definitely come—the challenge is for us to be prepared to win those moments. It's a challenge for every one of us to confront individually ... whether we head on to 4–1, or allow them to narrow the gap to 3–2.

Sixth Test, The Oval

McGrath & Healy Pty Ltd. They were a dynamic duo for Australia on tour.

His stumps scattered, Devon Malcolm departs—Michael Kasprowicz's seventh victim in the second innings of The Oval Test.

DAYS 1 & 2

So far, it's been a game of ebb and flow, on a wicket that's very uncharacteristic of The Oval. On this wicket with a difference, I lost the toss—for the first time in the series. Michael Atherton chose to bat, and so would have I. Usually the wicket at the Oval is hard and fast, with some moisture in it on the first day and some turn towards the end. In my experience it's been a wicket that's good for the quicks, but also a good wicket to score quickly on because the ball tends to come truly on to the bat. This time, it's different...

We're playing on a wicket that has been dry from the start—so dry, in fact, that now and then a ball has been bursting the surface. Scoring has been hard work, and winning the toss was a bonus for the Poms—not that they made the most of it. Thanks to a first-class contribution by Glenn McGrath (7-76) and some fairly ordinary batting by England, we thoroughly negated their advantage by bowling them out for 180. They came out obviously determined to be very positive, and went for their shots. In a number of cases that approach led to their downfall and we were delighted to have them all out for 180 on a wicket that is okay, if slow. It will get harder to bat on as the game progresses.

Our response on the first day was encouraging. At stumps we were 2-77—with yours truly extremely disappointed not to still be there. In my 38 I hit the ball as well as I have for the past 12 months and it was very disappointing to middle one off Phil Tufnell, only to see it go direct into the midriff of Mark Butcher in close. I had faced only 40 or so balls and was seeing it well—I'd even hit a couple of nice cover drives

Phil Tufnell (left) and Andy Caddick—England's heroes in the sixth Test at The Oval.

which is always an indication for me that my feet are moving well. Yep, I would have loved to be there overnight on that first day. But having said that, it was still a pretty good day for us—to have them out, and to be within 100 with eight wickets in hand.

The second day, however, wasn't all that I'd hoped it would be. Probably everyone expected us to muster 350–400, which we were hoping for too. Instead their left arm orthodox spinner Tufnell got among us, bowling very well and ending up with 7 for 66. We let him dictate to us, which is not the way we normally play the game. Most of the attacking came from him, and he sent down some very good deliveries and claimed the rewards. Greg Blewett made 40-odd, Ricky Ponting 40, and we were out for a very modest 218—a lead of 38. Not a lot, but on this low-scoring wicket, it might be handy. If we'd made 300 we would have been unbeatable. As it is, we've still got a fight on our hands even though we had them 3-50 at stumps on the second day, with Atherton, Stewart and Butcher back in the pavilion.

I felt personally sorry for Mike Atherton (even though we were happy to get him!) when he went for eight. He's been under plenty of pressure through this series, and especially so in recent times with all sorts of people calling for his head. Some of the headlines in the tabloids have been downright scandalous and disgraceful. It seems a lot of people have very, very short memories, conveniently forgetting times when they were ready to acclaim him as a hero. The fact is that the guy has been captain of his country for 46 Tests, a record for the England side which he claimed from Peter May at the Lord's Test. Mike Atherton is deserving of more respect, and his commitment to the cause more consideration. Whatever you think of him as a person or a player he's certainly given everything he can to his country as a cricketer, and he's captained the team through a very, very tough period during which success hasn't come easily.

It's been easier for me. I've captained Australia through a particularly good period in which I've had many fine players to work with. I have found the personal pressure enormous at times—but I've always had the comfort of the side doing well. Mike Atherton hasn't had that. When his personal form has slipped, he has rarely had any reinforcement from the collective achievement of his team.

Remarkably, this Test could be over tomorrow—the third day. If we can bundle them out, and then chase a target well, we're going to get a result and give the series an early mark. I don't think either side would been too disappointed with that. The series has been a long grind.

Shane Warne is going to be a key for us on a wicket that's turning. But Shane twinged a groin muscle late in the afternoon and there is some concern about how well he'll come up. Time will tell whether the injury will be a crucial factor in deciding the outcome of the match.

SIXTH TEST, THE OVAL, DAY 3.

Well, I got it right. The Test is over with. But unhappily the report tonight is that the side I had in mind to win the game has been beaten. Us—by a few runs after what was certainly a high-octane Test for the fans who watched these three days in London. Warnie did well despite difficulties, getting rid of Nasser Hussain in his first over. Mark Ramprakash and Graham Thorpe batted positively to put on 80 useful runs before we got rid of them. From that point we wrapped up the tail pretty quickly—and were left with 124 runs to win the Test. Sadly, it's in the record books now that we were bundled out for 104, and lost the sixth Test by 19 runs—a slightly disappointing postscript to the Ashes series. In the end it's 3–2, and that disappoints me personally, as I don't believe it's an accurate reflection of the respective strengths of the sides. In my view, it flatters England to an extent. The fact is that we had clearly the better of it in four of the six Tests, with one (this one) a photo finish. With just a shade of difference here and there (Lord's, The Oval), it could have been a 5-1 series, but that would have flattered us. So 3-2 is just a little disappointing, although I wasn't exactly pulling my hair out as the afternoon unfolded. After all, the Ashes were secured, and that's what we came to do. But it's a slightly sour aftertaste that we haven't finished on a high.

Today I scored 18, Matthew Elliott let one go on four, Greg Blewett was given out caught behind on 19, and Ricky Ponting was unlucky to be given out on 20. Gradually the match ebbed away from us. England bowled and fielded very well, spearheaded by Andrew Caddick (five wickets) and Phil Tufnell (four). When all is said and done they probably deserved their victory. I'm just a little disappointed that we didn't play better.

The fact that we lost dead rubber games in each of this season's Test series (West Indies, South Africa and England) is an indication, I believe, of the intensity of the cricket we're involved in. In each campaign (in Adelaide, Port Elizabeth and Trent Bridge) when the winning of the series hinged on one match, we came up trumps. Each time we responded outstandingly well to the challenge to clinch the series. Those victories I believe were the ones that showed the true quality that exists in this Australian team. When the chips were down, we won the big games. When there was not too much at stake we tended to take our foot off the pedal—despite our best intentions. If we let ourselves down a little in the dead rubber games—and we did to an extent—I would suggest there was no effect on the overall outcome ... a pass with distinction for the Australian cricket team in season 1996–97.

My Year

An up and down year, and one that I won't forget—there are plenty of tags you could put on this year of my own personal struggle. The strangest thing of all is that my batting form started well (India) and finished well (here in London). Without being in any way boastful it's probably reasonable to suggest that I was pretty close to our best batsman in India, with a one-day century, and solid starts in the innings of a Test in which we performed disappointingly. Here at The Oval I hit the ball very well again—my cover drives and pulls were good, while my feet moved in harmony with the rest of me, and I saw the ball well. It was in between those two Tests—Delhi and London—that I was in trouble. For fair lumps of that period I have felt—to put it bluntly—plain bloody awful. My footwork wasn't functioning, and I wasn't seeing the ball well. Why? The only answer I can give lives in the truism that cricket is a huge mental game. The simpler and more free of thoughts that you can keep your mind, the easier the game is. Under pressure, my mind cluttered by desperate thoughts of trying to get out of the personal rut—along with the myriad of other things I have to do as captain—I struggled.

The Party's Over

On the last evening of the last Test I sat with Mike Atherton and enjoyed a beer or two. We stayed at the ground until around 11.30 and the Poms were there until at least 10.30. We mixed together and enjoyed each other's company the way sporting teams that share mutual respect should. I had a long yarn with Athers; the word was out that he was contemplating retirement from the England captaincy, but I'm not so sure he will now that they've beaten us in this Test. I think if we'd got the 124 comfortably, won the match and taken the series 4–1, he may very well have pulled the plug.

But cricket is a funny game which turns on small events, like when Dean Jones dropped me on one, at Derbyshire. I told Mike I reckoned he should only stand down from the England captaincy if he felt that England are going to be a better side with him *not* captain, or if he believed that by standing down it would benefit his own game and therefore make England a stronger side. My view is that they do not have a better leader than him available at this stage.

Alec Stewart is the only bloke who I think could take over as skipper at this stage. But if I was in charge in the England side I wouldn't want to be sending a new leader to the West Indies for England's next campaign. That promises to be a very tough tour, and stability at all levels in the side will be important. Eventually Stewart could be an interim captain for England while they blood the heir apparent—whether it be Nasser Hussain or Adam Hollioake or whoever.

It's odd how Atherton's form has been almost a *reverse* of mine. At the start of the summer he had very little pressure on him. His team won the three one-dayers impressively, and he made a hundred along the way. Meantime, I wasn't making runs—and the weight of the world was on my shoulders. Slowly it changed. I made a hundred at Edgbaston, and gradually started to graft some runs as the rest of the tour unwound. Meanwhile, Athers was going downhill. By the last Test he was batting as badly as I've ever seen him bat in any series in which we've played against him. His feet weren't moving, and almost every ball seemed troubling. And he's been getting out very, very easily—which is certainly unlike him. Maybe he's never going to be remembered as a *great* batsman—but he's always been a very solid, plucky one; a man who values his wicket extremely highly. That wasn't the case here at The Oval, where we got him cheaply twice with deliveries that were useful, but certainly not unplayable.

The decision on his future is his to make, just as mine is my own. If he believes that he'll be a better and more relaxed player if he doesn't have the Fleet Street pack baying at his heels every day, then he should stand down as captain and go out and enjoy his batting and see if he can help England more that way. He's been a good batsman for England, and a committed captain. If I was in his shoes, I wouldn't be standing down.

Doing it My Way

My own situation continues to attract just as much attention. At the press conference after the Test, Malcolm Conn from the *Australian* asked me four questions in a row about my plans. That was a bit disappointing considering the last ball had just been bowled in a long and testing Ashes series in which Australia had brought home the bacon. I wasn't surprised, though. Malcolm Conn has been the bloke who has been looking closest at me, and the question of the Australian captaincy. I just told him the truth—that I didn't really know at this stage what I was going to do in regards to the captaincy. Deep down, my gut feeling is to stay on. I am greatly encouraged by my more recent form, and feel that if I can strike the ball as well in the Australian summer as I did at the tail end of this tour, then I'll be making some useful runs and that being the case, there's no reason why I should stand down. Only time will answer the question as to whether the ACB or the selectors hold a different view to that.

Stumps

It's been a long slog—but bringing with it some rich rewards that made it worth all the effort. A lot of cricket, not much rest, and I think that was showing through fairly transparently by the time we reached The Oval. Take Mark Waugh, for example, and the fact that he's struggled in this series. Yet over in South Africa, at Port Elizabeth, he played one of the finest Test innings you'd ever want to see. Here he made only a couple of hundred runs in an Ashes series on turf where he normally blitzes them. Put it down to sheer tiredness.

I think we're all a bit like that—drained, to an extent, and needing a break from the game. Maybe I'm one of the few who have mixed feelings about that, considering that I've just started to middle 'em. But boy oh boy, I'm looking forward to not having to answer questions about the Australian cricket team all the time, about what I'm going to do or not do. The questioning has been endless but for now, it's over.

Maybe in time the feeling of being under siege for much of this year will fade in my memory, and I'll recall instead the many fine times of a rewarding and (largely) enjoyable year in which we accomplished what we set out to do. This third Ashes tour has been a wonderful experience, tapping into the tradition of what the Ashes battle has meant over so many long years. The crowds were huge—sellouts at all the Tests. Who said Test cricket was on its last legs? Play the game the right way and the crowds will come ... now and forever. Test cricket needs no trickery or sleight of hand. It just needs determined, hungry teams playing positively, and playing to win.

On face value the Aussie balance sheet is not sensational for the year past. Fifteen Tests, eight wins, six losses and a draw. People might sniff and say we're not doing much better than 50 percent. But take out the dead-rubber games and the score stands at 8-3. Fact was that we won 8 of 12 'live' Test matches (drawing one) and took the series we had set our sights on—against talented and motivated opposition. Only India, very early, sneaked under our guard, and obviously that's a score we plan to settle.

I reckon we've done our bit. We've kept Australia at, or near, the top of the world cricketing tree. We have played to win and I believe, played fairly—albeit with a tough competitive edge. We have played to entertain, too, and I hope the fans enjoyed what they saw. We've had some fun, won some games, lost a few, had our share of drama, and travelled countless thousands of miles in the cause of the great game of cricket.

Right now, I'm sure there's a fish waiting to be caught, a golf ball to be struck in something hopefully resembling a straight line, some mini-stumps to be set up for a backyard game or two with the kids. A breath to be taken, a pause to be enjoyed, some memories to be savoured. This particular captain's year, 1997, has been nothing if not eventful. But very special too. And in the brief respite that the Aussie spring will bring, I plan to fully enjoy the fact that I have been through something extraordinary in sport ... before it all begins again.

A CAPTAIN'S YEAR

THE SCOREBOARD, 1996–97

Mark Anthony TAYLOR

Cricket Career	M	Inn	NO	Runs	H.S	50	100	Avrge	Ct
First-Class	219	377	15	15194	219	82	36	41.97	300
Test Cricket	87	155	9	6116	219	34	15	41.89	123
New South Wales	87	152	3	6344	199	31	16	42.58	121
Sheffield Shield	73	128	3	5454	199	27	14	43.63	109
Domestic One-Days	27	27	-	915	84	9	-	33.89	17
Int'l One-Days	113	110	1	3514	105	28	1	32.24	56

Australian Limited-Over Internationals (August 1996 - September 1997)

DATE	VENUE	OPPONENT	RESULT FOR AUSTRALIA
1996 IN SRI LANKA			
26/08/1996	Colombo	Zimbabwe	Won by 125 runs
30/08/1996	Colombo	Sri Lanka	Lost by 4 wkts
06/09/1996	Colombo	India	Won by 3 wkts
07/09/1996	Colombo	Sri Lanka	Lost by 50 runs
1996 IN INDIA			
19/10/1996	Indore	South Africa	Lost by 7 wkts
21/10/1996	Bangalore	India	Lost by 2 wkts
25/10/1996	Faridabad	South Africa	Lost by 2 wkts
01/11/1996	Guwahati	South Africa	Lost by 8 wkts
03/11/1996	Chandigarh	India	Lost by 5 runs
1996–97 IN AUSTRALIA			
06/12/1996	Melbourne	West Indies	Won by 5 wkts
08/12/1996	Sydney	West Indies	Won by 8 wkts
15/12/1996	Adelaide	Pakistan	Lost by 12 runs
01/01/1997	Sydney	Pakistan	Lost by 4 wkts
05/01/1997	Brisbane	West Indies	Lost by 7 wkts
07/01/1997	Hobart	Pakistan	Lost by 29 runs
12/01/1997	Perth	West Indies	Lost by 4 wkts
16/01/1997	Melbourne	Pakistan	Won by 3 wkts
1997 IN SOUTH AFRICA			
29/03/1997	East London	South Africa	Lost by 6 wkts
31/03/1997	Port Elizabeth	South Africa	Won by 7 wkts
03/04/1997	Cape Town	South Africa	Lost by 46 runs
05/04/1997	Durban	South Africa	Won by 15 runs
08/04/1997	Johannesburg	South Africa	Won by 8 runs
10/04/1997	Centurion	South Africa	Won by 5 wkts
13/04/1997	Bloemfontein	South Africa	Lost by 109 runs
1997 IN ENGLAND			
22/05/1997	Leeds	England	Lost by 6 wkts
24/05/1997	The Oval	England	Lost by 6 wkts
25/05/1997	Lord's	England	Lost by 6 wkts

ONLY TEST 1996–97 INDIA v AUSTRALIA

Feroze Shah Kotla Ground, Delhi. October 10,11,12,14, 1996.
Toss: Australia. India won by 7 wkts.

AUSTRALIA

MJ Slater c & b Kumble	44	(2)	c Azharuddin b Johnson	0
MA Taylor (c) lbw Prasad	27	(1)	c Rathore b Kapoor	37
RT Ponting b Kapoor	14		b Prasad	13
ME Waugh c Dravid b Joshi	26		c Mongia b Kumble	23
SR Waugh c Mongia b Kapoor	0		not out	67
MG Bevan lbw Joshi	26		c Azharuddin b Kumble	33
IA Healy (+) b Kumble	17		st Mongia b Kumble	12
GB Hogg c Rathore b Kumble	1		c Rathore b Kumble	4
PR Reiffel c Dravid b Kumble	7		lbw Kumble	6
PE McIntyre not out	6		lbw Prasad	16
GD McGrath run out	6		c Mongia b Prasad	0
EXTRAS (B 4, LB 3, NB 1)	8		(B 9, LB 6, W 1, NB 7)	23
TOTAL	**182**			**234**

FOW 1st Inns: 47 81 93 94 143 144 147 169 170 182
FOW 2nd Inns: 4 25 72 78 145 159 171 191 232 234

Bowling: First Innings: Prasad 12-4-34-1, Johnson 4-1-12-0, Joshi 23-7-36-2, Kumble 24-7-63-4, Kapoor 10-3-30-2. Second Innings: Prasad 13.3-7-18-3, Johnson 12-2-40-1, Kumble 41-12-67-5, Joshi 20-7-52-0, Kapoor 22-5-42-1.

INDIA

VS Rathore c Ponting b Reiffel	5	b Reiffel	14
NR Mongia (+) b Reiffel	152	lbw Reiffel	0
SC Ganguly c ME Waugh b Hogg	66	not out	21
SR Tendulkar (c) c ME Waugh b McIntyre	10	b McGrath	0
M Azharuddin b McGrath	17	not out	21
RS Dravid c Healy b SR Waugh	40		
SB Joshi c Ponting b McIntyre	23		
AR Kapoor c Ponting b ME Waugh	22		
AR Kumble lbw Reiffel	2		
D Johnson not out	0		
VBK Prasad b McIntyre	3		
EXTRAS (B 10, LB 1, NB 10)	21	(W 1, NB 1)	2
TOTAL	**361**		**3 for 58**

FOW 1st Inns: 13 144 169 199 260 303 341 353 354 361
FOW 2nd Inns: 1 25 26

Bowling: First Innings: McGrath 29-10-56-1, Reiffel 17-7-35-3, SR Waugh 13-5-25-1, McIntyre 37.4-7-103-3, Hogg 17-3-69-1, ME Waugh 18-0-62-1.
Second Innings: McGrath 7-2-30-1, Reiffel 6-2-24-2, McIntyre 0.2-0-4-0.

Umpires: S Venkataraghavan & P Willey

FIRST TEST 1996–97 AUSTRALIA v WEST INDIES

Brisbane Cricket Ground, Brisbane. November 22,23,24,25,26, 1996.
Toss: West Indies. Australia won by 123 runs.

AUSTRALIA

MA Taylor (c) b Walsh	43	(2)	c Browne b Benjamin	36
MTG Elliott c Browne b Ambrose	0	(1)	b Bishop	21
RT Ponting c Walsh b Benjamin	88		c Browne b Bishop	9
ME Waugh c Browne b Walsh	38		c Browne b Bishop	57
SR Waugh c Lara b Bishop	66			
MG Bevan c Samuels b Walsh	0	(5)	c (S)AFG Griffith b Ambrose	20
IA Healy (+) not out	161	(6)	not out	45
PR Reiffel c & b Walsh	20	(7)	run out	11
SK Warne c & b Bishop	24			
MS Kasprowicz c Benjamin b Bishop	6			
GD McGrath b Benjamin	0			
EXTRAS (LB 8, W 3, NB 22)	33		(B 1, LB 3, NB 14)	18
TOTAL	**479**		**6 dec**	**217**

FOW 1st Inns: 4 130 146 196 196 338 407 468 477 479
FOW 2nd Inns: 55 74 82 137 189 217

Bowling: First Innings: Ambrose 34-4-93-1, Walsh 35-6-112-4, Benjamin 33-6-97-2, Bishop 30-2-105-3, Hooper 19-3-64-0. Second Innings: Ambrose 18-2-47-1, Walsh 17-1-58-0, Bishop 13-2-49-3, Benjamin 15-1-52-1, Hooper 2-0-7-0.

WEST INDIES

SL Campbell c Warne b Reiffel	18	lbw Bevan	113
RG Samuels c Healy b McGrath	10	c Taylor b Warne	29
BC Lara c ME Waugh b McGrath	26	c ME Waugh b Reiffel	44
CL Hooper c Ponting b SR Waugh	102	c Healy b Bevan	23
S Chanderpaul c ME Waugh b Reiffel	82	b McGrath	14
JC Adams lbw Ponting	0	lbw Warne	2
CO Browne (+) c Healy b Reiffel	4	c Healy b McGrath	20
IR Bishop lbw Warne	0	c Ponting b Bevan	24
CEL Ambrose c(S)JN Gillespie b Reiffel	0	c Warne b McGrath	7
KCG Benjamin lbw Warne	9	lbw McGrath	1
CA Walsh (c) not out	0	not out	1
EXTRAS (LB 8, W 1, NB 17)	26	(B 8, LB 3, NB 7)	18
TOTAL	**277**		**296**

FOW 1st Inns: 30 43 77 249 255 267 268 268 277 277
FOW 2nd Inns: 54 118 154 187 202 241 281 293 293 296

Bowling: First Innings: McGrath 21-7-32-2, Reiffel 24.1-6-58-4, Kasprowicz 22-5-60-0, Warne 27-3-88-2, SR Waugh 8.1-1-15-1, ME Waugh 4-1-16-0, Ponting 1.5-1-0-1. Second Innings: McGrath 29.5-12-60-4, Kasprowicz 13-2-29-0, Warne 41-16-92-2, Reiffel 9-0-58-1, Bevan 14-3-46-3.

Umpires: CJ Mitchley & SG Randell (TV Umpire – PD Parker)

SECOND TEST 1996–97 AUSTRALIA v WEST INDIES

Sydney Cricket Ground, Sydney. November 29,30, December 1,2,3 1996.
Toss: Australia. Australia won by 124 runs.

AUSTRALIA

MA Taylor (c) c Chanderpaul b Bishop	27 (2)	c Lara b Bishop	16
MTG Elliott c Lara b Bishop	29 (1)	retired hurt	78
RT Ponting c Samuels b Walsh	9	c Browne b Bishop	4
ME Waugh c Lara b Walsh	19	c Browne b Ambrose	67
MG Bevan c Hooper b Benjamin	16	c Browne b Benjamin	52
GS Blewett c Adams b Walsh	69	not out	47
IA Healy (+) c Lara b Walsh	44	not out	22
SK Warne c Browne b Bishop	28		
MS Kasprowicz c Campbell b Walsh	21		
JN Gillespie not out	16		
GD McGrath lbw Adams	24		
EXTRAS (LB 10, W 1, NB 18)	29	(B 4, LB 10, W 3, NB 9)	26
TOTAL	**331**		**4 dec 312**

FOW 1st Inns: 54 68 73 94 131 224 245 283 288 331
FOW 2nd Inns: 51 67 209 274

Bowling: First Innings: Ambrose 25-5-73-0, Walsh 30-6-98-5, Benjamin 22-4-69-1, Hooper 14-6-15-0, Bishop 23-5-55-3, Adams 5.5-1-11-1. Second Innings: Ambrose 20-2-66-1, Walsh 19-6-36-0, Bishop 20-6-54-2, Benjamin 16-4-46-1, Adams 4-0-21-0, Hooper 27-7-75-0.

WEST INDIES

SL Campbell b Blewett	77	lbw McGrath	15
RG Samuels lbw McGrath	35	b Warne	16
BC Lara c Healy b McGrath	2	c Healy b McGrath	1
CL Hooper lbw Warne	27	c Taylor b Bevan	57
S Chanderpaul c & b Warne	48	b Warne	71
JC Adams c Bevan b McGrath	30	c Blewett b McGrath	5
CO Browne (+) c Blewett b McGrath	0	not out	25
IR Bishop c Elliott b Warne	48	run out	0
CEL Ambrose b Gillespie	9	b Bevan	0
KCG Benjamin b Gillespie	6	c Taylor b Warne	4
CA Walsh (c) not out	2	c McGrath b Warne	18
EXTRAS (B 4, LB 6, NB 10)	20	(LB 2, NB 1)	3
TOTAL	**304**		**215**

FOW 1st Inns: 92 108 136 166 229 229 243 286 298 304
FOW 2nd Inns: 33 33 35 152 157 176 176 176 183 215

Bowling: First Innings: McGrath 31-9-82-4, Kasprowicz 13-2-37-0, Warne 35.2-13-65-3, Gillespie 23-5-62-2, Bevan 11-0-35-0, Blewett 4-0-13-1. Second Innings: McGrath 17-7-36-3, Waugh 4-0-15-0, Gillespie 7-2-27-0, Warne 27.4-5-95-4, Bevan 14-2-40-2.

Umpires: DB Hair & DR Shepherd (TV Umpire - SJ Taufel)

THIRD TEST 1996–97 AUSTRALIA v WEST INDIES

Melbourne Cricket Ground, Melbourne. December 26,27,28, 1996.
Toss: Australia. West Indies won by 6 wkts.

AUSTRALIA

MA Taylor (c) b Ambrose	7	(2) c Hooper b Walsh	10
ML Hayden c Hooper b Ambrose	5	(1) b Ambrose	0
JL Langer run out	12	c Hooper b Ambrose	0
ME Waugh lbw Ambrose	0	lbw Walsh	19
SR Waugh c Murray b Bishop	58	b Benjamin	37
GS Blewett run out	62	c Murray b Walsh	7
IA Healy (+) c Hooper b Ambrose	36	b Benjamin	0
PR Reiffel c Samuels b Benjamin	0	lbw Benjamin	8
SK Warne c Campbell b Bishop	10	c Adams b Ambrose	18
JN Gillespie not out	4	lbw Ambrose	2
GD McGrath c Hooper b Ambrose	0	not out	5
EXTRAS (LB 8, NB 17)	25	(LB 4, W 1, NB 11)	16
TOTAL	**219**		**122**

FOW 1st Inns: 5 26 26 27 129 195 200 200 217 219
FOW 2nd Inns: 0 3 28 47 64 65 76 107 113 122

Bowling: First Innings: Ambrose 24.5-7-55-5, Bishop 11-1-31-2, Benjamin 19-2-64-1, Walsh 14-0-43-0, Adams 1-0-4-0, Hooper 5-1-14-0. Second Innings: Ambrose 12-4-17-4, Bishop 10-2-26-0, Benjamin 12.5-5-34-3, Walsh 11-4-41-3.

WEST INDIES

SL Campbell lbw McGrath	7	c Hayden b McGrath	0
RG Samuels c Taylor b Warne	17	lbw McGrath	13
S Chanderpaul c & b McGrath	58	b Reiffel	40
BC Lara c Warne b McGrath	2	c Hayden b McGrath	2
CL Hooper run out	7	not out	27
JC Adams not out	74	not out	1
JR Murray (+) c Reiffel b McGrath	53		
IR Bishop lbw McGrath	0		
CEL Ambrose b Warne	8		
KCG Benjamin b Reiffel	11		
CA Walsh (c) c ME Waugh b Warne	4		
EXTRAS (B 4, LB 7, NB 3)	14	(NB 4)	4
TOTAL	**255**		**4 for 87**

FOW 1st Inns: 12 62 71 86 107 197 197 215 230 255
FOW 2nd Inns: 0 25 32 82

Bowling: First Innings: McGrath 30-11-50-5, Reiffel 29-8-76-1, Warne 28.1-3-72-3, Gillespie 3-2-5-0, Blewett 9-3-19-0, SR Waugh 10-5-22-0. Second Innings: McGrath 9-1-41-3, Reiffel 9-2-16-1, Warne 3-0-17-0, Blewett 2.5-0-13-0.

Umpires: PD Parker & S Venkataraghavan (TV Umpire - WP Sheahan)

FOURTH TEST 1996–97 AUSTRALIA v WEST INDIES

Adelaide Oval, Adelaide. January 25,26,27,28, 1997.
Toss: West Indies. Australia won by an innings and 183 runs.

WEST INDIES

SL Campbell c Healy b McGrath	0		c Taylor b Bevan	24
AFG Griffith lbw Bichel	13		c SR Waugh b McGrath	1
S Chanderpaul c Taylor b Warne	20		c Taylor b Bevan	8
BC Lara c Blewett b Warne	9		c Healy b Warne	78
CL Hooper c ME Waugh b McGrath	17		lbw Warne	45
JC Adams c & b Warne	10		c ME Waugh b Bevan	0
JR Murray (+) c Blewett b Bevan	34	(8)	c Taylor b Bevan	25
IR Bishop c Healy b Bevan	1	(7)	c Bevan b Warne	0
CA Walsh (c) c Healy b Bevan	0		c SR Waugh b Bevan	1
CE Cuffy c Healy b Bevan	2		not out	3
PIC Thompson not out	10		c Hayden b Bevan	6
EXTRAS (B 4, LB 1, NB 9)	14		(B 2, LB 5, NB 6)	13
TOTAL	**130**			**204**

FOW 1st Inns: 11 22 45 58 72 113 117 117 119 130
FOW 2nd Inns: 6 22 42 138 145 154 181 192 196 204

Bowling: First Innings: McGrath 12-4-21-2, Bichel 10-1-31-1, Bevan 9.5-2-31-4, Warne 16-4-42-3. Second Innings: McGrath 17-4-31-1, Bichel 8-4-16-0, Bevan 22.4-3-82-6, Warne 20-4-68-3, Blewett 2-2-0-0.

AUSTRALIA

MA Taylor (c) lbw Bishop	11
ML Hayden st Murray b Hooper	125
JL Langer c Murray b Cuffy	19
ME Waugh c Murray b Hooper	82
SR Waugh c Hooper b Chanderpaul	26
GS Blewett b Cuffy	99
MG Bevan not out	85
IA Healy (+) c Lara b Thompson	12
SK Warne c Hooper b Bishop	9
AJ Bichel c Lara b Walsh	7
GD McGrath b Walsh	1
EXTRAS (B 2, LB 15, W 4, NB 20)	41
TOTAL	**517**

FOW 1st Inns: 35 78 242 288 288 453 475 494 507 517

Bowling: First Innings: Walsh 37.3-6-101-2, Bishop 34-6-92-2, Cuffy 33-4-116-2, Thompson 16-0-80-1, Hooper 31-7-86-2, Adams 8-0-23-0, Chanderpaul 3-1-2-1.

Umpires: SG Randell & DR Shepherd (TV Umpire - DJ Harper)

FIFTH TEST 1996–97 AUSTRALIA v WEST INDIES
W.A.C.A. Ground, Perth. February 1,2,3, 1997.
Toss: Australia. West Indies won by 10 wkts.

AUSTRALIA
ML Hayden c Lara b Ambrose	0	(2) lbw Hooper	47
MA Taylor (c) run out	2	(1) c Browne b Ambrose	1
GS Blewett c Browne b Simmons	17	b Ambrose	0
ME Waugh c Campbell b Ambrose	79	c Browne b Walsh	9
SR Waugh c Browne b Ambrose	1	c Hooper b Walsh	0
MG Bevan not out	87	c Simmons b Walsh	15
IA Healy (+) b Ambrose	7	c Chanderpaul b Walsh	29
PR Reiffel c Simmons b Ambrose	0	c Adams b Walsh	5
SK Warne c Browne b Bishop	9	c Simmons b Bishop	30
AJ Bichel c Browne b Bishop	15	c Samuels b Bishop	18
GD McGrath c Ambrose b Bishop	0	not out	2
EXTRAS (LB 10, W 2, NB 14)	26	(B 2, LB 8, W 6, NB 22)	38
TOTAL	**243**		**194**

FOW 1st Inns: 0   7 45 49 169 186 186 216 243 243
FOW 2nd Inns: 7 17 43 48 84 105 110 133 189 194

Bowling: First Innings: Ambrose 18-5-43-5, Bishop 18-5-54-3, Walsh 9-0-29-0, Simmons 20-5-58-1, Hooper 15-1-49-0. Second Innings: Ambrose 9-2-50-2, Bishop 12.3-1-44-2, Walsh 20-4-74-5, Simmons 3-0-9-0, Hooper 3-0-7-1.

WEST INDIES
SL Campbell c Healy b Reiffel	21	not out	16
RG Samuels c ME Waugh b Warne	76	not out	35
S Chanderpaul c Reiffel b McGrath	3		
BC Lara c Healy b Warne	132		
CL Hooper c Healy b Reiffel	57		
JC Adams c Healy b McGrath	18		
PV Simmons c ME Waugh b Reiffel	0		
CO Browne (+) c Warne b Reiffel	0		
IR Bishop c Taylor b Reiffel	13		
CEL Ambrose run out	15		
CA Walsh (c) not out	5		
EXTRAS (B 5, LB 10, W 1, NB 28)	44	(LB 2, W 1, NB 3)	6
TOTAL	**384**		**0 for 57**

FOW 1st Inns: 30 43 251 275 331 332 332 359 367 384
FOW 2nd Inns: n/a

Bowling: First Innings: McGrath 30-5-86-2, Bichel 18-1-79-0, Reiffel 26-6-73-5, Warne 19-8-55-2, Blewett 6-2-19-0, Bevan 5-0-31-0, SR Waugh 7-1-26-0. Second Innings: McGrath 4-1-14-0, Reiffel 5-0-24-0, Bichel 1.3-0-17-0.

Umpires: DB Hair & P Willey (TV Umpire - TA Prue)

FIRST TEST 1996–97 SOUTH AFRICA v AUSTRALIA
Wanderers Stadium, Johannesburg. February 28, March 1,2,3,4, 1997.
Toss: South Africa. Australia won by an innings & 196 runs.

SOUTH AFRICA
AC Hudson c Healy b McGrath	0	run out	31
G Kirsten c Healy b McGrath	9	b Warne	8
JH Kallis c ME Waugh b McGrath	6	b Warne	39
DJ Cullinan c Healy b McGrath	27	c Healy b Warne	0
WJ Cronje (c) c ME Waugh b Warne	76	c Healy b SR Waugh	22
JN Rhodes c Healy b Gillespie	22	lbw Warne	8
SM Pollock c SR Waugh b Bevan	35	not out	14
L Klusener c Taylor b Bevan	9	c Hayden b Bevan	0
DJ Richardson (+) not out	72	c Hayden b Bevan	2
AA Donald c Healy b Gillespie	21	b Bevan	0
PR Adams lbw Warne	15	b Bevan	0
EXTRAS (B 1, LB 3, W 3, NB 3)	10	(B 4, LB 2)	6
TOTAL	**302**		**130**

FOW 1st Inns: 0 15 25 78 115 165 183 195 253 302
FOW 2nd Inns: 36 41 46 90 108 127 128 130 130 130

Bowling: First Innings: McGrath 26-8-77-4, Gillespie 17-6-66-2, Warne 27.4-9-68-2, Bevan 17-1-64-2, Blewett 4-0-23-0. Second Innings: McGrath 10-5-17-0, Gillespie 11-4-24-0, Warne 28-15-43-4, Bevan 15-3-32-4, SR Waugh 4-1-4-1, ME Waugh 1-0-4-0.

AUSTRALIA
MA Taylor (c) b Pollock	16
ML Hayden c Cullinan b Pollock	40
MTG Elliott c Adams b Donald	85
ME Waugh c Richardson b Donald	26
SR Waugh c Richardson b Kallis	160
GS Blewett c Adams b Klusener	214
MG Bevan not out	37
IA Healy (+) c Kirsten b Adams	11
SK Warne b Cronje	9
JN Gillespie	
GD McGrath	
EXTRAS (B 1, LB 15, W 4, NB 10)	30
TOTAL	**8 dec 628**

FOW 1st Inns: 33 128 169 174 559 577 613 628

Bowling: First Innings: Donald 35-7-136-2, Pollock 32-3-105-2, Klusener 37-10-122-1, Kallis 21-4-54-1, Adams 52-7-163-1, Cronje 16.4-5-32-1.

Umpires: CJ Mitchley & S Venkataraghavan (TV Umpire - RE Koertzen)

SECOND TEST 1996–97 SOUTH AFRICA v AUSTRALIA
St George's Park, Port Elizabeth. March 14,15,16,17, 1997.
Toss: Australia. Australia won by 2 wkts.

SOUTH AFRICA

G Kirsten c Hayden b Gillespie	0	b Gillespie	43
AM Bacher c Elliott b McGrath	11	c McGrath b Gillespie	49
JH Kallis c Blewett b Gillespie	0	run out	2
DJ Cullinan c Warne b Gillespie	34	lbw Gillespie	2
WJ Cronje (c) b McGrath	0	c Healy b Bevan	27
HH Gibbs b Gillespie	31	c ME Waugh b McGrath	7
BM McMillan c SR Waugh b Warne	55	lbw Bevan	2
SM Pollock lbw Gillespie	0	lbw Warne	17
DJ Richardson (+) c McGrath b Warne	47	not out	3
AA Donald c & b Warne	9	c Warne b Bevan	7
PR Adams not out	5	c Taylor b Warne	1
EXTRAS (B 8, LB 8, W 1)	17	(B 1, LB 5, NB 2)	8
TOTAL	**209**		**168**

FOW 1st Inns: 13 17 21 22 70 95 95 180 204 209
FOW 2nd Inns: 87 98 99 100 122 137 152 156 167 168

Bowling: First Innings: McGrath 22-7-66-2, Gillespie 23-10-54-5, Warne 23.4-5-62-3, Blewett 4-2-3-0, Bevan 2-0-8-0. Second Innings: McGrath 13-3-43-1, Gillespie 18-4-49-3, SR Waugh 4.3-0-16-0, Blewett 7.3-3-16-0, Warne 17.4-7-20-2, Bevan 13-3-18-3.

AUSTRALIA

ML Hayden c Cullinan b Pollock	0	(2) run out	14
MA Taylor (c) c Richardson b Pollock	8	(1) lbw McMillan	13
MTG Elliott run out	23	c & b Adams	44
ME Waugh lbw Cronje	20	b Kallis	116
SR Waugh c Richardson b McMillan	8	c Cronje b Kallis	18
GS Blewett b Donald	13	b Adams	7
MG Bevan c Richardson b McMillan	0	c Cullinan b Cronje	24
IA Healy (+) c Bacher b Cronje	5	not out	10
SK Warne lbw Adams	18	lbw Kallis	3
JN Gillespie not out	1	not out	0
GD McGrath c Richardson b Kallis	0		
EXTRAS (B 1, LB 7, W 2, NB 2)	12	(B 11, LB 8, W 3)	22
TOTAL	**108**		**8 for 271**

FOW 1st Inns: 1 13 48 64 66 70 85 86 106 108
FOW 2nd Inns: 23 30 113 167 192 258 258 265

Bowling: First Innings: Donald 23-13-18-1, Pollock 6-3-6-2, Adams 4-0-5-1, McMillan 14-2-32-2, Cronje 14-7-21-2, Kallis 9.4-2-18-1. Second Innings: Donald 26-6-75-0, McMillan 21-5-46-1, Cronje 9.3-1-36-1, Kallis 16-7-29-3, Adams 21-4-66-2.

Umpires: RE Koertzen & S Venkataraghavan (TV Umpire - DL Orchard)

THIRD TEST 1996–97 SOUTH AFRICA v AUSTRALIA
Centurion Park, Pretoria. March 21,22,23,24, 1997.
Toss: South Africa. South Africa won by 8 wkts.

AUSTRALIA

Batsman	1st Innings		2nd Innings	
MA Taylor (c)	c Richardson b Klusener	38	c Richardson b Donald	5
ML Hayden	b Schultz	10	lbw Schultz	0
MTG Elliott	c Schultz b Donald	18	b Donald	12
ME Waugh	b Donald	5	b Symcox	42
SR Waugh	c Richardson b Schultz	67	not out	60
GS Blewett	c Richardson b Symcox	37	b Donald	0
MG Bevan	lbw Schultz	6	b Symcox	5
IA Healy (+)	c Richardson b Donald	19	c Richardson b Schultz	12
SK Warne	lbw Schultz	0	lbw Donald	12
JN Gillespie	not out	6	b Donald	0
GD McGrath	b Klusener	0	b Klusener	11
EXTRAS	(B 1, LB 4, W 7, NB 9)	21	(B 2, LB 6, W 4, NB 14)	26
TOTAL		**227**		**185**

FOW 1st Inns: 23 60 72 110 190 197 212 212 226 227
FOW 2nd Inns: 5 10 28 94 99 108 131 164 164 185

Bowling: First Innings: Donald 20-5-60-3, Schultz 20-4-52-4, Cronje 5-3-5-0, Klusener 14.5-4-23-2, Symcox 23-4-62-1, Kallis 7-2-20-0. Second Innings: Donald 18-5-36-5, Schultz 17-4-39-2, Klusener 14.4-1-40-1, Symcox 19-5-49-2, Kallis 5-1-13-0.

SOUTH AFRICA

Batsman	1st Innings		2nd Innings	
G Kirsten	c Healy b McGrath	16	c Taylor b Blewett	6
AM Bacher	lbw McGrath	96	c Elliott b Gillespie	5
BM McMillan	c Hayden b ME Waugh	55	not out	7
DJ Cullinan	b McGrath	47	not out	12
PL Symcox	c Blewett b Gillespie	16		
JH Kallis	c SR Waugh b McGrath	2		
WJ Cronje (c)	not out	79		
DJ Richardson (+)	b McGrath	0		
L Klusener	b Gillespie	30		
AA Donald	c Healy b Gillespie	8		
BN Schultz	c Healy b McGrath	2		
EXTRAS	(B 11, LB 16, W 1, NB 5)	33	(W 1, NB 1)	2
TOTAL		**384**		**2 for 32**

FOW 1st Inns: 26 128 229 252 255 262 262 330 367 384
FOW 2nd Inns: 11 15

Bowling: First Innings: McGrath 40.4-15-86-6, Gillespie 31-13-75-3, Blewett 5-0-19-0, Warne 36-11-89-0, Bevan 15-3-54-0, ME Waugh 7-1-34-1. Second Innings: Gillespie 3.4-0-19-1, Blewett 3-0-13-1.

Umpires: MJ Kitchen & CJ Mitchley (TV Umpire - RE Koertzen)

FIRST TEST 1997 ENGLAND v AUSTRALIA
Edgbaston, Birmingham. June 5,6,7,8, 1997.
Toss: Australia. England won by 9 wkts.

AUSTRALIA
MA Taylor (c) c Butcher b Malcolm	7	(2)	c & b Croft	129
MTG Elliott b Gough	6	(1)	b Croft	66
GS Blewett c Hussain b Gough	7		c Butcher b Croft	125
ME Waugh b Gough	5	(6)	c Stewart b Gough	1
SR Waugh c Stewart b Caddick	12	(4)	lbw Gough	33
MG Bevan c Ealham b Malcolm	8	(5)	c Hussain b Gough	24
IA Healy (+) c Stewart b Caddick	0		c Atherton b Ealham	30
JN Gillespie lbw Caddick	4	(10)	run out	0
SK Warne c Malcolm b Caddick	47	(8)	c & b Ealham	32
MS Kasprowicz c Butcher b Caddick	17	(9)	c Butcher b Ealham	0
GD McGrath not out	1		not out	0
EXTRAS (W 2, NB 2)	4		(B 18, LB 12, W 2, NB 5)	37
TOTAL	**118**			**477**

FOW 1st Inns: 11 15 26 28 48 48 48 54 110 118
FOW 2nd Inns: 133 327 354 393 399 431 465 465 477 477

Bowling: First Innings: Gough 10-1-43-3, Malcolm 10-2-25-2, Caddick 11.5-1-50-5.
Second Innings: Gough 35-7-123-3, Malcolm 21-6-52-0, Croft 43-10-125-3,
Caddick 30-6-87-0, Ealham 15.4-3-60-3.

ENGLAND
MA Butcher c Healy b Kasprowicz	8	lbw Kasprowicz	14
MA Atherton (c) c Healy b McGrath	2	not out	57
AJ Stewart (+) c Elliott b Gillespie	18	not out	40
N Hussain c Healy b Warne	207		
GP Thorpe c Bevan b McGrath	138		
JP Crawley c Healy b Kasprowicz	1		
MA Ealham not out	53		
RDB Croft c Healy b Kasprowicz	24		
D Gough c Healy b Kasprowicz	0		
AR Caddick lbw Bevan	0		
DE Malcolm			
EXTRAS (B 4, LB 7, W 1, NB 15)	27	(B 4, LB 4)	8
TOTAL	**9 dec 478**		**1 for 119**

FOW 1st Inns: 8 16 50 338 345 416 460 463 478
FOW 2nd Inns: 29

Bowling: First Innings: McGrath 32-8-107-2, Kasprowicz 39-8-113-4, Gillespie 10-1-48-1,
Warne 35-8-110-1, Bevan 10.4-0-44-1, SR Waugh 12-2-45-0. Second Innings:
McGrath 7-1-42-0, Kasprowicz 7-0-42-1, Warne 7.3-0-27-0.

Umpires: SA Bucknor & P Willey (TV Umpire - JW Holder)

SECOND TEST 1997 ENGLAND v AUSTRALIA

Lord's Cricket Ground, St John's Wood. June 19(no play),20,21,22,23, 1997.
Toss: Australia. Match Drawn.

ENGLAND

MA Butcher c Blewett b McGrath	5	b Warne	87	
MA Atherton (c) c Taylor b McGrath	1	hit wicket b Kasprowicz	77	
AJ Stewart (+) b McGrath	1	c Kasprowicz b McGrath	13	
N Hussain lbw McGrath	19	c & b Warne	0	
GP Thorpe c Blewett b Reiffel	21	not out	30	
JP Crawley c Healy b McGrath	1	not out	29	
MA Ealham c Elliott b Reiffel	7			
RDB Croft c Healy b McGrath	2			
D Gough c Healy b McGrath	10			
AR Caddick lbw McGrath	1			
DE Malcolm not out	0			
EXTRAS (B 4, NB 5)	9	(B 8, LB 14, W 1, NB 7)	30	
TOTAL	**77**		**4 for 266**	

FOW 1st Inns: 11 12 13 47 56 62 66 76 77 77
FOW 2nd Inns: 162 189 197 202

Bowling: First Innings: McGrath 20.3-8-38-8, Reiffel 15-9-17-2, Kasprowicz 5-1-9-0, Warne 2-0-9-0. Second Innings: McGrath 20-5-65-1, Reiffel 13-5-29-0, Kasprowicz 15-3-54-1, Warne 19-4-47-2, Bevan 8-1-29-0, SR Waugh 4-0-20-0.

AUSTRALIA

MA Taylor (c) b Gough	1
MTG Elliott c Crawley b Caddick	112
GS Blewett c Hussain b Croft	45
ME Waugh c Malcolm b Caddick	33
SK Warne c Hussain b Gough	0
SR Waugh lbw Caddick	0
MG Bevan c Stewart b Caddick	4
IA Healy (+) not out	13
PR Reiffel not out	1
MS Kasprowicz	
GD McGrath	
EXTRAS (B 1, LB 3)	4
TOTAL	**7 dec 213**

FOW 1st Inns: 4 73 147 147 147 159 212

Bowling: First Innings: Gough 20-4-82-2, Caddick 22-6-71-4, Malcolm 7-1-26-0, Croft 12-5-30-1.

Umpires: DR Shepherd & S Venkataraghavan (TV Umpire - DJ Constant)

THIRD TEST 1997 ENGLAND v AUSTRALIA
Old Trafford, Manchester. July 3,4,5,6,7, 1997.
Toss: Australia. Australia won by 268 runs.

AUSTRALIA

MA Taylor (c) c Thorpe b Headley	2	(2)	c Butcher b Headley	1
MTG Elliott c Stewart b Headley	40	(1)	c Butcher b Headley	11
GS Blewett b Gough	8		c Hussain b Croft	19
ME Waugh c Stewart b Ealham	12		b Ealham	55
SR Waugh b Gough	108		c Stewart b Headley	116
MG Bevan c Stewart b Headley	7		c Atherton b Headley	0
IA Healy (+) c Stewart b Caddick	9		c Butcher b Croft	47
SK Warne c Stewart b Ealham	3		c Stewart b Caddick	53
PR Reiffel b Gough	31		not out	45
JN Gillespie c Stewart b Headley	0		not out	28
GD McGrath not out	0			
EXTRAS (B 8, LB 4, NB 3)	15		(B 1, LB 13, NB 6)	20
TOTAL	**235**			**8 dec 395**

FOW 1st Inns: 9 22 42 85 113 150 160 230 235 235
FOW 2nd Inns: 5 33 39 131 132 210 298 333

Bowling: First Innings: Gough 21-7-52-3, Headley 27.3-4-72-4, Caddick 14-2-52-1, Ealham 11-2-34-2, Croft 4-0-13-0. Second Innings: Gough 20-3-62-0, Headley 29-4-104-4, Croft 39-12-105-2, Ealham 13-3-41-1, Caddick 21-0-69-1.

ENGLAND

MA Butcher st Healy b Bevan	51	c McGrath b Gillespie	28
MA Atherton (c) c Healy b McGrath	5	lbw Gillespie	21
AJ Stewart (+) c Taylor b Warne	30	b Warne	1
N Hussain c Healy b Warne	13	lbw Gillespie	1
GP Thorpe c Taylor b Warne	3	c Healy b Warne	7
JP Crawley c Healy b Warne	4	hit wicket b McGrath	83
MA Ealham not out	24	c Healy b McGrath	9
RDB Croft c SR Waugh b McGrath	7	c Reiffel b McGrath	7
D Gough lbw Warne	1	b McGrath	6
AR Caddick c ME Waugh b Warne	15	c Gillespie b Warne	17
DW Headley b McGrath	0	not out	0
EXTRAS (B 4, LB 3, NB 2)	9	(B 14, LB 4, W 1, NB 1)	20
TOTAL	**162**		**200**

FOW 1st Inns: 8 74 94 101 110 111 122 123 161 162
FOW 2nd Inns: 44 45 50 55 84 158 170 177 188 200

Bowling: First Innings: McGrath 23.4-9-40-3, Reiffel 9-3-14-0, Warne 30-14-48-6, Gillespie 14-3-39-0, Bevan 8-3-14-1. Second Innings: McGrath 21-4-46-4, Gillespie 12-4-31-3, Reiffel 2-0-8-0, Warne 30.4-8-63-3, Bevan 8-2-34-0.

Umpires: G Sharp & S Venkataraghavan (TV Umpire - JH Hampshire)

FOURTH TEST 1997 ENGLAND v AUSTRALIA
Headingley, Leeds. July 24,25,26,27,28, 1997.
Toss: Australia. Australia won by an innings & 61 runs.

ENGLAND
MA Butcher c Blewett b Reiffel	24		c Healy b McGrath	19
MA Atherton (c) c Gillespie b McGrath	41		c Warne b McGrath	2
AJ Stewart (+) c Blewett b Gillespie	7		b Reiffel	16
N Hussain c Taylor b McGrath	26		c Gillespie b Warne	105
DW Headley c SR Waugh b Gillespie	22	(8)	lbw Reiffel	3
GP Thorpe b Gillespie	15	(5)	c ME Waugh b Gillespie	15
JP Crawley c Blewett b Gillespie	2	(6)	b Reiffel	72
MA Ealham not out	8	(7)	c ME Waugh b Reiffel	4
RDB Croft c Ponting b Gillespie	6		c Healy b Reiffel	5
D Gough b Gillespie	0		c ME Waugh b Gillespie	0
AM Smith b Gillespie	0		not out	4
EXTRAS (B 4, LB 4, W 1, NB 12)	21		(B 6, LB 4, NB 13)	23
TOTAL	**172**			**268**

FOW 1st Inns: 43 58 103 138 154 154 163 172 172 172
FOW 2nd Inns: 23 28 57 89 222 252 256 263 264 268

Bowling: First Innings: McGrath 22-5-67-2, Reiffel 20-4-41-1, Gillespie 13.4-1-37-7, Blewett 3-0-17-0, Warne 1-0-2-0. Second Innings: McGrath 22-5-80-2, Reiffel 21.1-2-49-5, Gillespie 23-8-65-2, Warne 21-6-53-1, SR Waugh 4-1-11-0.

AUSTRALIA
MA Taylor (c) c Stewart b Gough	0
MTG Elliott b Gough	199
GS Blewett c Stewart b Gough	1
ME Waugh c & b Headley	8
SR Waugh c Crawley b Headley	4
RT Ponting c Ealham b Gough	127
IA Healy (+) b Ealham	31
SK Warne c Thorpe b Ealham	0
PR Reiffel not out	54
JN Gillespie b Gough	3
GD McGrath not out	20
EXTRAS (B 9, LB 10, NB 35)	54
TOTAL	**9 dec 501**

FOW 1st Inns: 0 16 43 50 318 382 383 444 461

Bowling: First Innings: Gough 36-5-149-5, Headley 25-2-125-2, Smith 23-2-89-0, Ealham 19-3-56-2, Croft 18-1-49-0, Butcher 2-0-14-0.

Umpires: MJ Kitchen & CJ Mitchley (TV Umpire - R Julian)

FIFTH TEST 1997 ENGLAND v AUSTRALIA

Trent Bridge, Nottingham. August 7,8,9,10, 1997.
Toss: Australia. Australia won by 264 runs.

AUSTRALIA

MTG Elliott c Stewart b Headley	69	(2) c Crawley b Caddick	37
MA Taylor (c) b Caddick	76	(1) c Hussain b BC Hollioake	45
GS Blewett c Stewart b BC Hollioake	50	c Stewart b Caddick	60
ME Waugh lbw Caddick	68	lbw Headley	7
SR Waugh b Malcolm	75	c AJ Hollioake b Caddick	14
RT Ponting b Headley	9	c Stewart b AJ Hollioake	45
IA Healy (+) c AJ Hollioake b Malcolm	16	c Stewart b AJ Hollioake	63
SK Warne c Thorpe b Malcolm	0	c Thorpe b Croft	20
PR Reiffel c Thorpe b Headley	26	c BC Hollioake b Croft	22
JN Gillespie not out	18	c Thorpe b Headley	4
GD McGrath b Headley	1	not out	1
EXTRAS (B 4, LB 10, W 1, NB 4)	19	(B 1, LB 11, NB 6)	18
TOTAL	**427**		**336**

FOW 1st Inns: 117 160 225 311 325 355 363 386 419 427
FOW 2nd Inns: 51 105 134 156 171 276 292 314 326 336

Bowling: First Innings: Malcolm 25-5-100-3, Headley 30.5-7-87-4, Caddick 30-4-102-2, BC Hollioake 10-1-57-1, Croft 19-7-43-0, AJ Hollioake 7-0-24-0.
Second Innings: Malcolm 16-4-52-0, Headley 19-3-56-2, Croft 26.5-6-74-2, Caddick 20-2-85-3, BC Hollioake 5-1-26-1, AJ Hollioake 12-2-31-2.

ENGLAND

MA Atherton (c) c Healy b Warne	27	c Healy b McGrath	8
AJ Stewart (+) c Healy b Warne	87	c SR Waugh b Reiffel	16
JP Crawley c Healy b McGrath	18	c Healy b Gillespie	33
N Hussain b Warne	2	b Gillespie	21
GP Thorpe c Blewett b Warne	53	not out	82
AJ Hollioake c Taylor b Reiffel	45	lbw Gillespie	2
BC Hollioake c ME Waugh b Reiffel	28	lbw Warne	2
RDB Croft c Blewett b McGrath	18	c McGrath b Warne	6
AR Caddick c Healy b McGrath	0	lbw Warne	0
DW Headley not out	10	c Healy b McGrath	4
DE Malcolm b McGrath	12	c ME Waugh b McGrath	0
EXTRAS (B 2, LB 6, NB 5)	13	(B 2, LB 6, NB 4)	12
TOTAL	**313**		**186**

FOW 1st Inns: 106 129 135 141 243 243 272 290 290 313
FOW 2nd Inns: 25 25 78 99 121 144 150 166 186 186

Bowling: First Innings: McGrath 29.5-10-71-4, Reiffel 21-2-101-2, Gillespie 11-3-47-0, Warne 32-8-86-4. Second Innings: McGrath 13.5-4-36-3, Reiffel 11-3-34-1, Gillespie 8-0-65-3, Warne 16-4-43-3.

Umpires: CJ Mitchley & DR Shepherd (TV Umpire - AA Jones)

SIXTH TEST 1997 ENGLAND v AUSTRALIA
The Oval, Kennington. August 21,22,23, 1997.
Toss: England. England won by 19 runs.

ENGLAND
MA Butcher b McGrath	5		lbw ME Waugh	13
MA Atherton (c) c Healy b McGrath	8		c SR Waugh b Kasprowicz	8
AJ Stewart (+) lbw McGrath	36		lbw Kasprowicz	3
N Hussain c Elliott b McGrath	35		c Elliott b Warne	2
GP Thorpe b McGrath	27		c Taylor b Kasprowicz	62
MR Ramprakash c Blewett b McGrath	4		st Healy b Warne	48
AJ Hollioake b Warne	0		lbw Kasprowicz	4
AR Caddick not out	26		not out	0
PJ Martin b McGrath	20		c & b Kasprowicz	3
PCR Tufnell c Blewett b Warne	1		c Healy b Kasprowicz	0
DE Malcolm lbw Kasprowicz	0		b Kasprowicz	0
EXTRAS (LB 8, NB 10)	18		(B 6, LB 10, NB 4)	20
TOTAL	**180**			**163**

FOW 1st Inns: 18 24 97 128 131 132 132 158 175 180
FOW 2nd Inns: 20 24 26 52 131 138 160 163 163 163

Bowling: First Innings: McGrath 21-4-76-7, Kasprowicz 11.4-2-56-1, Warne 17-8-32-2, Young 7-3-8-0. Second Innings: McGrath 17-5-33-0, Kasprowicz 15.5-5-36-7, Warne 26-9-57-2, ME Waugh 7-3-16-1, Young 1-0-5-0.

AUSTRALIA
MTG Elliott b Tufnell	12	(2)	lbw Malcolm	4
MA Taylor (c) c AJ Hollioake b Tufnell	38	(1)	lbw Caddick	18
GS Blewett c Stewart b Tufnell	47		c Stewart b Caddick	19
ME Waugh c Butcher b Tufnell	19		c Hussain b Tufnell	1
SR Waugh lbw Caddick	22		c Thorpe b Caddick	6
RT Ponting c Hussain b Tufnell	40		lbw Tufnell	20
IA Healy (+) c Stewart b Tufnell	2		c & b Caddick	14
S Young c Stewart b Tufnell	0		not out	4
SK Warne b Caddick	30		c Martin b Tufnell	3
MS Kasprowicz lbw Caddick	0		c AJ Hollioake b Caddick	4
GD McGrath not out	1		c Thorpe b Tufnell	1
EXTRAS (LB 3, W 1, NB 5)	9		(B 3, LB 4, W 1, NB 2)	10
TOTAL	**220**			**104**

FOW 1st Inns: 49 54 94 140 150 164 164 205 205 220
FOW 2nd Inns: 5 36 42 49 54 88 92 95 99 104

Bowling: First Innings: Malcolm 11-2-37-0, Martin 15-5-38-0, Caddick 19-4-76-3, Tufnell 34.3-16-66-7. Second Innings: Malcolm 3-0-15-1, Martin 4-0-13-0, Tufnell 13.1-6-27-4, Caddick 12-2-42-5.

Umpires: LM Barker & P Willey (TV Umpire - KE Palmer)